# Veils, Nudity, and Tattoos

# Veils, Nudity, and Tattoos

## *The New Feminine Aesthetics*

Thorsten Botz-Bornstein

LEXINGTON BOOKS
Lanham • Boulder • New York • London

Chapter 1 originally published as "Veils and Sunglasses" by Thorsten Botz-Bornstein. *The Journal of Aesthetics and Culture* 20:2, 2012.

Chapter 3 originally published as "Can the Veil be Cool?" by Thorsteon Botz-Bornstein. *Journal of Religion and Popular Culture* 25:2. © The University of Toronto Press, 2013. Reprinted with permission from Univeristy of Toronto Press (utpjournals.com).

Chapter 7 originally published as "From the Stigmatized Tattoo to the Graffitied Body: Femininity in the Tattoo Renaissance" by Thorsten Botz-Bornstein. *Gender, Place, and Culture: A Journal of Feminist Geography* 20:2. © Taylor & Francis, 2013. Reprinted by permission of Taylor & Francis Ltd, www.tandfonline.com.

Published by Lexington Books
An imprint of The Rowman & Littlefield Publishing Group, Inc.
4501 Forbes Boulevard, Suite 200, Lanham, Maryland 20706
www.rowman.com

Unit A, Whitacre Mews, 26-34 Stannary Street, London SE11 4AB

British Library Cataloguing in Publication Information Available

**Library of Congress Cataloging-in-Publication Data**

Botz-Bornstein, Thorsten.
Veils, nudity, and tattoos : the new feminine aesthetic / Thorsten Botz-Bornstein.
pages cm.
Includes bibliographical references and index.
ISBN 978-1-4985-0046-3 (cloth : alk. paper) -- ISBN 978-1-4985-0047-0 (electronic) 1. Body marking. 2. Tattooing. 3. Veils. 4. Body image. 5. Human body--Social aspects. I. Title.
GN419.15.B68 2015
391.6'5--dc23

2015021048

Printed in the United States of America

# Contents

# Acknowledgments

I would like to thank the following journals for having granted the permission to reprint revised versions of their articles: *Gender, Place and Culture: A Journal of Feminist Geography*, which published "From the Stigmatized Tattoo to the Graffitied Body: Femininity in the Tattoo Renaissance" (now chapter 7) in its 20:2, 2012 issue; the *Journal of Aesthetics and Culture*, which published "Veils and Sunglasses'" (now chapter 1) in its 5, 2013 issue; and the *Journal of Religion and Popular Culture*, which published "Can the Veil be Cool?" (whose much extended version is now chapter 3) in its 25:2, 2013 issue.

# Introduction

This is a philosophical book about two aesthetic devices that seem to be diametrically opposed: nudity and veiling. Tattoos settle somewhere in the middle between both. At first sight, tattoos, nudity, and veils[1] do not seem to have much in common except for the fact that all three have become more frequent, more visible, and more dominant in connection with aesthetic presentations of women over the last thirty years. Still there are links. In 2013, Nicola Formichetti, the new artistic director of the fashion brand Diesel, launched his first advertisement campaign called "Dieselreboot" using bold iconography employing tattoos, nudity, and veils. What can appear as an artistic whim is held together by profound relationships that this book attempts to reveal through a conceptual analysis.

In October 2011, twenty-year-old Aliaa El Mahdy posted her nude photo on her blogspot page, arousing the anger of the conservative part of Muslim society. In this photo, El Mahdy, dis-objectifies and desexualizes her body *not* through the device of decontextualization, but rather through an act of "semantic inversion" by presenting her body precisely in a way that is *normally associated with objectification*. This she has in common with many tattooed women and "re-veiled" women. The example shows that today more than ever it is necessary to think "woman" outside those boxes that attribute her to either conservatism or progressivism. In other words, tattoos, nudity, and veils need to be wrenched from essentialized discourses that look *either* for the authentic, natural, traditional, and morally correct expression *or* for its contrary.

The present book sketches the image of a woman who is not only sexually emancipated and confident, but also more and more aware of her cultural heritage. By doing so, she takes an unorthodox approach towards three phenomena that conventional ways of thinking tend to see as unrelated or even opposed.

What do tattoos, nudity, and veils have in common? All three concern the skin, are unconventional fashion objects, establish identity, and are linked to certain taboos. All three are private and public, humiliating and empowering, as well as backward and progressive according to the interpretation to which they are submitted. Furthermore, all three phenomena have considerably changed during the last thirty years, which makes comparisons possible. Nudity no longer represents a natural state of the body but rather detracts from nature. Still, it has a highly ideological value. On the radical feminist protest group FEMEN's posters, one can read "Naked Truth" or "Nudity Is Freedom." This book's purpose is to show that the veil has become part and parcel of a new script of body culture similar to nudity and tattoos. Though nudity still decolonizes the body, the nude can no longer be seen as "pure"; and tattoos and veils have developed in parallel with this cultural shift. As a result, all three phenomena need to be read in the same context. The chapters of this book will reveal many paradoxes revolving around respect, modesty, sexuality, female power, and female non-power. It will become clear that the only logic able to approach this world of paradoxes is the complex logic of Third Wave feminism that challenges dualism by recognizing diversity, particularity, and embodiment.

In order to understand the new constellations by which tattoos, nudity, and veils are determined, certain tropes need to be deconstructed beforehand. These include the trope of Western civilization vs. Oriental barbarism, the trope of the Muslim woman as the ultimate victim of an Islamic patriarchy, but also the trope of covering as an advancement of civilization. It is not enough to insist on tradition and to refuse so-called Western values.

Against this background, the questions asked in this book turn out to have a broad anthropological scope: What relationships do tattoos, nudity, and veils have with civilization? Is nudity itself "primitive" and does the covering (veiling) of nudity signify a step towards civilization or a step away from it? Do tattoos effectuate a shift from the primitive to civilization or does the untattooed, pure skin represent a supreme civilizational value even in contemporary postmodern culture? What will become obvious is that in contemporary culture neither the naked nor the nude can be seen as "pure." Nudity no longer functions as an ideal of civilization (or non-civilization) in the classical sense. As a consequence, the cancellation of essentialized notions of nature that were still current during modernity has also inaugurated a new approach towards tattoos and nudity.

Conventional comparative approaches might hold that tattoos and nudity are operating within the same system of signifiers because both have to do with the *baring* of the body and have sexual connotations for just this reason, while veiling consists of the *covering* of the body, and thus cancels those connotations. However, this view is simplistic because in terms of sexual economy, baring and covering are not antagonistic. As a matter of fact, critics of the veil often condemn the veil for the same reason for which others (or they themselves) condemn nudity—instead of reducing sexualization, the veil can foster sexualization. This becomes particularly clear in a 2001 article in *The Guardian*, where Polly Toynbee announces "that the veil arouses lasciviousness: more moderate versions of the garb dull, uniform coat to the ground and the plain headscarf have much the same effect, inspiring lascivious thoughts they are designed to stifle" (5 October, quoted from Afshar 2008: 420).

It is also possible to argue the opposite case by using another set of semantic links. For example, one can argue that tattoos and veils are similar because both emanate an uncanny power affronting "liberal" subjects and filling them with horror because both represent (relatively) permanent body alterations. (Of course, in the case of the veil this concerns only the public appearance of the body. See more on this below.) More radically, what tattoos and the veil have in common is that the covering they represent can be perceived as a device that displaces and destroys the items it covers. The tattoo as much as the veil "can be thought of as a poisoned name" (Fleming 1997: 36); that is, as the Socratic *pharmakon* or as "the Derridean supplement to the (interior) subject that is located on the surface" (39). Juliet Fleming says this about tattoos, but it applies also to veils (at least in the eyes of many people).

In this case, nudity seems to be the only remedy that frees us from both tattoos and veils; it seems to be the "natural" signifier that can cancel all "bad" connotations. Normally, nudity can reestablish the subject in its natural form and rearrange the distorted hierarchical order between surface and center. However, what this book shows is that in praxis, this kind of natural degree-zero nudity cannot be obtained either, because: (1) Tattoos and veils are indelible (tattoos cannot be deleted and veils cannot be taken off in public once they have been assumed by a devout subject), and (2) "Natural nudity," as a utopian vision of harmony between nature and civilization aspired by nudist movements emerging in the 1920 in Europe, has become a very difficult option because in a postmodern situation, nudity has become a supplement or poison in its own right. Nudity, in the way it appears today in the media, in the streets, in locker rooms, and on beaches, no longer represents the healthy natural state of the body but rather detracts from nature. This book provides examples, showing that at present nudity has become not more than the bleak vision of a utopian but impossible truth.

The theoretical conclusion is that we are very far removed from Plato's conception of the body as a covering of the soul. In a postmodern context, the body—no matter if tattooed, nude, or veiled—is merely one means among others of expressing cultural messages. All metaphysical conceptions suggesting that signs should always refer to a depth of meaning (situated in the soul) are overcome. The situation can be summarized through the sentence "The skin does not convey meaning; it stands in the place of meaning." The sentence is a paraphrase of Jacques Lacan's "Language does not convey meaning, it stands in the place of meaning" that has been taken up by Jean Baudrillard in another context (1990: 6).

By talking about veils, tattoos, and nude skin in a psychoanalytical context we approach indeed a concept that confirms the above reflections. It is psychoanalyst Didier Anzieu's concept of the skin as a thinking envelope underlying the formation of the ego. Also Anzieu complained that "since the Renaissance western thought is clouded by an epistemological theme: to know means to crack the bark in order to reach the kernel. But this theme has exhausted itself" (1995: 31).

The radical and paradoxical consequence is that within a semantic constellation that no longer recognizes the "absence of signs" as a natural and naked "degree zero" of the body, nudity is not different from veils. This is why Ruth Barcan writes about nudity: "For early thinkers, nakedness was often a lost purity, perhaps irretrievably corrupted, and clothes a sad necessity. For postmodern thinkers, both nakedness and clothing are "impure," but in a new sense: they are culturally and historically produced and experienced" (2004: 54).

The purpose of this book is to view the most recent developments of global culture as a coherent body in which resistance and humiliation of women are linked in an oftentimes curious fashion, and whose dynamics depends on those contradictions. As a result, the oppositions "veil vs. no veil," "covered vs. bared," "non-sexual vs. sexual," and "objectified vs. subjectified" are no longer pertinent in a contemporary context. In the same way, it is impossible to speak, as does French psychoanalyst Élisabeth Roudinesco, of the unveiled state as a "natural" psychological process and conclude that girls would lose "their feminine identity if their bodies could not be seen" (from J. Scott 2007: 158); or it is impossible to call the veil, as does Iranian dissident feminist Chahdortt Djavann, a form of "psychological, sexual and social mutilation" (ibid.). However, neither veil nor non-veil is nature, but both are culture. The veil is simply too similar to the tattoo, which has also been dismissed as being "against nature," but which seems to have been recuperated by contemporary youth culture *for just that reason*. Interestingly, the veil can also be conceived *as nature*, as is well demonstrated by a comment from the wife of an Amal militia member in Lebanon who held that "the veil reflects the natural differences between men and women" (Lazreg 2009: 69). This statement can be contrasted with French feminist Sarah Kofman's rebuttal of Sigmund Freud's idea that "in seeking to veil herself, the woman would only be imitating nature, which has always already covered over her genitals with pubic hair" (Kofman 1980/1985: 59). Kofman's claim will be discussed in chapter 4.

On the other hand, pro-veiling fanatics are just as mistaken as Roudinesco if they hold that veiling fosters civilization because it *overcomes* nature. What the no-veil position aims to obtain is not natural primitiveness, but a sort of civilized nudist innocence towards the unveiled body, which does not know any shame.

For all those reasons, in this book, veiling and nudity will not be presented as opposites, but as communicating branches of the same discourse. The temptation to see veils and nudity as opposites is great but represents a dangerous trap leading, for example, to the construction of "liberating nudity" and "oppressive veiling" as rigid concepts. However, the bikini is not necessarily more liberating than the veil. First it is important to understand that both veiling and nudity are unique expressions deriving their power from an inner self-contradiction. Both can be seen as humiliations and as empowerment. This they have in common with tattoos. Second, both possess metaphorical powers that are disproportionate with their original significations, especially when it comes to religio-metaphysical statements. "The naked truth" or "veiling the truth" are strikingly handy expressions, though they say nothing about nudity or veiling in concrete anthropological contexts. Their metaphorical power can easily be taken for reality, but this is a mistake.

At present, the symbolism of both nudity and the veil is increasingly stretched to include the realm of politics. It has been said, for example, that "Muslims are on a crusade to *veil* anything that threatens their faith, whether it be Western democracy, history (associated here with polytheism and powerful goddesses), or simply any form of change" (Majid Anouar: 329, my italics). The metaphor of nudity can be used in a similarly metaphorical way as a political expression. It is the radical character of those expressions that can make them either convincing or annoying.

## VEILS, TATTOOS, NUDITY

### Veils

While veiling[2] had once been almost done away with by many modernizing authorities in Islamic countries in the 1950s and could appear almost as a matter of the past by the 1970s in some countries, in the 1980s one could observe the beginning of a "re-veiling" process that would undergo different stages. During a first phase in the early 1980s, many women began to dress "like nuns before Vatican II" (J. Williams 1980: 73). However, something else changed soon afterwards. Islamic dress would be adapted to the modern fashion situation as young, urban, middle-class women began to cover themselves in a completely new style. Suddenly it became appropriate that "an

orthodox Muslim woman could with just as great propriety wear a simple
dress of modern type, with long sleeves, black stockings, and a nylon scarf
tied over her hair, especially if she did it without jewelry or make-up" (75).
In Turkey, so-called *tesettür* (veiling fashion) combines veiling with the
standards of beauty as well as of marketing methods intrinsic to modern
international fashion. In many Muslim countries, a new Islamic fashion industry offers "modern" (that is, "Western") clothes that are compatible with
religious standards of modesty. The phenomenon could be observed in many
places where this practice had previously been almost nonexistent, such as
Bangladesh (cf. Sandikci and Ger 2010: 11). The veil could even reach the
upscale areas of the fashion business. For example, since 2012, the New
York–based modeling agency Underwraps, set up by fashion designer Nailah
Lymus, specializes in Muslim females. In some way, the veil has undergone
a development similar to the tattoo, which went from counter-culture to
glamour.

In the eyes of some, all this has led to the "desanctification of the veil"
through which this symbol will end up being "just a piece of fabric" (Wassef
2001: 119). In the end, the veil might become an empty signifier helping to
insert the female body onto the world of consumer capitalism. International
lifestyle labels such as *Styleislam*, which distribute not only fashionable
street wear but also accessories like mouse pads and coffee mugs with Islamic messages, might indeed indicate such a banalization of religious references
in the lives of young Muslims. This is even more obvious in the music scene
where mainstream youth culture includes Muslim punk and hard rock or
even hip-hop as represented, for example, by the Danish band Outlandish.

At the same time, many women see the veil as a feminist tool of empowerment. In principle, the idea of the empowering veil is not new and can even
be found outside feminist contexts. The veil has often been related to sexual
seduction empowering women; and sometimes the mere fact of seeing without being seen has been perceived as an act of liberation. A Swedish woman
wearing an all-covering veil in Saudi Arabia has thus reported: "That was the
biggest sense of freedom I have ever had. . . . You are like a spy not taking
part and you can pull faces" (Franks 2000: 921). Many women point out this
kind of empowering effect. Even anti-Muslim campaigner Ayaan Hirsi describes her early experiences of veiling like this:

> The hijab I draped over my scrawny frame was overwhelmingly enveloping:
> there was simply nothing left to see except a small face and two hands. When I
> arrived in school, I took off my robe and folded it up inside my desk. Then, at
> the end of the day, I modestly unfolded it and put it on—and suddenly I was
> interesting, mysterious, powerful. (Hirsi 2007: 74)

## Tattoos

The increased use of tattoos by women in Muslim and non-Muslim countries has developed in parallel with the phenomenon of veiling and is just as striking. Tattoos are no longer restricted to biker and sailor culture but have been sanctioned by the mainstream of liberal societies. For the past thirty years, the West has been enjoying a "tattoo renaissance" (Rubin 1988) during which tattooing underwent a "transition from a (generally disvalued) craft to a (partially legitimated) art form" (Sanders 1989: 24). At present, tattoos are marketed as fashion items and to a large extent (though not exclusively), the fashion aspect of tattoos is responsible for the increase of female tattoos. While a woman with a full-sleeve tattoo might still be socially "out," society has become relatively tolerant towards smaller tattoos. In 1996, in America, tattoo parlors were among the top six growth businesses (American Business Information, Inc. 1996) and women made up almost half of those who get tattooed (Armstrong 1991: 215). In 2012, more women than men were tattooed in the United States (23% of women against 19% of men). (Lokke 2013).

However, in spite of their fashionable outlook, tattoos have not entirely lost their "mystical" appeal. In this sense they continue to stick out of mainstream culture. Though many people might wear tattoos merely as decorations (and are increasingly doing so), a "fundamentalist" spell continues to permeate the tattooing business. A recent tattoo e-handbook offering practical advice to anybody interested in tattoos overrides mere beauty arguments right at the beginning and lists the following as good reasons for getting a tattoo: "Self Expression, Tribal Identity, Spiritual Growth, For Spiritual Protection, Marking Important Events, Totem Symbols and Animals, As a Memorial, Enhancing Sexuality, To Make People Laugh" (Perry 1933: 14).

## Nudity

Like tattoos, nudity has become more visible than ever, especially on European beaches and on the internet. Obviously, we are talking here about public nudity and nudity as a social phenomenon and not about private nudity at home. On the internet, nudity often appears as pornography, which is today—in most countries—surprisingly easily accessed. Such a banalization of pornography would have been unthinkable only two decades ago. Female nudity is also more and more liberally used in advertising as well as in the media in general because "consumer culture permits and encourages the unashamed display of the human body" (Featherstone quoted in Barcan 2004: 61).

However, public nudity emerges also outside the realms governed by capitalist market economy. Having somehow disappeared from the countercultural scene where it was very present in the 1920s/1930s (in the form of nudist movements) as well as in the 1960s/1970s (in the form of a nudism amalgamated with "hippy culture"), nudity has most recently reappeared in the context of almost exclusively female protests such as those staged by the Ukrainian feminist group FEMEN. On the posters of FEMEN, one can read "Naked Truth," "Nudity is Freedom," "I Am a Woman, Not an Object," and "Undress and Win." As in the 1960s, this activism speaks out against the objectification of women and proclaims women's right to do what they want with their bodies. Now as before, nudity decolonizes the body. Based on this symbolical effect, it is also used to defend a whole range of other socio-political issues that are not immediately related to the body or to women's liberation. The concept of protest nudity reemerged also in so-called Slut Walks that have been held in major cities all over the world in recent years and whose aim is to point out that women held responsible for rape because of what they are wearing are not sluts because if they were, then all women would be sluts, since anyone can be victimized regardless of what they are wearing. The "International Go Topless Day" (or "International Go Topless Jihad Day"), held since 2008, has a similar function. It falls each year on the Sunday closest to Women's Equality Day. Even in China, Ai Xiaoming, 2010 laureate of the Simone de Beauvoir Prize for the liberty of women, posted nude photos of herself on the web in order to protest against the lax treatment of some rapists and pedophiles.

Public nudity can also be used in artistic contexts. Italian artist Vanessa Beecroft employs female nudity as an expression of female empowerment. Much of her performance art consists of the display of living nude young women, who look similar as they wear identical wigs, pantyhose, or shoes. Usually they stand motionless. In April 2005, one hundred women stood still in Berlin's Neue Nationalgalerie for three hours. In those performances, the nude women appeared very much as cold and severe angels: Their bored, indifferent, and impertinent look reduced the spectators to helpless, con-fused, and embarrassed beings (cf. Agamben 2011). One set of Beecroft's photographs presents a mock-fascist army of blonde, nude women in a dark space.

A remotely related concept of protest nudity is the Suicide Girls website (founded in 2001), which functions as a soft-porn website and at the same time as a woman-oriented interactive platform designed to inspire confidence and to help women build personality. Through its moral ambiguity, the site aspires to subvert the "traditionally gendered consumption of pornographic images" (Earle and Sharp 2007: 13) because (at least officially) Suicide Girls practices resistance as a part of the erotic aesthetic, which represents an attempt at freeing democratic society of the hypocritical and oppressive bar-rier to the nude body. The Suicide Girl phenomenon of "alternative erotica" will be examined in chapters 7 and 8.

Male nudity, on the other hand, as it has been presented in the media in recent years, does not empower, but more often disarms and embarrasses the *nude subject*. In 1997, an advertisement by Lee jeans showed a woman wearing stiletto-heeled boots with her toe resting on the naked buttocks of a prostrate man. The text reads: "Put the boot in." The pictures of naked, tortured males in Abu Ghraib prison had a similar effect, especially since the torturers—always fully dressed in military uniforms—were sometimes female. Beecroft has explored the possibilities of entirely male performances with the U.S. Navy in San Diego and with the U.S. Silent Service at the Gallery Intrepid in New York (in 1999 and 2000). However, those males were never nude. Though following similar principles, the photos differ from those obtained with female models because the encounter between models and audience is of another nature. Shame, expectations, interests, and power relations follow different rules when male bodies are encountered.

The most remarkable fact is that female protest nudity has also spread to the conservative Middle East. In October 2011, twenty-year-old Aliaa El Mahdy posted a nude photo of herself on her blog, asking those who oppose her act to burn their own bodies that they obviously so much despise in order to "rid yourself of your sexual complexes." A year later, in Turkey, four Ukrainian FEMEN activists staged their trademark bare-breasted protests in Istanbul to demonstrate against domestic violence in Turkey. Still six months later, in March 2013, Amina Tyler, a nineteen-year-old Tunisian woman posted two photos of herself topless on Facebook with the words "Fuck your morals" and "My body belongs to me and is not the source of anyone's honor" written in English and in Arabic across her chest. Meanwhile, El Mahdy has founded an Egyptian branch of FEMEN.

FEMEN has increasingly appropriated anti-Muslim themes, especially in their Paris-based actions. In the French television documentary *Nos seins, nos armes! (Our Breasts, Our Weapons!)* (2013) by Nadia El Fani and Caroline Fourest, one sees FEMEN activists crossing the Arab quarter of Paris, employing burqas in their performances. The burqa is declared to not be a dress for women but "a dress made by men for women, which thus symbolizes the negation of women." FEMEN have also demonstrated against the sharia. At the end of the documentary one sees the group of FEMEN demonstrators colliding with French far-right activists who beat them as the former invite themselves to a demonstration against gay marriage. The images, which are uncannily similar to what could be expected should FEMEN appear in Egypt or some other Muslim country, surprise the film's older feminist commentators who had led similar actions in Paris in the 1960s. At that time, nude protests were met with more tolerance.

The recent Arab revolutions must also be seen as sexual revolutions as the nudity theme plays a part in it. Paul Moreira, author of the French television documentary *Sex, Salafists and Arab Spring*, depicts sexuality in Arab countries with the revolution as a backdrop, and shows how much religious radicalization, male frustration, gender segregation, and harassment of women are linked. In his opinion, "political democracy, just as much as sexuality and the place of women, will be a determining element showing how much control Islamists can get over society."

It can be concluded that the veil is caught in a liberty-oppression (protection-imprisonment) paradox that academic discourses have great difficulties disentangling. However, in reality, the constellation is not really unusual as tattoos have been found to be caught in a similar paradox. Nancy Kang reports that tattooed women have been asked "to cover up your body art not for us but for yourself, for your own protection and feminine integrity" (Kang 2012: 66). The present analytical confrontation of the veil with nudity and tattoos attempts to clarify this situation. I show in this book that tattoos, nudity, and veils can be traced to similar social and psychological patterns and that it is possible to establish an ontology of veiling through comparisons with nudity and tattoos. This comparative concept is relatively new. As a matter of fact, in the past, corresponding parallels between tattoos, nudity, and veils have occasionally been evoked by scholars though none of them has analyzed them much further. Homa Hoodfar, for example, mentions the frequently encountered idea that women who veil might be "mutilating their bodies" (Hoodfar 2003: 26), which brings the veil indeed close to what some people believe to be the truth about tattoos. Marnia Lazreg detects a similarity between veiling and the presentation of nudity in magazines because both reduce women to their sex: "If advertising in the West thrives on depictions of naked or semi-naked women, it also finds fertile ground in representations of women with hijabs in Iran" (Lazreg 2009: 108). However, such analogies are not only rudimentary, they also simplify a reality in which the status and the use of tattoos, nudity, and veils is extremely complex.

## COOLNESS

The term "coolness" is central in this book and I use it in two ways. First it is derived from Marshall McLuhan's conceptual system of "hot" and "cool" media. Then it is based on the premises of African American thinkers who wrote about coolness as an aesthetical and ethical peculiarity necessitated by the African American cultural and economic situation. The aesthetics of cool developed mainly in the form of a behavioral attitude practiced by black men in the United States at the time of slavery and residential segregation. Joel Dinerstein sees as essential for cool behavior the control of emotions, to remain relaxed in a performance, to develop a unique style, and to be "emotionally expressive within an artistic frame of restraint" (Dinerstein 1999: 241).

The instances of veiling shown in this book—reaching from protest veiling in Western countries to slogans such as "Islam and the hip hop nation" or "transglobal hip hop umma" (Anderson 2005: 273)—demonstrate that coolness can be transferred across different cultural contexts. Muslim identity values *can* enter into a transcultural relation with a concept of coolness inspired by the African American struggle for freedom. In ideological terms, the resulting constellation is complex because here a non-Western female topic (veiling) is discussed in a context that cannot be limited to that of "Third World feminism" because the comparison addresses not merely other women but also men (that is, African American men who were operating with the concept of coolness) and above that, men who are living in the first world. I admit that such associations of feminist topics with a "masculinist" theme are rare but I do not see why it cannot be handled correctly in theoretical terms.

## THE CHAPTERS

Chapter 1 introduces the veil by submitting it to an analysis inspired by McLuhan's analysis of sunglasses. Both the veil and sunglasses aim to disrupt gazes, they enact a selective covering of the face, but in the former case only the eyes are uncovered whereas in the latter the face is visible while the eyes are covered.

Chapter 2 reflects upon those women who see their veiling as an act of resistance and liberation bearing a link with feminist strategies in general. My argument is that those pro-veiling positions can be much better understood when being read through Third Wave feminist thought. Both pro-veiling positions and Third Wave feminism[3] organize their fight by looking for means of empowerment in appearance and both contradict preceding anti-ideologies, which are anti-sex ideologies of earlier feminist generations for the former and hardline anti-veiling ideologies for the latter. The "complexity" as well as the "contradiction of lives" that Rebecca Walker puts forward as a subject of interest for Third Wave feminism need to be examined against the background established by the tattoo-nudity-veiling triangle. This is necessary especially today in a world where the arguably most famous Third Wave feminists are FEMEN. Also, Walker confirms that instead of perfect womanhood, feminism can only create "identities that accommodate ambiguity and multiple positionalities: including more than excluding, exploring more than defining, searching more than arriving" (Walker 1998: xxxiii).

In chapter 3, I compare veiling with some of the principle virtues of African American coolness: moderation and self-control. Can the veil function as a tool of cool? Does this piece of cloth maintain the crucial balance between visibility and non-visibility, assimilation and cultural resistance, submission and subversion, control and the inability to control?

Chapter 4 presents the debate on veiling through French feminist Sarah Kofman's (1934–1994) reflections on the "respect for women." In Kofman's opinion, the respect for women humiliates and elevates women at the same time because "the respect for women is always the moral and glorious flip-side of men's 'misogyny.'" The veil turns out to be a highly ambiguous item for exactly those reasons.

Chapter 5 explores the phenomenon of spatial segregation and compares African American segregated space with that of gender separation increasingly practiced in Muslim countries. My thesis is that in both cases segregation is resolved through the creation of a "cool space" of playful transgression.

With chapter 6 begin the reflections of the veil against tattoos and nudity. This chapter establishes parallels and differences in a systematic fashion.

Chapter 7 analyses the spectacularly rising popularity of tattoos by showing that they have become a spatial project in the largest sense: The participation of tattoos in the creation of social space is different from that of tattoos before the Tattoo Renaissance. What took place is a shift from tattoos to body graffiti.

Chapter 8 disentangles the notions of the "savage" and the "civilized" in the cultural discourse on tattoos. Aiming to examine the position that sees tattoos through the perspective of the savage as opposed to civilization, this chapter looks at the particular link that tattoos maintain with nudity. Contrary to what had happened in former times, tattoos are now used in order to reinstall the body as a civilized entity: The tattooed body is never entirely naked and can never be entirely savage.

Chapter 9 considers the role of men with regard to fetishism and nature.

I would like to end this introduction with a colorful picture of the new body culture drawn by Rebecca Walker, which summarizes the subject of this book:

> Whether it's multiple piercings, femme girls with no hair, two-foot-high head wraps, or skin covered with tats that the whole idea of "clear and blemish free" seems hopelessly naïve, it is obvious that as a result of artistic and political movements new and different scripts are being written. The body, the blank page waiting for words, and beauty, a subjective idea looking for a location have been liberated to meet up in a variety of unique and often surprising ways. Barbie, with her pert nose and shoulder-length blonde hair, no longer reigns supreme. (Walker 1998: xv–xvi)

It should be mentioned that, by now, Barbie has been submitted to a new aesthetics in her own right, this time based on Muslim culture. The Muslim Barbie comes with *abaya* and prayer rug. Trying to escape Western ideologies of consumption and moral laxness, the veiled Barbie follows the rules of religious correctness and piety. Interestingly, a Muslim woman interviewed by Emma Tarlo points out that a Barbie doll scheme is not alien to, but *inherent* in Muslim ideologies. According to her, it is not simply imposed by the West: "The 'Muslim world' is guilty of distorting women's roles by promoting either 'the self-sacrificing mother' or 'the Barbie doll thing,' both of which she feels miss the essence of Islam's real emphasis, which is on gender balance and complementarity" (Tarlo 2007: 26). Is Barbie really more Muslim than Muslim clerics are ready to admit?

## NOTES

1. Though I attempt in this book to cancel the ideological weight clinging to the term "veil" and to examine the phenomenon in purely aesthetic and phenomenological terms, I decided not to reject the term veil altogether and to replace it with the word "headscarf"or "covering" (though these terms would certainly be more appropriate in the Turkish context that will be evoked). The reason is that the metaphorical power of the word "veil" is essential to the present argument. The word "hijab," which will also be used, is here defined as the headscarf worn in an Islamic way covering also the neck and leaving only the face visible.

2. In general, when talking about the veil in this book, my intention is not to establish an idealized version of the "veiled woman" in the way in which "ethnocentric universalism"—so much criticized by feminists like Chandra Talpade Mohanty—tries to invent the group of prototypical "Third World Women" as if they were "an already constituted, coherent group with identical interests and desires, regardless of class, ethnic, or racial location, or contradictions" (Mohanty 2003: 21). As a matter of fact, media and culture industry do already enough to erase class, ethnicity, nationality, piety, sexuality, and politics in terms of gender (cf. Gökariksel and McLarney 2010: 6). It is clear that the veil has different meanings for different people.

3. The generally accepted time periods for the three feminism waves are 1848 to 1923 for the first wave, 1960 to 1979 for the second wave, and 1995 to the present for the third wave. Though occurring successively, the waves do of course interpenetrate. The above scheme also shows that there have been long transitory phases between the waves. First Wave feminism emerged from women's discontent during the Industrial Revolution, expanded women's citizenship rights, and disrupted the separation of male and female spheres that was particularly typical for Victorian culture. Second Wave feminism expanded women's equality with men in public activities and further modified traditional gender roles. It also protested against conventional-feminine trappings such as bras, cosmetics, and high-heeled shoes, along with the moral obligations of women to bear children and be pleasing to men. Third Wave feminism emerged within a social situation where much equality had already been achieved. It began to combine rebellious-masculine qualities with conventional-feminine qualities, that is, to make wearing lipstick compatible with women's fights for greater freedom and empowerment.

*Part I*

# Veils

*Chapter One*

# Veils and Sunglasses

The purpose of this book is to show that the veil, just like the nude body, no longer exists as a simple, essentialist, coherent, unified, and eternalized concept. And since the perception of nudity has obviously evolved a great deal since modernism, it has become necessary to interpret the veil in a similar "postmodern" context. To begin with, I examine the veil by reflecting it against a conceptual system developed by Marshall McLuhan with regard to the analysis of sunglasses and their function as "hot" and "cool" media.

Both the veil and sunglasses aim to disrupt gazes. This is especially true in the case of the *eye-covering* veil where the effect is similar to that of sunglasses. Here the subject cannot be gazed at but adopts the role of a mere spectator. The veil has been compared to the *mashrabiyya*, the wooden latticework enclosing oriel windows of traditional Arab houses thus permitting women observing *purdah* to look outside without being seen, or to the Indian *jharokha*, which serves the same purpose (Figure 1). To see without being seen is an act of empowerment and liberation. In the 1980 British drama-documentary *Death of a Princess*, Saudi women on a desert raid sit inside a vehicle taking advantage of their covering for promiscuity. The car stops: outside, men dance as if they want to be chosen by the princess. Being covered is here a sign of empowerment. Veiling is associated with traditional Arab notions of power relations like "who has the right to be seen by whom" (cf. El Guindi 1999: 94). In a different context, Frantz Fanon writes about colonized Algeria that "this woman who sees without being seen frustrates the colonizer. There is no reciprocity. She does not yield herself, does not give herself, does not offer herself" (Fanon 1967: 169). The problem is that the person who is completely veiled is *too* invisible for others as a person and cannot always fully participate in the social game played.

## THE FACE, VEIL, AND SUNGLASSES

Both the veil and sunglasses enact a selective covering of the face, but in the former case only the eyes are uncovered whereas in the latter the face is visible while the eyes are covered. The face-covering veil impairs communication (the woman is less audible because her voice is dampened by the veil and the covering of the ears impairs her hearing) but her eyes leave her considerable possibilities to communicate with the outside world. It is perhaps equally difficult to interact with somebody wearing very dark glasses as it is to interact with a veiled woman whose only visible facial part are the eyes. But the difficulties can be traced to different reasons.

McLuhan has analyzed sunglasses and their relationship with his system of hot and cool media. McLuhan's definition of "cool" bears no explicit link with typical African American elaborations of the term that will be the topic of chapter 3. He rather operates with an interesting opposition of "hot" *presence* to a more elusive but inspiring "cool" semi-presence. In studies on African American culture the "cool mask" as "an extension of the instinct to survive" (Majors and Billson 1992: 60) is often linked to the use of sunglasses. Joel Dinerstein reports that Lester Young's "second contribution to

**Figure 1.1.   A *Mashrabiyya*. Courtesy: Thorsten Botz-Bornstein**

individual self-expression on the bandstand was the strategic use of sunglasses. . . . Young recognized the use of shades as a mask to deflect the gaze of others without causing conflict" (Dinerstein 1999: 250). It seems that since then the cool pose of supreme indifference has become "eyes hidden behind shades" (Fraiman 2003: xi) able to symbolize habits of transgression and irreverence as a worldview. The subject of "veiling and coolness" will be examined at length in chapter 3.

For McLuhan, "hot" is any kind of information that is highly defined or that "leaves not much to be filled in" (McLuhan 1964: 37). Hot media favor analytical precision, quantitative analysis, and sequential ordering and are usually linear and logical, while "cool" media leave the transmitted information open to interpretation or even partly unexplained. Speech is thus "cooler" than highly defined images. A cool person wearing dark glasses lacks the "articulation of data" (42) because the glasses "create the inscrutable and inaccessible image that invites a great deal of participation and completion" (44). McLuhan could have made identical points about the veil because the veil also evokes an elusive semi-presence. However, is the veil just as "cool" as sunglasses?

The face defines the person's identity in a private as well as in an official fashion (passports, etc.). It is both an intimate and a legally responsible part of the body. The eyes are certainly the most private and most "unofficial" part of the face as they are closely connected to the brain and thoughts become manifest more directly through the eyes than through other facial features or body movements. It is relatively easy to fake a smile using the mouth and other facial muscles, but it is difficult to entirely control the expression of the eyes. Professional poker players wear the "poker face" but in addition, they often wear dark glasses because the eyes can unwillingly betray spontaneous reactions. Aldous Huxley was intrigued by dark glasses, whose popularization he could observe in his youth:

> This extraordinary notion that the organ of light perception is unfitted to stand light has become popular only in the last twenty years or so. Before the war of 1914 it was, I remember, the rarest thing to see anyone wearing dark glasses. . . . As a small boy, I would look at a be-goggled man or woman with that mixture of awed sympathy and rather macabre curiosity which children reserve for those afflicted with any kind of unusual or disfiguring physical handicap. Today, all that is changed. The wearing of black spectacles has become not merely common, but creditable. Just how creditable is proved by the fact that the girls in bathing suits, represented on the covers of fashion magazines in summer time, invariably wear goggles. Black glasses have ceased to be the badge of the afflicted, and are now compatible with youth, smartness and sex appeal. (Huxley 1974: 29)

Huxley traces this "fantastic craze for blacking out the eyes" to weakness: "This addiction has its origin in the fear of light." Paul Virilio, in a comment on Huxley, takes the problem from the opposite end. He does not interpret the wearing of dark glasses in terms of a weakness but rather of "coolness" because, for him, the wearer of dark glasses becomes *stronger*: "The wearer of dark glasses knows that the protectors-propagators of bodies and images are loaded weapons. He veils therefore prudently his retina and particularly the area of the macula. . . . His fear of being surprised by the sudden onset of the image, the intense illumination of projectors . . . is magnified when he finds himself in a place that is naturally dark or crepuscular" (Virilio 2009: 60). Robert Murphy, in an article from 1964 on Tuareg culture, synthesizes both opinions when interpreting the sunglass phenomenon as a "means of defense and withdrawal" which is particularly popular "among West African emirs and Near Eastern potentates. . . . They are commonly used in Latin America, where, indoors and out, heavily tinted glasses are the hallmark of the prestigeful as well as those aspiring to status, for they bestow the aloofness and distance that has always been the prerogative of the high in these lands" (Murphy 1964: 1272).

The wearer of dark glasses is protected against light even at night (who has not been blinded by a car flashing its high-beam headlights in the night?) as well as against the look of the other. The other's look into my eyes can be hypnotizing and thus disabling and the protection through glasses will make me more powerful. As a consequence, the wearer of dark glasses is cool: no grimaces, no frowns, no signs of strain and tension even when exposed to extreme light or hypnotic stares.

Though both sunglasses and veil present a combination of presence and non-presence creating the effect of mystification, in both cases the mysteries are "resolved" in different ways. The person wearing dark glasses reveals important parts of her face though she obliges us to retain any final judgment about these expressions because the gaze is missing. We have to content ourselves with the "official" signal sent out by the rest of the face but are unable to look "behind" it in order to interpret the face in the light of the more "real" intentions signaled by the eyes. In its totality, the face remains "cool" in McLuhan's sense because the meaning can never be construed.

The veil, too, incontestably does construct a mystery. It is not without reason that it has been a main symbol of the "inscrutability of the East" (Secor 2002: 7) for centuries and this not only for women. Murphy finds that also the face veil of Tuareg men "promote[s] this atmosphere of mystery and apartness and the Tuareg, whether in town or in his native desert, has often been remarked upon for his penchant for appearing the master of all he surveys" (1964: 1266). However, the mystery created by the veil is entirely different from that created by sunglasses. The face of the woman who is wearing the face veil is like being put on a psychological operation table exposing only the most important parts of her psyche: her eyes, which remain analyzable, hypnotizable, and vulnerable. The eyes give us access to "hot" information because, as long as we see the eyes, we can decipher her state of mind (is she afraid, shy, defiant, etc.).

It is true that the protection and hiding of the mouth does have equally strong symbolical connotations. Murphy, in his study of the Tuaregs, points to Freudian literature, which "gives extensive documentation to the female symbolism of the mouth, its vulnerability to penetration, and to the unconscious association between the eyes and the male generative powers" (1272). However, in no way is *this* kind of covering related to the grammar of coolness. The plugging of bodily orifices for fear of penetration is not an expression of coolness, while the hiding of information as well as the disruption of one's own stare definitely is. For this reason, the "hot" exposure of the woman's eyes does not permit the expression of real coolness. Above that, while the woman can communicate emotions relatively directly through the eyes, she is given no chance to formulate her message "officially" through other facial expressions. All this contradicts the concept of the face veil as a vehicle of coolness.

Apart from the prevention of potential penetration, the covering of the mouth has other important symbolical (and practical) consequences. In conversations, the mouth is the main communicator and to see a person's mouth while speaking can be crucial especially when there is background noise or when the person speaks the language poorly. The "mystery" of the face veil is in the hiding of the official information that is supposed to complement the intimate one. This explains why the veil has so often been evoked in the context of erotic intentions because here the intimate message is sent out without being complemented by any official confirmation. Attractive eyes invite the gaze to further scrutiny. A general but relatively profound attraction is effectuated first, which will then create the desire to discover the rest of the face.

The perceptual mechanics of dark glasses works the other way. Here the official part of the face is freely exposed but it loses a part of its attractiveness because the deeper or "real" meaning of the features cannot be fully construed and, in many cases, is not supposed to be construed at all. The result is mystery but not primary eroticism. I am not saying that the (male or female) wearer of sunglasses cannot be erotic, but s/he will not be erotic *because* she is wearing sunglasses. The sunglasses themselves are not erotic because they divert the gaze instead of encouraging it to further scrutiny. This is the reason why they are cool and especially much cooler than the veil. Sunglasses create a diffuse sort of interest and occasionally they arouse the feeling of being intrigued, which can also include erotic intentions; but they do not attract.

The above pattern explains why sunglasses worn together with a face-covering veil do not have the same effect of coolness that is usually attached to sunglasses. What is needed in order to be cool is the interplay of official messages with more or less construable unofficial messages.

The question arises whether the annulment of the signifying power of the eyes (which do not attract) produces seduction or not. Jean Baudrillard would probably support the idea of "seductive sunglasses" because for him seduction is *always* the annulment of signs, whereas a "seductive look" is literally non-seductive just because its signifying power is too strong. Baudrillard writes:

> Seduction lies with the annulment of the signs, of their meaning, with their pure appearance. Eyes that seduce have no meaning, their meaning being exhausted in the gaze, as a face with makeup is exhausted in its appearance, in the formal rigor of a senseless labor. Above all, seduction supposes not a signified desire, but the beauty of an artifice. (Baudrillard 1979/1990b: 76)

Once again, it is not the sunglasses that seduce but the interplay produced by the juxtaposition of hidden eyes and other facial signifiers. Therefore, for Baudrillard, sunglasses seduce. The (uncool) glance of the veiled face, on the other hand, which is so straightforward, is *not* seductive. The cool glance can seduce just because it is neither active nor passive but, according to Dick Pountain and David Robins, it is "rather detached—it expresses an indifference that challenges the other to attempt to attract its interest" (Pountain and Robins 2000: 116).

Not everybody will agree with Baudrillard (or rather with my interpretation of what Baudrillard would make of the difference between veils and sunglasses). Many will probably hold that sunglasses worn by women cannot have strong erotic connotations because in this case, the male gaze will not be supported by desire and seduction cannot take place. However, Baudrillard's point is that, just because the gaze can never become subjective but will keep hovering between objective and subjective expressions, it *can* produce seduction.

Saudi Arabian clerics who claimed in 2011 their right to cover women's "tempting eyes" (Keyes 2011) clearly adhere to the former position and would certainly not support Baudrillard's argument. On the other hand, should the covering of the eyes ever happen in Saudi Arabia, it will most likely not happen through the use of sunglasses. The generalized wearing of sunglasses would definitely make Saudi women look cooler—perhaps too cool. Interestingly, there is no Islamic veil covering *only* the eyes, while in Western culture there is. Occasionally worn at funerals, women wear this veil because it can hide the emotions communicated by the eyes. At the same

**Figure 1.2.  The woman can communicate emotions relatively directly through the eyes. Courtesy: Peet de Rouw**

time it makes possible the communication of more official emotions and messages by displaying the facial region around the mouth.

It can be concluded that the veil covering *everything but the eyes* is not cool. By hiding in an apparently "cool" way official facial expressions, the resulting play with desire and attraction makes the veil rather hot in the McLuhanian sense because the eyes are the "hottest" component of the face and any vestimentary aesthetics limiting facial expressions to this hot part cannot be considered cool.

It remains to be said that the eroticism of veiling works along the lines of the Lacanian scheme of the paradox of desire as it has been explained by Slavoj Žižek. The perception of the veiled object is "supported, permeated, and distorted by desire" or it is even "posited by desire itself" (Žižek 1992: 12). Desire is sparked when *something* (its object-cause) embodies or gives positive existence to its *nothing*—that is, to its void. What does the desire want? It wants an official confirmation that the desired object (the rest of the face) "really" exists and possibly desires us.

In some particular situations the observer might decide not to reconstruct the rest of the face and make those items that are visible the final focus of his fascination. Sometimes he might fear that the discovery of the entire face will involve a deception. The woman in Figure 1.2 attracts because her "hot" eyes

**Figure 1.3.    The "hot" information sent out by the Tuareg's eyes suggests defiance and aggressiveness. Courtesy: Eric Lafforgue**

actively engage in seduction. Her expression of seduction is so much emphasized that we do not *necessarily* feel the desire to have our impression "officially" sanctioned by unveiling the rest of the face. We might simply take her seductive look for granted.

The male wearing of the veil can follow the same perceptual pattern. The Tuareg man in Figure 1.3 might look cool but not because interesting facial elements have been hidden in a "cool" fashion, but rather because the "hot" information sent out by his eyes suggests defiance and aggressiveness. Again, we do not necessarily desire to discover the rest of his face.

## THE VEIL AS A FETISH

The veil becomes a fetish when the feminine attraction is suppressed in a way that the subject will definitely refuse to discover what is underneath the veil; he will be attracted only by the veil. In this case, the veil itself becomes "hot." French nineteenth-century writer Gerard de Nerval was convinced "that it is the veil itself and not the woman concealed beneath it, that attracts" (Dobie 2001: 127), and Orientalist appreciations of the veil have suggested that the woman is not "the interior that needs to be protected or penetrated. Her body is not simply inside of the veil: it is of it; she is constituted in and by the fabrication of the veil" (Yeğenoğlu quoted in Sedira 2003: 70). Faegheh Shirazi notes a similar pattern with regard to those cases where "the veil is exploited to galvanize fantasies of Oriental licentiousness in the reader. The object of desire is the woman under the veil. In some photographs, however, the veil itself functions as object of desire. It becomes a fetish" (Shirazi 2001: 38). Shirazi also thinks of the veil in situations where it is depicted "as a fetish signifying oriental submissiveness." Then "its purpose is to sexually arouse the consumers of *Penthouse* and *Playboy*" (55).

The fetishized veil can also be transformed into a clichéd symbol of unequivocally negative perceptions of Islamic culture. An example is the veil as seen in the propaganda posters of the Western right-wing anti-Muslim movement, which combines a veiled woman with missiles and war motives. It is certainly no coincidence that hoods and balaclavas are also worn by (extremely uncool and "hot") terrorists.

Veiling can either disrupt the process of female fetishization or work in the service of fetishization. Which option is most likely in which situation? Like in the case of tattoos, there is a big difference between a man forcing a woman to wear a veil and a woman who decides to do so on her own, though in the latter case she might still have given in to self-fetishization. Baudrillard writes that women can either be turned into fetishes or they can decide to "perform this labor of continual fetishization on themselves" (1993: 102). When the woman choses to fetishize herself, she will do so by choosing a form that remains appealing to the male. A man putting a veil over a woman is able to control her desires. On the other hand, it is impossible to imagine a man becoming impotent simply because he is confronted with a veil. The woman who decides to get a tattoo clearly disrupts the process of her own phallicization because she destroys her skin's blank surface. Contrary to tattoos (which are practically never applied to penises) the veil emphasizes smoothness and combines a phallic shape with doll-like attributes.

# SPIKES IN THE GULF

A phenomenon clearly confirming the above thesis is the "spike aesthetics" or studded clothing trend that is particularly current in the Arabic/Persian Gulf region. This aesthetic can be interpreted as a "hairy" anti-fetishization device. What interests us most here is that the phenomenon reinforces the link between the veil (which covers hair) and tattoos because, as will be shown, the "spike aesthetics" has ontological functions similar to those of the tattoo.

Within the Middle East, spike fashion is most popular in the Arab United Emirates. True, the edgy fashion trend exists also in the West; however, in conservative Arab countries, studded or spiked jewelry and grommets are attached to the traditional and smooth *abaya*,[1] which gives those spikes a particularly strong metaphorical power. First, the juxtaposition is surprising because, normally, spikes and grommets will be associated with rougher materials such as leather or jeans. Even more surprising is the fact that in Western mainstream fashion the threatening metal hardware is overall more "modest" than in the Gulf. It is in Dubai's malls that the shoulders of devout *abaya*-wearing sisters bear the most exaggerated forms of stegosaurian edginess.

The metaphor of "dangerous hair" could hardly be spelled out more clearly. Where hair cannot be shown, spiky stubbles signal "attention, dangerous woman." The smooth surface of the veil is roughened by explicitly (though probably unconsciously) referring to a fashion vocabulary borrowed from "tough" protagonists such as punks and bikers—thus from those who are also intimately linked to tattoo culture. The spikes are not only shocking and scary, they also represent the most consistent antithesis of the smooth surface as they go symbolically "against the grain." Just like tattoos, those protest spikes must be considered as "anti-fetishization" devices. A further—and perhaps more than metaphorical—link with tattoos is established by the fact that fetishistic and sadomasochistic imagery (which has become more and more visible globally in the last ten years) involves piercing, tattooing, as well as spikes.

The conclusion is that those spikes are hair and tattoo substitutes in a culture where the exposure of both female hair and tattoos remain restricted because the body is consistently covered. In other words, once the veil has made women too smooth, they may apply spikes to make up for the loss of hair. And they might decide to do so because spikes, just like tattoos, interrupt the process of fetishization.

Unwittingly, those young Arab women relate themselves to Muslim punk movements such as the subgenre of punk music dealing with Islam called Taqwacore. Frequently, Muslim punks use spiky hijabs. The combination of Muslim culture with punk is actually more current than most people would

**Figure 1.4.   Spiky *abaya* fashion in the Gulf. Courtesy: Thorsten Botz-Bornstein**

suspect, and Taqwacore is only the arguably most famous example. The Taqwacore movement is inspired by Michael Muhammad Knight's 2004 novel *The Taqwacores*, which was made into a film in 2010. Taqwacore is composed of *taqwa*, which is the Arabic word for piety or "to be God conscious," and "core" like in hard-core punk. Both novel and film are about a Muslim punk collective in Buffalo, New York, consisting of rocambolesque characters: Muslim gays, a burqa-clad punk girl who wrestles with mohawked Sufis, Indonesian skaters, and Muslim skinheads on drugs who use pizza boxes as prayer rugs.[2]

## CONCEALING, CROPPING, CUTTING

The difference between veils and sunglasses should have become clear. The mystery created by sunglasses disrupts fetishization in a much more unequivocal way than the veil because it does not reenact the person in the form of a blank screen. The libidinal economy of sunglasses comes thus closer to that of tattoos. In the case of sunglasses, there is no direct path leading from the glasses to the control of the wearer's desire, while with regard to veiling, such a path exists. Of course, also sunglasses and tattoos *can* become objects of fetishization, but compared to the veil they are much more unlikely to become fetishes.

Sunglasses are thus "cooler" than veils for mainly two reasons: First, the covering of the eyes mystifies the person in a "cooler" way than does the

**Figure 1.5.    Spiky *abaya* fashion in the Gulf. Courtesy: Thorsten Botz-Bornstein**

covering of the mouth. Second, the covering of the eyes is not prone to
fetishization while veils (and this concerns also those veils which leave the
face uncovered) can easily become fetishes. Some might still argue that the
veil can appear as cool because it suppresses information about the face in a
way similar to the technique of cropping (frequently used on Facebook profile pages). Veiling is cool because it makes the person's face appear mysterious. However, first, the cool cropping effect has been designed for the
alteration of immutable *pictures* and not of faces in real life. In pictures, the
look appears to be more stable and much more inscrutable than in real life to
the point that the frozen photo face can function as a cool mask in itself. The
reductive cropping of portraits draws attention to the eyes and makes the
appearance of the face more mysterious; but it becomes so only *as a picture*.
We remember Roland Barthes' desperate attempts at searching the look (in
the eyes) of Japanese General Nogi, victor over the Russians at Port Arthur,
and his wife for signs testifying to the anticipation of their imminent death.
The photos had been taken right before their suicide which they chose because their emperor had died. However, there is no sign of anger in their
eyes, "no adjective is possible, the predicate is dismissed, not by the exemp-
tion of Death's meaning" (Barthes 1993: 94). As they are *posing* for the
photo their pose becomes a cool pose. The conclusion is: A cropped (or

**Figure 1.6.　Taqwacore poster, by Mila Aung-Thwin. Courtesy: Mila Aung-Thwin**

veiled) face *in real life* is not necessarily as cool and mysterious as a cropped face on a photo.

At the same time it must be admitted that cropping techniques, when integrated into the practice of veiling, have the highest potential of producing an effect of "cool veiling" simply because here the veil is allowed to overcome the logic of mere concealing. On the other hand, the logic of the concealing veil is difficult to overcome because, in its history, the veil has most often been construed as a concealing item. In the Franco-Algerian war, for example, the veil could even conceal bombs as its purpose had become to mask the woman in her revolutionary activity. The colonizer strove to unveil the Algerian woman and to remove the concealing item.

The notion of hiding seems to stick to the veil because, obviously, being even more than a dogma, this is its basic purpose. In principle, "hiding" is not even associated with female concepts of shame or honor that many people are inclined to quote immediately when asked about the reasons for veiling. The proof is that the hiding paradigm occurs also with regard to male veiling. Murphy writes this about the Tuareg males who veil: "Given the particularly threatening quality of the interaction situation, the actor is enabled to maintain autonomy and self-esteem. In a very real sense, he is in hiding" (Murphy

1964: 1272). Interestingly, a Tuareg man explained also why males must veil while females don't: "We warriors veil our faces so the enemy may not know what is in our minds, peace or war, but women have nothing to hide" (Brooks 1996: 22). This clearly reverses the common Islamic male and female ethos without discarding the ethos of veiling.

Though the notion of the "concealing veil" is very solid, the concept of the "cropping veil" attempts to deconstruct it. By its nature, cropping follows the logic of cutting much more than that of concealing. Cutting as an act of stylization, that is, as a gesture able to transform any subject into an *aesthetic* subject, has been very much analyzed in the context of Japanese aesthetics and is known as the aesthetics device of *kire* (切れ), which means "cut" in Japanese. In a haiku for example, a line will be cut at a certain point and the stylistic cut invites us to anticipate what "exists" beyond the cut. The purpose of the cut is thus not to *hide* a part of the verse, but rather to produce a new "virtual" verse by cutting off the preceding verse. In this sense the *kire* technique comes close to cropping. It comes also close to Derrida's concept of the frame as a site of meaning (Derrida 1987) that will be explained in chapter 8. The aesthetics of framing sees all art as "inside" a frame simply because it is distinguished from all outside matter and events. The frame highlights, stylizes, and gives symbolical power to the object simply by applying the device of spatial limitation. The limiting "cut" comes also close to what has been rendered in the West most generally as "stylization."

The result of *kire* can be that of the sublime Japanese cultural style called "iki," a phenomenon that has fascinated several Western thinkers including Martin Heidegger.[3] *Iki* is a traditional Japanese aesthetic term often translated as "chic" or "stylish." The word became widespread in modern intellectual circles through Kuki Shūzō's book *The Structure of Iki* (1930). What is "cut off" through *kire* (and which can produce *iki*) is the "everyday context" of an item or a situation, which produces a new and more interesting aesthetic situation. The "cut off" part continues to "exist" but it appears in the form of more stylized and sublime instances.

Sunglasses follow the logic of cutting much more than that of hiding, especially if we think of the unconscious association between the eyes and the male generative powers that have been pointed out by Murphy. This is a further reason why sunglasses are cooler than the veil, which is—in most cases—merely concealing. Like in the case of *kire*, tattoos and sunglasses attempt to disrupt the gaze by disturbing existent structures; they do not merely hide the body's surface, but involve parts of the body in a playful act of stylization.

However, it is not entirely impossible to push also the veil towards such mechanisms of cutting and cropping, though, in general, this remains a difficult undertaking given the religious dogma clinging to the veil as an item whose primary purpose is to protect the woman by hiding parts of her body.

The way many Iranian women wear the veil at present involves an act of stylization that does not seem to be limited to mere concealing. Also, the Indian *sari* attracts because, in the words of Roxanne Gupta, "it is a veil that covers but does not hide" (Gupta 2008: 62). Finally, one can look at the headscarf worn by Western women such as Katharine Hepburn, Jackie Onassis, Brigitte Bardot, Sophia Loren, and Grace Kelly in the 1960s. Here the headscarf relies more on stylization than on hiding; it does not establish a rigid separation between the wearer and the spectator, but functions rather like an accessory similar to jewelry, purses—or sunglasses.

The same is true—though to a lesser extent—in contemporary Muslim "veiling fashion," which attempts to reenact the veil in a modern context through fashionable devices. It is true that in most Muslim countries most veiled women no longer look like nuns before Vatican II. As mentioned in the introduction, the new appropriation of the veil often manages to deconstruct the rigid form of the veil to some extent, especially in Turkey, whose *tesettür* (veiling fashion) is the pet subject of academic researchers. However, the creative input should not be overestimated. In principle, the veil as a religious symbol is incompatible with fashion because fashion is playful by definition. Playing or being playful means to be submitted to the constraints of the game but to be also able to step out of the game (to take off the veil) at any moment. Otherwise it's not a game but work. Anthropological and philosophical definition of games from Johan Huizinga to Mary Midgley highlight this voluntary and liberal stance as one of the fundamentals of the definition of games. It has been said that "play" in a fashion context can never pursue, as Özlem Sandikci and Güliz Ger say about *tesettür* women, a matter of entirely "asexual femininity" freed "from the predatory gaze" (2010: 40). This is the reason why the Muslim veil will always remain "more" than merely a fashion article: It will never be *merely* playful; and this is a problem when it comes to questions about its potential coolness. For "Perihan Mataraci and Serap Cebeci, two covered designers, *tesettür* fashion has been under the dominance of male businessmen who dress women according to their own understanding of religiously appropriate dress" (Olgun 2005, quoted in Sandikci and Ger 2007: 206). According to the same author, "Most of the brand-name *tesettür* companies market clothes that are devoid of elegance, beauty, and aesthetics and force women to dress in a tasteless and uninspiring way" (ibid.). Rajaa Alsanea, Saudi author of the popular novel *Girls of Riyadh*, should thus be taken seriously when making her protagonist Michelle express "how hideous hijab-wearing women usually looked and how the hijab restricted a girl from being fashionable because it also required covering her arms with long sleeves and her legs with long pants or skirts" (Alsanea 2007: 244). Religion is simply too serious and "uncool" to be involved in the game of fashion. A way out of this dilemma is to transform religion into culture or to see religion in less dogmatic terms but more in terms of cultural conventions. An adequate treatment of this subject would require preliminary definitions of religion and culture as well as their relationships, which would transcend the scope of this book.

The headscarf worn by Western women such as Katharine Hepburn has been able to add value to the overall appearance of the woman. The reason is that like tattoos and sunglasses, this veil disrupts the gaze by weaving it into an aesthetic game that the wearer engages in, in order to explore diverse stylistic possibilities. Being coordinated with the rest of the clothes, this headscarf helps create a stylistic unity that can be read in multiple ways, including that of lightness, sport, or cuteness. Most probably it will not lead to one-dimensional readings of the veiled woman in terms of a mere fetish.

The *hijab bo tafkha* ("puffy hijab") is another example of how the veil can be used as a restructuring device by "cutting" or restylizing fixed and traditional structures. It is created with the help of a hairclip to which are attached one or two decorative flowers worn underneath the hijab which yields the impression of having a huge amount of hair. Banu Gökariksel and Anna Secor call it the "bonnet," which enables women "to play with the shape of the veiled head, thus giving rise to the controversial faux bun. To give the veiled head an elongated shape, some women stuff their bonnets with another scarf or other padding. The effect is that of a large bun of hair piled on the back of the head under the scarf" (Gökariksel and Secor 2012: 854).

## CONCLUSION

The hijab worn in the traditional way by many women today in Middle Eastern countries, on the other hand, does not imply a very pronounced act of stylization but is most often limited to mere hiding. Here the veil often *deforms* instead of adding value to the overall stylistic appearance. One problem is that the strict adherence to tradition does not permit the playful attitude necessary for the creation of a personal style found through the veil. Because important parts are simply hidden, the woman's face can adopt a rigid, artificial, waxy, or empty expression. The sculpture-like appearance can easily become sinister. Other ways of applying the veil in a more stylistic way as a means of cool disruption should be explored.

## NOTES

1. The *abaya* is a traditional all-covering black cloak always worn together with the hijab.
2. For more analyses of the Taqwacore phenomenon, see Botz-Bornstein 2014, "Revelation and Seduction: Baudrillard, Tillich, and Muslim Punk."
3. Kuki's *The Structure of Iki* (Kuki Shūzō, *Reflections on Japanese Taste: The Structure of Iki*) has become famous beyond the community of Japanologists mainly because of Heideg-

ger's essay "Aus einem Gepräch über die Sprache" (Heidegger 1959). See also Ohashi 1992 and Botz-Bornstein 1997.

*Chapter Two*

# Veiling and Third Wave Feminism

## *Playing with Fire*

### THE ECONOMY OF THE GAZE

In this chapter, the preceding observations about the distancing aesthetics of the veil will be extended by considering the complex social conditions surrounding the phenomenon of veiling. Coolness, which, in the preceding chapter, was mainly derived from McLuhan's theories of communication, will here be anchored in the African American context from which it evolved in the first place.

Literature on the veiling of women in Muslim contexts is controversial in feminist circles. Some trace the veil back to Islam's "constant highlighting of the conflict between the divine and the feminine" (Mernissi 1991a: 83). Others criticize Western ethnocentric views of the veil and defend it as a symbol of resistance or as a means to bring about equality between the sexes. As mentioned, for some Muslim women "veiling also symbolizes an element of power and autonomy and functions as a vehicle of resistance" (El Guindi 1999: xvii). Those women wear the veil out of protest in order to manifest their rejection of Western pseudo-values such as materialism, consumerism, and commercialism (cf. Minces 1982; Ahmed 1982; Williams and Vashi 2007). In Iran of the late 1970s, in Egypt of the 1980s as well as in Turkey and Algeria, but also, more recently, in Western countries with high rates of Muslim immigration (especially in France), women chose the veil in order to reject Western models of "emphasized femininity" and replace them by a "combative model of femininity" (Moallem 1999: 330). In 1981, Fadwa El Guindi found that "the veil has been adopted by some feminists partly as a symbolic shield against their being treated as sex-objects" (El Guindi 1981:

466). The mothers of those "re-veiled" women did often not veil or had even fought for the right not to veil.

It cannot be denied that many veiled women are oppressed and that others see their veil as neither a symbol of oppression nor of liberation but as a symbol of religious or traditional conformity. In this chapter I want to reflect upon those women who see their veiling as an act of resistance and liberation bearing a link with feminist strategies in general. While much feminist critique defines freedom for women as freedom from veils, it is also possible to define freedom for women as the freedom *to wear* veils. The veil can be seen as an affirmative element, which does not make the woman disappear but more visible. For example, when the stylish magazine *Azizah* presents young veiled women in a modern fashionable context it is said to shape "an American Islamic feminist discourse while creating the beauty and gloss of *Vogue*" (Karim 2005: 169).

My argument is that those pro-veiling positions can be much better understood when being read through Third Wave feminist thought that emerged in late capitalism with a generation of women for whom established, old-school feminists appear out of touch with the contemporary culture of women. The above "freedom to wear veils" theme parallels very precisely the Third Wave theme, which *Bust* magazine editor Debbie Stoller has put like this: "Expecting women to be sexy is one way of oppressing women, while not allowing women to look sexy is another way" (from an interview in Rowe-Finkbeiner 2004: 91).

Third Wave feminism arose in the 1980s and attempted to redefine women and girls as assertive, powerful, and in control of their own sexuality. In principle, one strove "to resist the all too easy oversimplification of second wave feminisms, and . . . to address with frank honesty the difficult and contradictory questions of desire, pleasure, and guilt" (O'Brian 2004: 123). While Second Wave feminists suggest "that oppressive female roles and docile female role-models are still being pushed upon vulnerable female adolescents" (Hopkins 2002: 10) and thus need to be altered, Third Wave feminists accept the social improvements brought about by older generations of feminism but at the same time embrace "the pleasures of 'girliness' and exaggerated femininity" (ibid.). This is how they try to create a new subjectivity in feminist matters. Third Wave feminists reject "the so-called victim feminism of Catherine MacKinnon and Andrea Dworkin with its focus on the danger of rape and women's lack of agency" (Henry 2004: 14) as old-fashioned, moralistic, and too conservative. Instead, they celebrate a right to pleasure, are sexy and strong, and reject the binary logic that opposes feminine and feminist; but they do so by investing a solid amount of flexibility and irony in their discourses and actions. Rebecca Walker writes that the "new feminist loves misogynist hip-hop music, still speaks of her father that abused her, and gets married." The new feminist finds it "too tedious to always criticize world politics, popular culture" (Walker 1998: xxxii–xxxiii).

Apart from the original agenda on sexual politics, Third Wave feminism continues to pursue classical Second Wave feminist issues such as wage discrimination and domestic violence. Today, arguably the most famous Third Wave feminists are FEMEN because they attribute distinct qualities to women and to typically feminine protest, which is incompatible with the positions of Second Wave feminism.

Though "exaggerated femininity" and veiled "combative femininity" appear as antagonistic terms at first sight, parallels become obvious as soon as one adopts a less dogmatic perspective. The "rejection of men" theme, often attributed to Second Wave feminists, is commonly refused by both Muslim and Third Wave feminists. Sajida Alvi explains that "Muslim women are not like those feminists in the West who reject men; they do not wage a war against Muslim men. They are simply becoming more aware of their rights and are learning to be more assertive" (Alvi 2003: 175). Still it is wrong to draw an East–West line and to attribute certain kinds of feminism to certain regions. The idea of Iranian Islamic reformer Zahra Rahnavard that "after all Islam does not demand beauty from a woman" (*Beauty of Concealment and Concealment of Beauty*) sounds very much like Second Wave command. And it is equally wrong to see Third Wave feminism, which sprang very much from a culture of punk-rock and hip-hop, consumerism, and the internet, as being opposed to a culture of veiling as if the latter culture would be current only in self-enclosed and backward areas. Veiled feminists are living in a globalized world that is in many respects similar to that of any feminists. Within this world, feminists of all geographical regions challenge normative gender roles and enrich the range of possibilities that liberated womanhood can obtain.

It is in this context that the combination of "Muslim female assertiveness" with typical Third Wave themes has become an interesting option and has also become more and more visible on the horizon of the international feminist scene. Egyptian feminist Leila Ahmed finds that

> in terms of the level of intellectual liveliness, ferment, and activism, the era we are in today seems to be one that most directly parallels and resembles, in relation now to Muslim American women, the era of extraordinarily dynamic activism and cultural and intellectual productivity which American feminism more broadly—Christian, Jewish, secular, and to some extent Muslim—underwent when second wave feminism vigorously emerged in the 1960s and 1970s. (Ahmed 2011: 278)

Against this background it becomes clear that, though "girliness" and pro-veiling feminism adopt completely different ways of expressing themselves, they do follow similar abstract rules and patterns. In the present chapter I detect parallels between Third Wave feminism and pro-veiling feminism that can be summarized in four points.

First, both organize their fight by looking for means of empowerment in appearance. Veiling is about clothes and also in Third Wave feminism fashion plays a central role, "both in terms of literal fashion—that is, style of dress—and in terms of the desire to be 'in fashion' in a larger sense" (Henry 2004: 124). Still, neither Third Wave nor pro-veiling feminists (see Rahnavard's statement) want to be judged merely by their beauty.

Second, both Third Wave feminism and pro-veiling feminism contradict preceding anti-ideologies, which are anti-sex ideologies of earlier feminist generations for the former and hardline anti-veiling ideologies for the latter. Both decide to invent new ways of organizing their own feminism. In other words, both overemphasize certain stereotypes without becoming "fundamentalist." When Third Wave feminists fight against anti-masculinist ideologies of Second Wave feminists, they claim that "using make-up isn't a sign of your sway to the marketplace and the male gaze; it can be sexy, camp, ironic" (Baumgardener and Richards 2004: 60). In a similar vein, the wearing of the veil by feminists does not necessarily signify that they have given in to blunt Islamic claims. Just like Third Wave feminists use self-exploitative stances in a playful way, self-veiling can refrain from religious seriousness and see itself as an integral part of fashion, identity advertisement, as well as subtle social protest. This is also the reason why a reading of pro-veiling feminism through the Third Wave makes sense in the light of the Third Wave's link with poststructuralist thought. For poststructuralist theory of interpretation, texts and words have no fixed and self-evident meaning; and the veil is not supposed to deliver clear and ultimate meanings either. Very often, the veil, as it is applied in modern life, deconstructs binaries of power and oppression as well as essentialist visions of women and certain feminist positions. Third Wave feminism intends to do exactly this.

Third, Third Wave feminism challenges the Second Wave's unilateral definitions of femininity, which it criticizes as being limited to upper-middle-class white women. It emphasizes the fact that women are of many colors, ethnicities, nationalities, religions, and cultural backgrounds. Also, pro-veiling feminists attempt to find their own way of feminist expressions, paying tribute to their particular history and ethnic conditions. In this sense, parts of pro-veiling feminism should be integrated into Third Wave feminism just like elements of queer theory, anti-racism, postcolonial theory, transnationalism, ecofeminism, or transgender politics have been integrated into Third Wave thought. Nancy Hirschmann regrets that Western feminists commit all too frequently the error "to treat women in different cultures as if they were simply variations on a basic theme defined by white Western middle-class experience" (Hirschmann 1997: 464). Like Western Third Wave feminists, Islamic feminists are critical of any feminism that claims to be inscribed into a global, rationalist, and universalistic order; and both revise the universalism of feminism by introducing elements of cultural diversity. Since Chandra Mohanty's article "Under Western Eyes: Feminist Scholarship and Colonial Discourses" (1988), "postcolonial" branches of feminism have criticized the dominant Western feminist discourse, which reproduces colonial representations of women. Coalitions between Third Wave and Third World women's feminist concerns are desirable and, as writes Denise DeCaires Narain, "the remit of Third Wave feminism needs to be actively reshaped by Third World women's texts and its agenda revived by their interventions" (DeCaires Narain 2004: 250). Some people believe that this is clearly not the case: "If anything can be said with certainty about third wave feminism, it is that it is mainly a first-world phenomenon generated by women who, like their second-wave counterparts, have limited interest in women's struggles elsewhere on the planet," writes Winifred Woodhull (2003, quoted from DeCaires Narain: 242).

The present research thus clearly enters the territory of "Third World feminism," which refuses to take the conditions proposed by first world feminists for granted. I do not prescribe Western feminism as a norm but believe that it needs to be examined whether certain streams of Third World feminism (Islamic feminism, for example) can be integrated as a subgroup into Third Wave feminism. Third World feminism, like postcolonial feminism, focuses on unfamiliar forms of feminism (Jolly 1996:185) and attempts to theorize feminist experiences from the embodied perspectives of third-world women. The present reflection on Third Wave feminism and veiling is doing exactly this. Postcolonial feminism in particular undertakes cross research into gender, race, and class problems. The typically "postmodern" slant questioning the notion of a unitary self-aware subject capable of making unambiguous and universal choices, in a word, the weakening of the subject, is part of this project.

Fourth, while the "weakening of the subject" is meant to deconstruct dualisms without inviting brainwashing, both Third Wave and pro-veiling feminisms are in constant danger of succumbing to diverse forms of false consciousness. Deborah Siegel mentions

> hundreds of younger women [who] dress like Playboy bunnies (minus the tail), posing, some might say, as feminists, flaunting their hot pants and peek-a-boo thongs as proof of their empowerment, French kissing other women while male "guests" watch. An outside observer might ask whether this new empowerment is any different from the old objectification. Why call such sexed-up behavior "liberated" and "feminist" and not what it looks like: false consciousness or even, to use an even more outdated-sounding term, "oppression?" (Siegel 2007: 157)

For two reasons the paradigm of the "veil as protest" can result in similar racialized and commodified forms of "feminism": First, it can be hijacked by fundamentalism; second, like any feminism, it can be reduced to mere life-style and fashion choices. Companies specializing in veiling fashion produce consumerist micro-trends for the global Islamic market propagating a certain type of femininity.

It is also important to insist that in many parts of the world veiled women (and even "self-veiling" women) do *not* refrain from religious seriousness. I am not saying in this book that all veiling is "Third Wave Veiling," but only that this phenomenon *can* exist. In some countries "self-veiled" women do *not* see themselves as an integral part of fashion, identity advertisement, or subtle social protest but perceive veiling in religious terms. In chapter 3, Kuwait will be presented as such a place. Apart from that, the "self" in "self-veiling" is a rather ambiguous entity and should never be taken for granted either.

Nor am I suggesting that the Western Third Wave and pro-veiling feminism are historically linked. Historically, both phenomena cannot be compared. The causal inferences that have led Western countries from one wave of feminism to the other do not exist in the Middle East. According to Third Wavers, old style feminism became pointless in the West while in the Middle East, Second Wave feminism is far from being pointless. Feminism in Middle Eastern countries is overburdened with the double task of simultaneously contesting global capitalism *and* historically entrenched Islamic patriarchies. However, it is just because these matters are so complex that I find a discussion of Third Wave motives, such as the ironic play with objectification, useful and, finally, conducive to the realization of a progressive (i.e. democratic, anti-patriarchal, and anti-imperialist) feminist agenda in this region. Through the logic of Third Wave feminism we can understand that the veil *can* be empowering (or also the contrary). Sex-positive feminism and veiling-positive feminism are not binary oppositions but both borrow from each other and are related by a sense of irony as well as a certain fractured consciousness.

It is clear that any comparison of Third Wave feminism with veiling practiced in Islamic culture is bound to simplify Third Wave feminism. Third Wave feminism is not a unified movement but evolves on a constant basis through internal discussions. One issue raised by critics of Third Wave feminism is its apparent lack of a single cause. However, in the context of the present project, common intellectual patterns can be crystallized only by extracting, in a schematic fashion, from Third Wave feminism its most principal features.

## "PRO-VEILING FEMINISM"

The term "pro-veiling feminism" is my own invention. It became necessary in order to address a particular pattern that is not entirely covered by, and does not cover, certain branches of feminism. In spite of the overlaps pointed out previously, the Middle Eastern world has created its own feminisms without merely deriving its ideologies from Western models. In principle, Western and Middle Eastern feminisms are confronted with very different social contexts, which let women's issues in Middle Eastern cultures follow different historical paths. While in the West, questions of universal suffrage and women's right to education and work are no longer acute, Muslim feminists still negotiate issues of identity, mobility, and independence. However, the different contexts also produce different views of the relationship between men and women. Minoo Moallem explains, for example, that "while Western egalitarian feminism emerged claiming a subject position within the pervasive masculinism . . . , Islamic fundamentalism opposes the assimilatory forces of modernity, modernization, and Westernization to claim cultural uniqueness and difference" (1999: 324). It is clear that critiquing Western masculinism and critiquing anti-Western Islamic masculinism inspired by religious fundamentalism are two different things.

First of all, pro-veiling feminism is not the equivalent of Islamic feminism. Islamic feminism emerged in the early 1990s when some Muslim feminists began to interpret feminist problems through rereadings of the Qur'an and other religious texts and attempted to reconcile Islamic faith with international human rights. Asma Barlas, Leila Ahmed, and Fatima Mernissi are Islamic or Muslim feminists. Islamic feminism has always valued religion, which makes it very different from Western feminism. Using readings of the Qur'an, they argue that Islam is inherently gender-equal. They go back to a prestate Islam, in which women were influential in shaping the religion and its rules. Islamic feminism exercises considerable influence via the dissemination of publications and through grassroots social movements (Read and Barkowski 2000: 398).

Still, Islamic feminism should not be seen as a Third Wave movement, especially not in the light of extremely conservative initiatives that call themselves "feminist" in Saudi Arabia and that are different from the Islamic feminism practiced by Ahmed and Mernissi. John Bradley reports of

> those women—a cross section of doctors, businesswomen, professors, artists, housewives, and social workers—[who] want to reach back to the ancient roots of Islamic law, viewing the Prophet's era as the golden age of women's rights. Before Muhammad, women on the Arabian Peninsula were considered chattel, inherited along with land or livestock. Some Saudi historians who are women now believe that the Prophet's own tribe initially opposed elevating their status. His favorite wife, Aisha, led men in battle. (Bradley 2005: 178)

Sherin Saadallah wants to see Muslim (Islamic) feminism "as a third wave feminist movement" (2004: 218). The reason is that Islamic feminists have always very radically argued for full gender equality and empowerment of women not only in the public but also in the religious sphere (Badran 2009: 33).

However, not all feminists in Islam are Islamic feminists. The second trend in Muslim feminism is secular and explicitly part of the movement to modernization and democratization. Muslim secular feminists (who engage with international human rights and whose discourse is entirely grounded outside religion) predate Islamic feminists. As a matter of fact, it was Muslim secular feminists who coined the term Islamic feminism (Badran 2009: 9). Muslim secular feminists favor the separation of civil laws from religious rules and insist on gender equality also with regard to marriage, divorce, child custody, and inheritance.

Of course, mixtures of both ideologies are frequent and radicalism is not the rule. Further, the task of identifying feminist values is complicated by internal contradictions. There are self-veiled women who touch upon themes most typically embraced by feminist sensibilities but who refuse to identify with any sort of feminism. In Turkey, for example, the commonly called "veiled feminists . . . do not want to be called feminists, and neither do they want to emphasize gender in their way of thinking" (Sakaranaho 2008: 53). Ideas that "feminism describes a war against men and Islam, waged by Western and Westernized bourgeois women, advocating sexual promiscuity" (Rhouni 2010: xi), or that Western feminism has alienated women from their true nature because it is merely fighting against men, are still current in Muslim countries. More paradoxically, there are others who have achieved feminist goals by employing counter-feminist strategies or by fraternizing with the patriarchal enemy. Margot Badran explains that "women, normally excluded from the Islamic establishment, have joined the ranks of more radical, populist fundamentalist movements. The women leaders in such movements have taken on daring social and political roles while acquiescing in an ideology that contradicts their own conduct as activists" (Badran 2009: 45). Similar to this category is Islamist (not Islamic) feminism which emerged from the socially and intellectually conservative Islamist movement Al Harakat Al-Islamiyya and which understands women to be "oppressed precisely because they try to be 'equal' to men" (Saadallah 2004: 218). The Islamist arguments are reflections of "neo-patriarchal attitudes, delineating a conservative rather than a progressive attitude to change" (ibid.).

It needs to be pointed out that there is also a Western pro-veiling feminist position, which remains linked to Second Wave patterns and which is not a movement but rather an often-voiced position. This position is adopted by Western feminists who defend veiling on a feminist basis. Martha Nussbaum is such an example. In her often-quoted article "Veiled Threats?" she commits a strange inverted *tu quoque* fallacy (which could be called the *nos quoque* fallacy) by equating plastic surgery with veiling, saying that since *we* remodel our faces, we cannot criticize *them* because they are veiling: "Isn't much of this done in order to conform to a male norm of female beauty that casts women as sex objects? Proponents of the burqa ban do not propose to ban all these objectifying practices. Indeed, they often participate in it" (Nussbaum 2010). True, plastic surgery is bad (in many cases at least) and worse than veiling. However, Nussbaum's radical opposition of objectification versus non-objectification does not indicate an exit out of this situation beyond mere confrontation.

The landscape sketched above makes clear that links between feminism and the veil are not straightforward but complex. Not all Muslim feminists who veil are Islamic feminists. Many of those who call themselves Islamic feminists are even opposed to veiling (most prominently Fatima Mernissi and Margot Badran). An interesting phenomenon is Huda Sha'rawi's early and metaphorical "feminist hijab" described by Badran. Egyptian feminist pioneer Sha'rawi, famous for publicly removing her face veil in 1923, also removed her head covering but, interestingly, kept it for her "official" portrait (Badran 2009: 230). The term "pro-veiling feminists" includes all those who self-veil on grounds that can be identified as feminist in the broadest sense.

## IRONY AND AMBIVALENCE: THE METAPHORICAL VEIL

As mentioned, Third Wave feminism defines women as assertive and powerful but at the same time as being in control of their own sexuality. A certain ambivalence is thus at the root of Third Wave's own definition. Third Wave feminists do not imitate men but empower themselves by asserting their own feminine attributes, that is, by distinguishing themselves from men in the most obvious manner. This can result in the cute but powerful girl-woman but also in other established strong female types like the femme fatale. Even girliness can be a source of power, which used to be unthinkable for earlier generations of feminists. In a similar vein, pro-veiling feminists present women as assertive and powerful but use a visual vocabulary that Second Wave feminists would have found incompatible with any sort of feminist thinking: the veil.

Metaphorically speaking, Third Wave feminists do re-veil: they put on the veil of femininity that their Second Wave mothers had once shed. By taking off the veil of femininity, Second Wave feminists believed to reveal the universal truth of the equality of the sexes. Third Wave feminists put the veil of femininity back on their heads but not before redefining it as a sign of empowerment instead of oppression. They believe that the unveiled state of their personalities had constrained their individuality and that their femininity had been curbed by Second Wave's long list of rules and regulations. Third Wave feminists believe that the feminine veil will make their feminine nature more manifest, which they interpret as a sign of empowerment.

Third Wave feminism is against the objectification of women; still, they chose to assert their female attributes, an assertion that Second Wave feminists had once read as an act of objectification. Even the objectification of fashion models is seen by some Third Wave feminists as potentially empowering (cf. Hopkins 2002: 104). Slut Walks illustrate this new feminist logic. The first Slut Walk took place in Toronto on April 3, 2011, in response to Toronto police officer Michael Sanguinetti's statement that "women should avoid dressing like sluts in order not to be victimized." The protests, which have since been held in cities all over the word, took the form of a march, mainly by young women, many of whom dressed provocatively. The purpose of Slut Walks is to clarify that victimized women are *not* sluts because if they were, then all women must be sluts, since anyone can be victimized regardless of what they are wearing. Third Wave feminists who participate in Slut Walks overemphasize thus in an ironic fashion a negative stereotype. The strategy is current in certain parts of Third Wave feminism where the connotations of sexist words such as "spinster," "bitch," "whore," and "cunt" are changed into positive terms, as has most obviously been shown by Elizabeth Wurtzel in her book *Bitch: In Praise of Difficult Women* (1998).

The following chapter on veiling and coolness will show that pro-veiling feminists follow a similar strategy: Pro-veiling feminists use the practice of veiling, which has "historically underpinned patriarchal oppression, to subvert patriarchy and assert themselves as autonomous believers" (Hoodfar 2001: 421, quoted from Laborde 2006: 366) and subvert masculinist practices "by turning its norms against itself" (Hirschmann 1997: 486). In other words, in order to encounter sexism, the re-veiled woman sexualizes herself even more, which is exactly how Third Wave feminists suggest reading objectification during a Slut Walk. In Third Wave feminism, it is important that the semantic reversal takes place in a context of irony: "Various aspects of girlie culture use the humorous reappropriation of traditions and symbols to craft identities in the context of structural disempowerment" (Heywood and Drake 2004: 16). Humor is the key to success.

It has been said that "Third Wave co-opt the male gaze" as they appropriate "signifiers of masculine power for their own amusement" (Owen, Stein, and Vande Berg 2007: 126) and that for Third Wavers the "male gaze is now internalized" (Zaslow 2009: 58). Self-veiling follows the same pattern: The patriarchal perspective is adopted (though along ludic lines) and can even be pushed through stances of (Western) fashion and makeup that are normally incompatible with traditional ideologies of veiling. Second Wave foremothers told their daughters that any fashion interest signifies that they are dupes of patriarchy. For Second Wave fundamentalist anti-fashion ideologists the only way leading towards the equality of sexes was "to reject Barbie and all forms of pink packaged femininity" (Baumgardener and Richards 2004: 61). This is how Second Wave feminists burned bras and high heels—but their Third Wave daughters put all those items back on. Similarly, an earlier generation of Islamic feminists had taken the veil off, while at present their daughters put it back on. In both cases the "enemy" is the (capitalist, imperialist or Islamic, fundamentalist) patriarch. The "re-veiled" woman contests the soundness of the pseudo-liberated woman associated with Westernization and goes for a positive identity brought about by veiling. This parallels the arguments that Third Wave feminists hold against their Second Wave mothers. At the same time, Third Wave feminists refuse to succumb to fundamentalist attitudes declaring war on all men. Instead of becoming Puritans, they establish their own code of moderation, which functions very much through the devices of irony and moral ambivalence.

## PLAYING WITH FIRE

At first sight, pro-veiling feminism and Third Wave feminism appear as opposites. Pro-veiling feminists cover themselves, while Third Wave feminists are able to include the taking off of clothes into their repertory of most efficient strategies. Third Wave feminists are not modest, while in Islam, covering is perceived as modest. It is true that in many contexts, those oppositions still pertain. In French immigrant ghettos, for example, young women are forced to veil (most of the time by their brothers) and see the wearing of fashionable, revealing clothes as a sign of protest. If they *have* to wear the veil, "make-up has become for them a sort of war paint, a sign of resistance" (Amara 2004: 50), which can, once again, be interpreted in terms of a confrontation of veiling and Third Wave feminism.

However, in a postmodern context, those opposites are beginning to be deconstructed. Tuula Sakaranaho writes that educated women, by veiling themselves, "blur the clear-cut opposition between religion and modernity and also question the notion of women's emancipation" (Sakaranaho 2008: 52). This means that the veil as a means of empowerment is no longer necessarily a gesture of mere modesty. Pamela Taylor complains that much of political Islam believes that the hijab "is all about modesty, not about rejecting the objectification of women or about her demanding to be viewed on the basis of character" (P. Taylor 2008: 124). Here there is a parallel with Third Wave feminism. There are further parallels that are even more directly linked to "Islamic" themes such as gender segregation. "Girl Power [feminists] endorse and value female friendships, even over and above the pressure to get (and bother about) boyfriends," says Christine Griffin (2004: 33), which does not seem to be incompatible with "modest" pro-veiling attitudes. Even the punk-related Riot Grrrl underground feminist movement has insisted on gender separatism (Rosenberg and Garofalo 1998). As a matter of fact, here both pro-veiling and Third Wave join discussions that were typical for typical Second Wavers who also suggested gender segregation.

Another apparent opposition that needs to be deconstructed is the idea of Third Wave feminists as of women who are "at war with men," which is one of the reasons why feminism in general is held as suspicious by many women in Middle Eastern cultures. Surprisingly, Third Wave sympathizer and writer Naomi Wolf extracts from bridal magazines the concept of a mystical "Brideland" that stylizes brides as princesses and in which "men worship the goddess of female sexuality once again." Wolf compares the veil worn by brides with the hymen and claims that "the dream of a formal wedding . . . demonstrates on some level how barren the world is for women when female sexuality is stripped of its aura." In this article that has been published in an academic book, Wolf suggests that we have perhaps "lost the sense of value of female sexuality" (Wolf 1995: 340). Wolf's highlighting of women's modesty in the context of (Third Wave) feminism is surprising, to say the least. Is it along those complicated lines that Third Wave feminism and pro-veiling feminism might finally join hands?

All feminists have in common that they want to be recognized as equal with men. Being invisible in the company of men, or being visible only as sex symbols and not as rational beings is unacceptable. Pro-veiling feminists cover their heads for that purpose. Third Wave feminists do not refuse to be visible as sexual beings but they make it clear that their sexuality is highly self-controlled: It is only a "veil." This is how they attempt to obtain their status as equal partners. Third Wave feminists use their "sexuality" merely as a marker and not as an objectified commodity because they are able to interpret sexuality in a twofold manner. Pro-veiling feminists use the veil as a marker and hope that it will not be perceived as an objectified commodity. It is clear that both are playing with fire: Both veil and sexuality can easily switch from devices of liberation to devices of oppression. Pro-veiling-feminist Pamela Taylor donned the veil because she saw it as a "proactive, feminist statement." However, she is aware that many other Muslims perceive the hijab "not as a liberation from objectification, but merely as a substitute for its other forms" (P. Taylor 2008: 124). She knows that many people will simply put her down as oppressed. In parallel, Third Wave feminists are aware that people might treat them as "real" sluts.

## "WOMEN ARE DANGEROUS"

Both Third Wavers and pro-veiling feminists put forward signifiers of femininity in order to empower themselves. Here *both* are opposed to Second Wave feminists who attempt to eliminate their femininity and see the masculinization of the feminine as the primary goal through which the equality of genders will be established. Third Wave feminists put forward their sexuality, which is well controlled but still clearly visible. Seen from this perspective, Third Wave feminists can appear as the opposite of pro-veiling feminists: The latter's sexual appeal appears as reduced to the level of Victorian women who were powerless because they were "told that all sexual impulse is wrong," as writes historian Peter Stearns (Stearns 1994: 18). However, even in this case, the conclusion must be that *if* they are veiled in order to hide their sexuality, they are still sexual beings in the first place.

It has been shown above that it is possible to overcome the erroneous view that establishes veiling and Third Wave feminism as opposites, the view which holds that veiled women hide their feminine attributes under a modest veil while the latter are simply showing them off. In order to continue the comparison of empowerment through the emphasis of female attributes on the one hand, and veiling on the other, it will be necessary to distinguish two kinds of pro-veiling feminists: those who believe that the veil needs to be worn in order to protect women from men (PWM) and those who believe that the main purpose of the veil is to protect men from women (PMW). In an Islamic context, the PWM coalition perceives women as a source of *awrah* (shame) while the PMW coalition believes that women are a dangerous source of *fitna* (roughly translated as "chaos" provoked by women's sexuality).

Traditionally, in Islamic culture the female body has been seen as a source of both *fitna* and *awrah* and veiling has been recommended for both reasons. The "protect women from men" view, expressed by many pro-veiling militants when calling attention to the uniquely masculine penchant for untamed sexual activity, approaches positions of Second Wave feminists because they define men as dangerous and require women's protection. Curiously, this means that Second Wave feminism shares here some of the positions of patriarchal anti-feminism. An obsession with rape and rape prevention is indeed what Second Wave and Islamic fundamentalists have in common.

The Protect Men from Women position, on the other hand, holds that women are dangerous. It rests on the idea that men and society are threatened by women, by women's nature, as well as by women's desires and the related temptations. "The 'dangerous feminine' has been central to the scholars' view of gender relations in the past, and it remains the heart and staple of conservative discourse today," writes Lynda Clarke (Clarke 2003: 125). "Dangerous hair" (see chapter 1) plays a prominent role here.

The PMW view can easily adopt double standards because, in the end, men might not be held responsible for *their own* "dangerous" acts: it is rather the unveiled woman who sparked the poor man's instincts. To "protect men from women" often means to charge women with taming men's sexuality and accusing them should they not succeed. The PMW position can appear as the contrary of PWM, but in reality both are linked and represent a unity.

In principle, the PMW position (together with its paradoxical alliance with the PWM position) is not peculiar to Middle Eastern culture. Sarah Kofman has shown that both Immanuel Kant and Jean-Jacques Rousseau believed that women "have the tendency to dominate and the tendency to please, and this mainly in public (in a way that makes it possible to liken the second character trait to the first: by trying to please, the woman always wants to prevail over any rival)" (Kofman 1982). Men best address this danger "by introducing a separating distance between themselves and women, by forcing themselves to stay clear of women." More precisely, men must place "women on a throne by making them goddesses or queens." The hypocritical play with PWM and PMW (or with *awrah* and *fitna*) in a Western context will be examined in chapter 4 by relying on Kofman's reflections.

At the same time it is true that the PMW position manifests similarities with Third Wave feminism. Abolhassan Banisadr, Iran's first elected post-revolution president allegedly shared the PMW position when saying that "concealing female hair says more about men's sexual anxiety than about the seductive power of women" (Zahedi 2008: 259). Faegheh Shirazi confirms this by writing that "by focusing on the proper hijab for female protagonists, the government censors reveal their concern for the purity of the male spectator" (Shirazi 2001: 69).

The "women are dangerous" view can even be extended to the concrete social sphere reaching beyond sexual metaphors. Islamic feminist Bahithat al-Badiya believes that men are afraid of women because "the day we are educated we shall push them out of work and abandon the role for which God created us" (Badran 2009: 81). Muslim women in French ghettos who are forced by their brothers to veil appear to be trapped in exactly this constellation, as has been very graphically shown by French activist Fadela Amara in her book *Ni Putes ni soumises* (2004).

However, before developing this line of thought, it is necessary to contrast the above branches of pro-veiling patriarchisms (both PWM and PMW) with the curious stance of what can be called "anti-veiling patriarchism." In 2003, French president Jacques Chirac pointed out in a speech that "wearing the veil, whether it is intended or not, is a kind of aggression." Joan Scott interprets Chirac's anti-veiling statements not in merely political terms (as a defense of secularism) but reads it in terms of *fitna*. For Scott, there is "an oblique reference to the hidden danger of women's re-pressed sexuality. Out there to see, women's sexuality was manageable; unseen, it might wreak havoc" (Scott 2007: 158). What is dangerous is not sexuality but *repressed* sexuality. The sexual economy should be more transparent; otherwise it becomes dangerous. Further, Scott believes that Chirac perceives veiling as an act of "denying (French) men the pleasure—understood as a natural right (a male prerogative)—to see behind the veil. This was taken to be an assault on male sexuality, a kind of castration. Depriving men of an object of desire undermined the sense of their own masculinity" (159). The "veil as castration" paradigm is original. Here the veil becomes such a powerful instrument because men perceive women's hiding of the body as an attack of their masculinity. If with anything, this "castrating" attitude is more compatible with certain Second Wave feminist approaches than with Third Wave feminism. And it seems to be a peculiarity not expressed by feminists but occurring in Western male perceptions of the veil.

It is necessary to analyze the particularly ambivalent character of veiling at the moment it is justified by *fitna*. Similar to the Christian assumption of the temptress nature of Eve, Islam assumes that women are "powerful and dangerous beings" (Mernissi 1991b: 19), that they can be a source of corruption to the social order and should therefore be confined in a separate sphere: "Learned Islamic texts and popular belief hold that women possess enormous sexual appetites (far greater than those of men), and that women's whole being, body and voice constitutes a sexualized entity," writes Badran (2009: 170). Mernissi identifies a theory that has an *active* conception of female sexuality from which men must be protected (Mernissi 1991b), though she also points out that Islam's explicit theory of female sexuality considers it to be passive.

Passive? It has been shown above that passivity itself is ambivalent. Female passivity can be guided by the will to power and even its most "innocent" charm is related to sexuality. This is also part and parcel of Western culture. Kofman explains that women are bound to win "precisely because of their weakness; it's the weakness that disarms men, forces them to respect them and deliver a whole series of other compensations; women buy the right to respect through their weakness, a protective measure that the strong impose upon the weak" (Kofman 1982). The conclusion is that women are *really* dangerous. This is why the ruling Iranian fundamentalists seem to consider "the individual identity of women as the most perilous threat to their enduring power" (Kar 2006: 32).

While any intention to cover women because they equate danger and chaos sounds anti-feminist, it is also certain that the concept of *fitna* contradicts the objectification of women by definition. As a matter of fact, it depicts women as active and powerful agents who *cannot* be objectified. Objects are passive but women (even when veiled) remain powerful and active subjects. The equation of women with *fitna* implies a sex-positive statement and is thus, in principle, compatible with Third Wave feminism. True, Third Wave feminists want to openly celebrate the sex-positive aspect while pro-veiling feminists (must) hide their sexuality under a veil. However, both strategies can and often do imply elaborate ironic enactments. As has been explained above, Third Wave feminists wear their sexuality *like a veil*. In parallel, pro-veiling feminists can wear their veil *as sexuality.*

The "women are dangerous" theme is current in Third Wave feminism and has even appeared in exaggerated ways in popular perceptions. A certain cultural shift to a new aggressive woman in popular films and advertisements as well as a "cultural fascination with images of women who know how to shoot and fight," (McCaughey 1997: 5) especially in Japanese *manga*, has been noted. An article by the BBC called "Men Cringe as Adverts Show 'Girl Power,'" shows sexist advertisements by Lee jeans in which dominant women are threatening men. A woman wearing stiletto-heeled boots rests her toe on the naked buttocks of a prostrate man. The text reads: "Put the boot in." Similarly sexist ads have been published by Nissan, whose advertising agency defended the strategy by stating that "it's about saying women are feeling much stronger than ever before and if they want to react in the way they choose then they are free to do that" (BBC 1997).

In spite of the crudeness of the message one should not forget that this is only an advertisement and an image, and that it does not openly proclaim female violence against men. In Rebecca Walker's Third Wave classic *To Be Real*, Naomi Wolf provides the more straightforward example of young Indian women who have armed themselves with baseball bats in order to defend a train's women-only section and who "beat the shit out of any men who tried to enter the women's section. First World feminism has to take that basic step" (Wolf 1995: 340). And Veena Cabreros-Sud, in her article from the same volume entitled "Kicking Ass," plays with the idea of a "woman's response to violence with violence" (Cabreros-Sud 1995: 44). More recent books combining feminist theory with women's self-defense in order to make "feminism physical" (cf. McCaughey 1997) confirm this tendency.

It is probably concepts like these that deter Islamic feminists from Western feminism, which they often construe as a "war of women against men." In the Lee jeans advertisement, women are using their (sexual) power in order to dominate men and, for obvious reasons, the BBC reporter links this strategy to Girl Power. However, the "war against men" theme is rather a Second Wave motive. Third Wave feminism is not as violent as the above examples pretend but, as mentioned, the "sexuality as veil" technique uses irony and play as primary devices.

How does *pro-veiling feminism* handle irony and play? If men veil women because they believe them to be dangerous, the result will be a one-dimensional model of patriarchy. However, if women voluntarily don the veil because they deem it necessary to protect men from themselves, the strategy becomes highly ironic because this sort of veiling implies two messages at the time: (1) be assured because I have put on the veil and will not attack you sexually; (2) don't you ever forget that I *am* dangerous, which is the reason why I put on the veil. The two kinds of veiling parallel the two kinds of objectification pointed out by Third Wave feminists: objectification with power and objectification without power (cf. Zaslow 2009: 58). The "veiling with power" scenario looks very much like that of a sexually aggressive man who is openly wearing a chastity belt. The message is twofold: I cannot rape you because I am wearing the belt; but the fact that I am wearing this belt in the first place clearly advertises my primary sexual intentions.

Self-veiling with the aim of protecting men overlaps very much with the general tendency of Third Wave feminist strategies. Pro-veiling feminists reinforce the assumption that women are *fitna*. However, would the veil merely de-eroticize the female body, it would follow the pattern of Second Wave feminism or Mao-suits of the Chinese cultural revolution. It would attempt to establish the woman as an equal partner through this very act of de-feminization. However, because the veil simultaneously sexualizes the body, it works in the service of feminine empowerment through sexualization, which is part and parcel of Third Wave feminism.

The fallacies of veiling motivated by *awrah*, on the other hand, have frequently been pointed out. Similar to Rousseau only much later, the Persian poet Hussayn al-Azri (1880–1954), after explaining that male–female relations are basically like wolf–lamb relations, recommends women outside their homes to ignore men and give men short and polite answers in order to protect themselves. In reaction to this text, Faegheh Shirazi wonders how a "meek lamb can prevent a wolf from ravishing her just by ignoring him or by giving him short and polite answers" (Shirazi 2001: 140). Shirazi shows how the cofounder of the Egyptian national movement, Qasim Amin (1863–1908), "reverses al-Azri's binary oppositions of seducer/seduced, hunter/hunted, and strong/weak [and] makes women the seducers, the hunters, and the strong" (143).

The moral input on which self-veiling depends must be seen as ambivalent, a point that brings it so close to Third Wave feminism. Naturally, the woman is endowed with a fatal attraction, which she perfectly controls to the point of no longer employing her power with the intention of attracting men. Would she want to attract men, this would indeed objectify her and possibly make her dependent. However, the pro-veiling feminist, just like the Third Wave feminist, does not really want the man—her aim is merely to demonstrate sexual power, as says Susan Hopkins: "It's not about trapping a man; it's about demonstrating personal power" (Hopkins 2002: 102). Third Wavers do not care what men might think of them. High heels and makeup are conceived of as self-sufficient expressions of power. What matters most is the display of power over men as an end in itself: "The power of being 'attractive' is no longer fixed to heterosexual practices and desires. Beauty techniques such as make-up and fashion are appreciated as power strategies in their own right" (Hopkins: 93).

Pro-veiling feminism and Third Wave feminism are not opposed to each other because the former would hide the woman's sexual power under the veil while the latter intends to expose it. Both base their entire economy on the fact that the woman *is* sexually powerful and potentially dangerous for men. And both want to exercise this power without having the intention to "trap a man." This is why Joan Scott interprets the veil as "a sexual provocation and a denial of sex, a come-on and a refusal" (Scott 2007: 60).

The assumption that women are dangerous for men is unacceptable for Second Wave feminists, who would identify such assumptions with patriarchal positions. For Second Wavers it is *men* who are dangerous: "Much of the lesbian feminism and cultural feminism that came out of this movement increasingly focused on the dangers of male sexuality and the need to protect women from its harm" (Henry 2004: 86). The curious overlap of this segregative ideology with that of patriarchal Islam has been previously pointed out. It shows that an Islamic feminist like Leila Ahmed, who insisted already in the 1980s that segregated society "allows men considerably less control over how women think" (cf. Ahmed 1982: 528), can best be identified as a Second Wave feminist; but her perspective is also highly incompatible with Third Wave points of view. More discussion on segregation in various societies will come in chapter 5.

Third Wave feminists agree with patriarchs that women are dangerous but instead of hiding their fangs they put forward their femininity with all its "dangerous" implications. In other words, they use *fitna* not in order to provoke general chaos but, first of all, to provoke the patriarchal order. Some self-veiling women have chosen exactly this approach, and this brings them close to Third Wave feminism.

Both Third Wave and pro-veiling use *fitna* in an ironic fashion, a strategy that many patriarchs have difficulties to grasp. Second Wave women mean really "no" when they say "no" and they are annoyed when their "no" is interpreted as a "yes." Third Wave women say "yes" but they mean "no." Similarly, pro-veiling feminists use the veil as "a sexual provocation and a denial of sex, a come-on and a refusal" (Scott 2007: 60).

Third Wavers reply to their Second Wave mothers that they are wearing their femininity merely like a veil, which means that this femininity is not supposed to be "real." It is rather to be read as a game full of ambivalence and ironic connotations. Pro-veiling feminists might wear the veil with similar intentions: not as a "real" item charged with past connotations. Since the veil no longer *necessarily* promotes Islamic-style submission (or even sexual exploitation) it is not exaggerated to say that in some cases the veil has become the equivalent of a tattoo. Consider this comment from a twenty-five-year-old American woman:

> On my upper left arm I have a six-inch long tattoo of a voluptuous cowgirl. One of her hands rests jauntily on her hip. The other is firing a gun. An earlier feminist might frown upon my cowgirl's fringed hot pants and halter top as promoting sexual exploitation, and might see her pistol as perpetuating male patterns of violence. Yet I see this image as distinctly feminist. Having a tattoo signifies a subculture that subverts traditional notions of feminine beauty. (Owen et al. 2007: 106)

The woman's tattoo presents female sexuality combined with combative violence, not shying away from the presentation of a phallic pistol for feminist purposes. Yet the entire metaphor comes packaged in the form of a tattoo, which is, in itself, a highly ambivalent symbol of female emancipation. As I have shown, the veil, when used as an identity-loaded fashion item, can follow similarly torturous lines of signification.

## VEILING AND NUDISM

Girl Power, Slut Walks, tattoos, and sexist advertisement humiliating men might appear to be a far cry from what happens in the Muslim world today, but the above explanations have shown that pro-veiling feminism can indeed be interpreted as a sort of Girl Power. Further scrutiny will demonstrate that the lines along which female empowerment works in Arab societies run even more closely in parallel with Third Wave empowerment than one would assume in the first place. In October 2011, a twenty-year-old Egyptian feminist woman named Aliaa El Mahdy posted a nude photo of herself on her Facebook page, asking those who oppose her act to burn their own bodies that they obviously so much despise in order to "rid yourself of your sexual complexes." Three months later, a young Iranian actress living in France, Golshifteh Farahani, posed half naked for *Madame Figaro* magazine and appeared topless in a short video clip produced by the French fashion photographer Jean-Baptiste Mondino. Both women put forward their public nudity as an act of liberation and emancipation claiming the ownership of their bodies. El Mahdy declared on her blog:

> Women are objects in many conservatives' views. Things that can be owned and used for a man's pleasure when he desires and when he wants. This is why we have seen the growth of polygamy, the shoving aside of a woman's ability to choose her life's goals, and the unending "debate" over the causes of sexual harassment and sexual assault.

El Mahdy keeps a questionnaire about the hijab on her website, which shows how closely her nudity is linked to the theme of veiling (or rather un-veiling). In her article "Who Is Afraid of Aliaa's Nudity?" blogger Sara Emiline Abu Ghazal does not hesitate to analyze El Mahdy's actions in terms of female empowerment. El Mahdy has also received various comments, and those who put forward the threatening and dangerous character of the female body (in a critical or affirmative way) are numerous.

Naked protests are closely linked to Slut Walks, and El Mahdy's strategy must be read within the logic of Third Wave feminism. Lesbian Third Waver Jocelyn Taylor explains the meaning of nudity as a means of protest when fantasizing

> about riding an army of naked women on horseback down Constitution Ave. in Washington, DC. The nudity is an important part of the fantasy because it's a strong and fearless image that we do not believe that our bodies are inferior or ugly, or open to assault of any kind. An army of women is a force that will not lie on its back passively while others eroticize and differentiate. (J. Taylor 1995: 234)

El Mahdy perceives clothes (as well as veiling) as items that sexualize and objectify the normally not sexualized body. There she is in company not necessarily with Third Wavers but rather with classical European nudists from the 1920s who insisted that "shamefaced petit bourgeois and religious attitudes toward the body had to be discarded" (J. Williams 2007: 25). El Mahdy's thoughts, sparked by her uproar against prudish Egyptian society, are also similar to those that have been expressed in the context of Islamic veiling debates. Marnia Lazreg finds that when a mother "wraps a scarf over her young daughter, [she] conveys to her the belief that her body is an object of shame" (Lazreg 2009: 29).

Both Third Wave feminists and El Mahdy dis-objectify and desexualize their bodies not through the device of decontextualization but rather through that of "semantic inversion" by showing it precisely in a way that is *normally associated with objectification and sexualization*. As a matter of fact, El Mahdy is not entirely nude on the photo but wears stockings and red ballet shoes, which brings her aesthetics very close to that of girliness and Girl Power and moves it away from the aesthetics of European naturist ideologies of the 1920s. El Mahdy deconstructs the paradigm of "nudity out of protest," and overcomes the modern equations of "taking off clothes equals modern" and "covering equals non-modern," an equation that has been coined, as will be shown in chapter 7, in modernity. This is why her black-and-white nudity establishes the same kind of distance that is also aspired by the veil. Her aesthetics can also be compared with Vanessa Beecroft's performances with nude women who are not entirely naked either, but wear pantyhose, shoes, or wigs (see introduction). The disarming distance created by this device is similar in both cases. For El Mahdy, like for Beecroft's nudes, "nudity is not a state but an event." Giorgio Agamben writes this about Beecroft: It is an "event that never reaches its completed form, . . . and that does not allow itself to be entirely grasped as it occurs" (Agamben 2011: 65).

At the same time, El Mahdy's gesture should never be read outside the context of pro-veiling feminism because there is something that unites both, which is precisely the logic of Third Wave feminism. It has been said above that both pro-veiling feminism and Third Wave feminism show female empowerment for its own sake, that they want power without projecting "to trap a man." They pose nude but not as objects. Jocelyn Taylor, for example, asks for "public eroticism as activism rather than as objectification" (J. Taylor 1995). The conclusion is that naked protest and pro-veiling feminism are not opposites. They can appear as opposites only as long as one believes, as the classical nudist movement did, that nudism attempts to liberate sexual behavior from mystification, ignorance, and irrationality, and that clothing (and therefore also veiling) produces the contrary. Views like these are very current among both Islamic and Western intellectuals. Psychoanalyst Élisabeth Roudinesco defends the unveiled state as a "natural" psychological process because "the visual appreciation of women's bodies by men brought women's femininity into being. In this view, girls were lost to their feminine identity if their bodies could not be seen" (from J. Scott 2007: 158). Similarly, Iranian dissident feminist Chahdortt Djavann has called the veil a form of "psychological, sexual and social mutilation" (ibid.). However, while nudist nakedness was indeed supposed to help "people to rise above their primitive urges [and] to liberate themselves from bourgeois morality" (J. Williams 2007: 64), veiling is supposed to do exactly the same. Nawal El-Saadawi's comment that the woman who wears a veil is even explicitly drawing attention to her body as much as the woman who wanders the streets naked, adopts here a new meaning. The pro-veiling ideology does not appear as diametrically opposed to those ideologies advocating the veil since, as will be shown in chapter 7, in 1931 the German Nudist Federation's stated aims were to impose through nudism an "'educational method for moral strictness,' abstinence from alcohol and nicotine and the rejection of makeup and jewelry" (J. Williams 2007: 28).

The slogan popularized by Iranian Islamicists, that "if unveiling is a sign of civilization, then animals must be the most civilized" (Shirazi 2001: 107), misses the point because what the no-veil position aims to obtain is a sort of nudist innocence towards the unveiled body, which animals, who do not have to overcome any shame, do not need to learn. Animals know neither clothes nor their bodies in relationship with civilization and therefore do not need to learn mutual respect or the sublimation of desires either. The analogy is thus extremely weak. But nudism, in the sense propagated by the classical nudist movements of the 1920s and 1930 as well as El Mahdy's nudism, are supposed to teach humans (and not animals) all those things.

As will be shown, classical European nudism found that "civilization has stolen the purity of nakedness" (Ross 2004: 5). El Mahdy will say that it was religion who stole it, which does not make a big difference. Nobody, neither El Mahdy nor Muslim religion, desires the negation of civilization but both propagate the construction of a higher form of civilization. For nudists this is a civilization in which nudity can exist in a "pure" state. In the early twentieth century, nudity could symbolically equate modernity, which was understood as a higher form of civilization. The "intellectually awakened, worldly experienced woman" would be defined in a way that both El Mahdy and Third Wave feminists would support: "The nudist woman, sexually emancipated, chaste, naked, confident and self-aware, would gradually lead the nation to greater glories through her natural maternal instincts" (Ross 2004: 131).

Modernity has been introduced into Islamic countries by using very similar words, also insisting on the de-eroticization of the body. Compare the passage from Ross with the following passage from feminist Afsaneh Najmabadi about how Iranians were supposed to liberate themselves from backwardness and to catch up with the West:

> The woman of modernity, thus crafted through the construction of a veiled language a disciplined de-eroticized body, as well as through the acquisition of scientific sensibilities, could now take her place next to her male counterpart in public heterosexual space. Instead of being envisaged as a threat to social order, her very disciplined language and body became the embodiment of the new order. Unlike her traditional Other who was scripted not only illiterate but crudely sexual, a shrew if not a whore, she could now be imagined unveiled. (Najmabadi 1993: 510; quoted from Majid 1998: 336)

One veil is supposed to replace another veil. The unveiled woman must have a veiled (= civilized) language, she must have veiled (= civilized) manners. For Anouar Majid, who quotes this passage, this represents not more than a "hollow conception of freedom advanced by women trapped in the discourse of modernity." However, Majid also recognizes that the de-eroticizing approach towards the body "would, ironically, be taken at face value by Islamists in the post-1970s period, when the veil was mistakenly revalorized as the true symbol of chastity" (ibid.).

El Mahdy's approach, on the other hand, looks much more like a real sexual revolution and not like a pseudo-modernization controlled by public authorities. She fully deconstructs the opposition between clothes and nudity, between bodies fully covered and nude bodies and everything in between. Like this, she reverts to a radical non-dress (neither nude nor clothed) that is, in fact, similar to the tattoo. As will be shown, both nudity and tattoos can claim to bring about civilization, which means that covering cannot be rejected in terms of nudity and nudity cannot be rejected on the grounds of a "better" covering. Civilization means that we are always partially nude and partially covered. And this is the whole difficulty of the problem of veiling.

## CONCLUSION

This chapter has shown that the oppositions "veil vs. no veil," "covered vs. bared," "non-sexual vs. sexual," are no longer pertinent in contemporary contexts. The complex logic of Third Wave feminism is the only logic with which a complex phenomenon such as pro-veiling feminism can be approached. On the other hand, it has become clear that pro-veiling feminism should learn from Third Wave not to take itself too seriously. Both pro-veiling and anti-veiling discourses have often essentialized the veil as the authentic, traditional, and morally correct form of Islamic dress for women. Only humor and play (to be learned from Third Wave feminism) can relativize this essentialization.

*Chapter Three*

# Can the Veil Be Cool?

In this chapter, the observations about the distancing aesthetics of the veil that have been demonstrated in chapter 1 will be extended by considering the complex social conditions surrounding the phenomenon of veiling. Coolness, which, in chapter 1 was mainly derived from McLuhan's theories of communication, will here be anchored in the African American context from which it evolved in the first place. The preceding chapter has shown that literature on the veiling of women in Muslim contexts is abundant and diverse. It reaches from Leila Ahmed's critique of ethnocentric views of the veil (1982) to Fatima Mernissi's attempts to trace the veil back to the "almost phobic attitude towards women" that she believes to be characteristic of Islam because of its constant highlighting of the conflict between the divine and the feminine (Mernissi 1991a: 83). During the last hundred years, the veil has been interpreted as a symbol of both oppression and resistance, as a means to bring about equality between the sexes as well as the exact contrary; it has been said to confine women to a more ethical social space but has also been accused of facilitating flirtation and adultery. It has been seen as a symbol enhancing Islamic values and as the reduction of these same values, and decisions to veil have been supported by feminist justifications as well as by explicitly antifeminist rationales.[1] Add to this that the veil has been interpreted as a desexualizing device and at the same time as a means to raise women's sexual appeal. Ayatollah Morteza Motahari, ideologue of the Islamic Revolution, pointed out that Eastern women were no longer alluring precisely because they had abandoned the veil: "With their attempt to emulate Western women they unveiled themselves and decreased their sexual appeal" ("The Issue of Veiling," quoted from Naficy 2003: 184).

The semantics and functions of the veil are extremely diverse within different geographical locations and historical periods. First, this might be

surprising for any Western observer because the black *abaya* and head cover
that is now worn all over the Middle East (and which is so strongly reminiscent of the dress of Christian nuns) seems to excel through its unifying power
to *erase* all cultural differences. To some extent this is even true. The all-
black tenure stems from the remote region of Najd in the center of Saudi
Arabia and had once been imposed by the ruling Sauds upon women in other
Saudi regions in order to emphasize the cultural unity of the newly founded
Saudi Arabia. Hijazi women, for example,

> were obliged to wear concealing external clothing that, among other things,
> obscured any possible regional variations between Saudi women coming from
> different regions of the kingdom. When some Hijazi women sought relief from
> the heat of Jidda by walking along the Red Sea coast wearing attire typical of
> that worn in the late Ottoman era, the Saudi authorities condemned them for
> immodesty. (Ochsenwald 2007: 29)

On the one hand, instead of strengthening local traditions, the black *abaya* or
*chador* has thus erased other local (religious) clothing traditions (cf. Hammadou 1999). On the other hand, the veil remains polysemic simply because not
everybody sees the same thing when seeing a veil. The preceding chapters
have pointed out the double function of the veil as an instrument of both
concealing/hiding and cropping/stylization. The primary function of any veil
is certainly protection from the climate, the male gaze, etc. However, in spite
of such common primary functions, the veil can have multiple secondary
functions and meanings, which may remain determined by cultural contexts.

The secondary meanings are indeed as diverse as the contexts. For an
Egyptian woman living in Cairo, the veil has a different meaning than for an
Afghan woman who grew up in a war zone. For an Iranian woman living
during the Islamic Revolution, the veil represented "a gendered invitation to
political participation and as a sign of membership, belonging, and complicity" (Moallem 2005: 110). The veil has also had a very distinct meaning for
Arabs in colonial Algeria, where French soldiers forcibly unveiled women
and thus "raped" the country (or for Uzbek women who were suffering from
similar strategies at the hands of the Soviet regime). It has still another
meaning for a Pakistani English woman living in Britain who chooses to turn
the veil into an intercultural issue of identity politics. In Canada, "some
mothers felt powerless to deny their daughters' decision to veil" and "two
fathers, after failing to convince their daughters not to veil, refused to talk to
them for several months" (Hoodfar 2003: 15). And the veil has a still different status in India where it is—at least traditionally—more strongly linked to
"erotic allure and spiritual awakening" (Grace 2004: 3). It does not help that
the veil has been charged with even more extended metaphorical meanings
urging us, for example, to take note of colonial perceptions of Muslim states
as "veiled, obliterated, nonexistent" (Mernissi 1991a: 23) or to link, as did

the U.S. administration (as well as the French government in the famous national veil debate) the unveiling of women to the fight against terrorism.

No thinkable scenario is missing: men put veils on women; women take off their veils against men's will; men take off women's veils against women's will; women put on veils against men's will; men take veils off women with their ostensible agreement (as did Americans in Afghanistan).

As a result, the veil has become so highly charged with religious, historical, and ideological symbolisms that its socio-functional aspects can easily disappear behind debates on related matters. If it is discussed, this often happens in terms of either cultural essentialism or relativism or, as Fadwa El Guindi has criticized, the explanation will be limited to either the "origin type" or the "utilitarian type" (El Guindi 1999: 124). Often these approaches fail to explain the reality of the veil as it is experienced in contemporary societies. To avoid symbolical as well as historical or deterministic shortcuts, I attempt in the present chapter to grasp the function of the veil inside a social game that I attempt to grasp through the following question: How can the veil function as an instrument of coolness in modern Islamic or non-Islamic societies?

## "WHY DO YOU VEIL?"

The question "Why do you wear the veil?" has often been posed but, today more than ever, the answers "I have been forced to wear it" and "It was my free decision to wear it" should not be perceived as dichotomous. As Marnia Lazreg points out, though the subject believes to have "freely" chosen the veil, her act was perhaps not "based on decisions in full knowledge of one's motivations and the consequences of one's acts, after weighing the pros and cons and considering alternatives" (Lazreg 2009: 86). This is true for the wearing of the veil as well as for not wearing it. However, to classify anybody who is "not fully aware of all options" as brainwashed would be equally wrong. In the contemporary situation the notion of "free will" is more complex than ever. "Adaptive preference" (cf. Laborde 2006: 358) is a euphemism concealing unjust background conditions. Rigid historical materialism does not recognize that any "false consciousness" (which was for Karl Marx the proletariat's internalization of certain patterns of thinking under heavy ideological control) *can* have been submitted to diverse influences that are, in a postmodern context, manifold without following coherent schemes. Most generally, those powers are "cultural influences" which can emanate from the Islamic tradition and from capitalist consumer culture alike. Even in the context of "religious" practices such as veiling, the subject is, as pointed out by Lila Abu-Lughod, submitted to "forms of power that are rooted in practices of capitalist consumerism and urban bourgeois values and aesthet-

ics" (1990: 50, quoted from Mahmood 2005: 6). And those practices normally include more "freedom" than religious practices. Antonio Gramsci came
thus closer to our present scenario than Marx when insisting on the active
role of consciousness in history, explaining that the proletariat is not merely a
passive receiver but at any moment has the ability to influence the existing
social reality.

The other side of the coin is that within this constellation of elements,
*absolute* liberty is inexistent. Correspondingly, much research on the veil has
shown that the enlightened, autonomous, rational, and freely choosing subject is an illusion. The French idea of an unencumbered, autonomous—and
necessarily unveiled—individual that arose during the famous "veiling debate" in the 1990s is a similar kind of illusion. In the end, the question "Why
do you wear the veil?" turns out to be almost redundant because the whys are
multiple, partly conscious, partly unconscious, never allowing the crystal-
lization of a clear cause.

This probably explains the contradictory results of much empirical research on the veil. Ahmed finds that "from El Guindi through Williams to
MacLeod and Zuhur . . . the decision to veil was the result of women's own
choices, [while] the findings of researchers studying the Islamist movement
more broadly suggest rather that veiling spread because Islamist male leaders
conceived of veiling as strategically important to their movement" (Ahmed
2011: 131). It is true that many—often opposing—meanings that the veil has
accumulated through its use in different locations and historical periods remain attached to this piece of cloth. It is also true that, within an increasingly
globalized world, a renewed search for cultural, ethnic, religious, or national
identity has become necessary for many people and that many revert to the
veil because of its traditional and conservative input. However, at the same
time, young peoples' everyday life experience is constituted by religion, the
customs of traditional society as well as by an aggressive consumer culture
displaying international fashion, Western lifestyles, or music. Many women
who veil consider themselves "Western" because they grew up in Western
countries. Today, many young Muslim women have to negotiate the hijab
between *niqab* and Lady Gaga. Since few of them seem to be willing to
recede to an idealized Islamic past, do they perhaps want to create a sort of
alternative modernity propelled through youth culture in the way it has been
done by African American young people before them? Drawn by the appeal
of things Western, they still harbor a militant sense of local culture and
national pride. At the other end of the spectrum is fundamentalist religion
with its rigid and unreflected imperatives.

## "NEW WORLD MODERNITY"

The question is: Does the Islamic culture of veiling suggest a sort of "New World Modernity" in the way in which the African American philosopher Cornel West attempts to see the "New World African"? West explains in his book *Keeping Faith: Philosophy and Race in America* that African Americans first "proceeded in an assimilationist manner that set out to show that black people were really like white people—thereby eliding differences (in history, culture)" (West 1993: 17). However, in the end, New World African moderns would become the exponents of an original African American modern culture that does not simply imitate Euro-American modernity.

Very similarly, in the 1990s, opponents of the French anti-veiling law insisted that the "headscarf" (which is supposed to be slightly different from the traditional veil) must be taken as thoroughly *modern* even though it does not conform to current concepts of "French modernity." More precisely, the headscarf should be recognized as the expression of "the autonomy of a newly urbanized youth" (Chafiq and Khosrokhavar 1995: 163, from Joan Scott 2007: 138). Many observers would indeed agree with Emma Tarlo that "the proliferation of new Islamic fashions in Western metropolitan cities is not necessarily a sign of increased religious conservatism, but it may also signal the emergence of new material expressions of Islamic cosmopolitanism" (Tarlo 2007: 29). This means that the project of modernity has never been abandoned by those young people, but that "false models and false friends are being questioned," as John Williams already wrote in 1980 (Williams 1980: 85). Islam is not a mere community ideology which cuts Muslims off from modernity but it can be seen as a modernity communicating with other sorts of modernity.

The parallel between African Americans and Muslims can even be taken a step further. Exactly like Cornel West's African Americans, inhabitants of Muslim countries were first confronted with modernity in the form of an alien power. Modernity was the project of the "Turkish state, which, formed from the ashes of the Ottoman Empire in 1923, did indeed aspire to create a 'new man' and a 'new woman' through a process of 'reculturation' that used dress reform to corporeally inscribe (or to 'embody') the new principles of the regime" (Secor 2002: 5). Again similar to African Americans, Muslims had to face the historical teleology of Western social Darwinists who believed that "non-Europeans are still at the stage of European childhood but will eventually replicate European 'progress' toward modern forms of organization, sociality, economics, politics, and sexual desires" (Massad 2007: 49). The "new style" that has emerged since the 1980s can indeed be read as an Islamic version of African American "cool" modernity. A fact supporting this argument is that this veiling movement is rather urban and not linked to autochthonous folklore; as a matter of fact, it has often been installed in society from top to bottom, which disqualifies it as a popular folk movement. Williams observed how in Egypt "in small towns, women still seemed to be discarding traditional dress for modern dresses or pantsuits. Even in the cities, the daughters of poorer families save their piasters in order to have a dressmaker make them something modish and foreign-looking" (Williams 1980: 75). Here the veil did *not* catch on. Veiling in the proper sense has been an urban phenomenon to begin with: In Iran, as elsewhere, "urban women wore the veil, whereas rural and tribal women covered their hair with long and wide scarves" (Sedghi 2007: 88). As a consequence, unveiling was also first enforced in larger cities. Interestingly, Williams predicted as early as in 1980 that a new Egyptian revolution would take place for precisely those reasons. The revolution would be sparked by the clash of those two cultures. Williams also anticipated that "the Muslim brotherhood will try to win as much advantage for itself as it can from the new situation" (ibid.).

It is possible to say that the critical type of modernity, labeled "New World Modernity" by Cornel West within an African American context, is present in the Muslim world in the form of "veiling fashion." This might appear as surprising if one considers that in general, fashion is the ultimate symbol of materialism and secularism. However, contrary to what seems to flow out of fundamentalist theology, in the fashion world, Islam is not necessarily construed as a movement unable to absorb modern influences. The Islamic "New World Modernity" does not come along in the form of a "jihad": In principle, there is no clash of tradition with the global consumer world or of constraints with freedom, but only a "clash" of ethicized modernity with globalized modernity.

Fashion designers have long developed the veil into something trendy, as shown by Maliha Masood in her accounts of travels through Cairo, Damascus, Amman, and Beirut (Masood 2008). Also, in Turkey, "veiling-fashion, with its array of brands and ever-changing styles, has been on the rise in the past decade" (Gökariksel and Secor 2012: 848). Already in Afghanistan of the 1970s, designer Hamida Sekander transformed the burqa into an exquisite, carefree, pleated dress, "its square bodice tailored from the veil's crocheted eyepiece and cap" (Heath 2008: 11).

Most often, attempts to redefine the veil at least partly as a fashion item have been made in the context of studies of overseas Muslim communities. Here Rhys Williams and Gira Vashi find that "wearing hijab has a fashion dynamic that cannot be fully accounted for by religious motivations or social, ethnic, or class backgrounds" (2007: 284). In general, "hijab fashion" follows certain trends and might even represent fashion cycles on its own. American Muslim "girls and young women talk about hijab with each other as if they were talking about their clothes from the mall" report Williams and Vashi (285).

Of course, tensions remain. "Fashion shows, as [Islamic fashion designers] point out, are an instrument of capitalism, designed to motivate people to consume more" (Sandikci and Ger 2007: 195) while *tesettür* is about modesty and should not be abused as a marketing tool. This is why the above authors believe that the only thing that remains constant is that, in spite of the insertion of the veil into the "fashion game," the veil remains "a visible marker of a Muslim identity" (2010: 12). For some, this means that the veil has become firmly linked to the Islamist fundamentalism, which would, of course, cancel the legitimacy of the above idea of an Islamic New World modernity.

## ISLAMIC FASHION AND COOLNESS

When it comes to the veil, religious, political, aesthetic, and personal values are constantly mixed and any attempt to disentangle them can too easily be foiled by the bias of the observer. The question "Can the veil be cool?" encourages debate on the kind of values "cool" is supposed to incorporate. Condemnations of the veil because it "limits women's capacity for self-determination in their bodies as part of their human development" and are thus "detrimental to women's advancement" (Lazreg 2009: 10) are as unhelpful as the lauding of the veil as a catalyzer of emancipation. The point is that women might simply have chosen to veil because they find it cool, subsequently attributing more or less specific meanings to their personal concept of coolness. In principle, the veil *is* (represents, signifies) nothing that can be spelled out in terms of fixed symbolisms, but it will only *function* in a certain way.

These are the reasons why the question "Why do you wear the veil?" should shift to "Do you find the veil cool?" Attempts to understand veiling "from the inside," that is, as a phenomenon developing its own dynamics without reducing it to a restrictive practice imposed upon women by "outside" authorities, have most recently been undertaken by Hama Hoodfar (2003), Saba Mahmood (2005), and Leila Ahmed (2011).[2] The particular point that those authors are trying to convey is that veiling should be seen neither as actions of *passive* victims suffering from constraints issued by *active* forces, nor as emanations of mere "activism" designed to resist paternalism or totalitarianism. The "dynamics of veiling" settles somewhere in the middle.

For Ahmed, renewed research on the veil consisted mainly in understanding how "the veil, widely viewed as the emblem of Islamic patriarchy and oppression, had come now to signal a call for gender justice (of all things) and a call for equality for minorities" (2011: 211). Mahmood points to "feminine virtues, such as shyness, modesty, and humility" (Mahmood 2005: 6)

that are constantly put forward in Islamic political, religious, and social contexts and explains that any attribution of such attitudes to the old-fashioned
categories of "false consciousness or the internalization of patriarchal norms
through socialization" (ibid.) is inadequate. She finds that any resistance
through subversion necessitates a twofold agenda: "How do women contrib-
ute to reproducing their own domination, and how do they resist or subvert
it?" (ibid.). Mahmood undertook extensive empirical research within the
Egyptian "Mosque Movement" or "Piety Movement," which is organized
exclusively for women. There she learned that "an analysis of the historical
and cultural particularity of the process of subjectivation reveals not only
distinct understandings of the performative subject but also the perspectival
shifts one needs to take into account when talking about politics of resistance
and subversion" (167).

Meanwhile, the dangers of religious brainwashing subsist. In the same
book Ahmed describes pro-veiling propaganda functioning through the more
classical, inception-style indoctrination: "In contrast to the Iranian regime,
which imposed veiling, the quiet revolution that the Sunni Islamists were
setting in motion in Egypt was seemingly rather implanting in women the
will and desire to wear hijab" (2011: 116).

## WHAT IS COOLNESS?

The veil might be cool, and if it is, then it seems to be the one thing that the
larger public has the most difficulty understanding and accepting. It is at least
more difficult to understand than conventional explanations of veiling
through paternalism or false consciousness. Hoodfar writes that what "the
Canadian community at large, fail[s] to appreciate are the decidedly modern
contours of the hijab as a twentieth-century adaptation of traditional modest
dress" (Hoodfar 2003: 92).

It is necessary to define the notion of coolness in a more general manner.
As mentioned, the aesthetics of cool developed mainly in the form of a
behavioral attitude practiced by black men in the United States at the time of
slavery and residential segregation. A cool attitude helped slaves and former
slaves to cope with exploitation or simply made it possible to walk streets at
night. Overt aggression of black people was punishable with death. To be
cool means to remain calm even under stress, and for African Americans "to
be cool" represented a "paradoxical fusion of submission and subversion"
(Holt 1972: 153) appearing as an only *apparent* submission constantly bor-
dering on insult. During slavery, any provocation had to remain on the level
of passive resistance, reuniting within one frozen, imperturbable—though
ironic—state of mind participation and non-participation. In this sense,
African American cool is a classic case of resistance through creativity and

innovation (see Botz-Bornstein 2011 for the history and definition of coolness from which this paragraph has been adopted).

There is another meaning of cool, which is almost opposed to the preceding one: Cool can also be a consumer value. "Cool today, mass tomorrow," says Nick Southgate (2003: 455). In fashion, marketing mechanisms hijack large parts of the cool aesthetics (that very often originates in black America) and extend them into the sphere of consumer society where "cool items" will be readily available in shops. Of course this is paradoxical because, first, cool cannot be manufactured (Gladwell 1997), and, second, to be cool means not to be duped by the world around and to escape manipulation. In the end, cool becomes synonymous with "popular" and "fashionable."

## DIGRESSION: CAN WOMEN BE COOL?

Talking here about coolness in the context of the veil, that is, as applied to women, some reflections are in place regarding the question if women can be, or are supposed to be, cool at all. Many people hold that cool is a masculine quality. Susan Fraiman finds that "coolness is primarily a mode of masculinity" and that cool women "resemble men who precede them in affirming a kind of dissent, hip masculinity, which typically phrases itself over against a more conventional 'feminine'" (Fraiman 2003: xii). "Women and control" is a topic that Western civilization has often been unable to handle serenely. John Stuart Mill held that "all women are brought up from the very earliest years in the belief that their ideal of character is the very opposite to that of men; not self-will, and government by self-control, but submission and yielding to the control of others" (Mill 1985: 15, quoted from Laborde 2006: 369). The question is: Are women allowed to pass from "feminine" submission to "masculine" self-control? By *literally* imitating the masculine cool, cool women might indeed lose something of their womanhood; however, they can design coolness in their own way by reproducing the concept without following its concrete manifestations. Dick Pountain and David Robins, in their book on coolness, single out Greta Garbo, Barbara Stanwyck, Marlene Dietrich, Lauren Bacall, Billie Holiday, Nico, and Chrissie Hynde (2000: 23) as cool women. Among those examples we might indeed find Joel Dinerstein's main qualities of coolness, which are a relaxed sense of control as well as smooth, fluid, and easy motion. These qualities are thus not necessarily masculine.

Baudrillard has perhaps looked deeper into the matter than others when writing about Nico, the singer of the rock group Velvet Underground, that "Nico seemed so beautiful only because her femininity appeared so completely put on. She emanated something more than beauty, something more sublime, a different seduction. And there was deception: she was a false drag

queen, a real woman, in fact, playing the queen" (1979/1990b: 13). Is this the
prototype of feminine coolness? A woman playing at being a fake woman?
This seems to be precisely what Baudrillard thinks: "If femininity is a principle of uncertainty, it is where it is itself uncertain that this uncertainty will be
greatest: in the play of femininity" (12). And since "woman is but appearance," the depth of woman cannot be obtained by imitating masculine depth
but rather by "playing" her own—women's—appearance: "And it is the
feminine as appearance that thwarts masculine depth. Instead of rising up
against such 'insulting' counsel, women would do well to let themselves be
seduced by its truth, for here lies the secret of their strength, which they are
in the process of losing by erecting a contrary, feminine depth" (10). The
same would then go for coolness.

Apart from that, there are similar rules for both men and women. What
distinguishes the macho from the cool male is that the former displays a
compulsive masculinity, rigid prescriptions of sexual promiscuity, manipulation, as well as thrill-seeking, and violence (cf. Majors and Billson 1992: 34),
while the latter is able to assert and at the same time control his desires.
Feminine coolness can only be developed along the same lines. Today, for
the Girl Power movement as well as for Third Wave feminism, feminine
coolness is of particular importance, as has been pointed out by Susan Hopkins: "She may play at being vulnerable or passive, the image which prevails
is one of an iron perfection—cool, detached and seriously ambitious" (Hopkins 2002: 103).


## VEILING AND COOLNESS


Nilüfer Göle has brought forward, in her article on modernity and veiling, the
'Islam is beautiful' slogan (Göle 2000: 482), which obviously echoes the
'Black is Beautiful' slogan of the 1960s. According to her, the slogan has
gained credence among Muslims as a cool device rather than as a political or
religious program. Journalist Emily Wax has been surprised that some pro-
fessors from major American universities referred to identity questions when
asked about the new veiling phenomenon at their institutions and encouraged
her to "think of the expression 'Black is Beautiful' during the late 1960s"
(from Ahmed 2011: 209). Ahmed also tells about a staff member on the
campus of Wayne State University in Detroit, Michigan, who wanted to
support Muslim women by pulling "a scarf over her dreadlocks," explaining
"I'm wearing it because I understand how it marks you as an object for
someone else's hatred" (206). Similar ideas resonate in slogans such as "Islam and the hip hop nation" or "transglobal hip hop umma" (J. Anderson
2005), which illustrate new, transcultural relationships between Muslim
identity values and a concept of coolness inspired by African American

struggles for freedom. Ted Swedenburg reports, "Hip-hop activism has been an important arena for anti-Islamophobic mobilization for both French and British Muslims" (Swedenburg 2002, quoted from J. Anderson). First of all, this shows that coolness (originally very much linked to African American culture) can be transferred across different cultural/historical contexts. When Muslim women wear the veil out of protest, the veil can reaffirm their identities and manifest their rejection of Western anti-values such as materialism, consumerism, and commercialism (Minces 1982; Ahmed 1982; El Guindi 1999; Williams and Vashi 2007). The parallelism of modern Islam with African American culture is even continued in the recent Gallup study of Islam where the authors compare anti-Islamic attitudes with anti-black racism and where they refer, in particular, to the American Civil War and the Watts riots of 1965 (Esposito and Mogahed 2007: 146).

All this has, of course, much to do with James Scott's ideas expressed in *Domination and the Arts of Resistance* (1990), where the author shows that those who are oppressed might accept their domination but always question their domination offstage. Iranian women who chose the veil rejected Western models of "emphasized femininity with their sexual objectification of women . . . and replaced [them] by a 'combative model of femininity'" (Moallem 1999: 330). In Turkey, veiled "educated women blur the clear-cut opposition between religion and modernity and also question the notion of women's emancipation" (Sakaranaho 2008: 52). Especially after 9/11, many a Muslim woman living in a Western country wearing traditional dress wished "to tell the world that she is not afraid of diffuse hostility toward Muslims, that she is willing to confront it head on by sporting her identity" (Lazreg 2009: 53). In Britain, "in order to wear Islamic dress . . . today, they have to be bold and intrepid," suggests Myfanwy Franks (2000: 920). In this sense, the veil is indeed cool. In France, a sociologist once suggested "that for young dissidents in the twenty-first century, identifying with Islam was the functional equivalent of the Maoism of the 1960s and 70s" (Joan Scott 2007: 32); and for some young French Muslim women, wearing the veil "is a way of talking back" (137). Often veiling has nothing to do "with religion itself, but represent[s] an attempt by young and immigrant populations to counter their deprivation and exclusion from active political agency and from effective, meaningful citizenship" (Ivekovic 2004: 1117).

A major trait of coolness is to adopt an "unexpected attitude catching society off-guard and conquering defiantly with its own and inimitable style" (Williams 1994: xii), and it is safe to assume that these women's decision to return to the veil took large parts of non-Muslim and even Muslim societies off-guard. The idea of "forced veiling" *in non-Muslim countries*, on the other hand, seems to be overstated, as displayed by many studies (Read and Bartkowski 2000: 396).

In linguistics, the phenomenon is known as "semantic inversion" through which hip-hop artists use, for example, the n-word by turning it into something positive. When Lazreg writes that she "would have expected this younger generation of women to come up with a new way by which to identify their religiosity" (Lazreg 2009: 91), she is missing the point. In those countries, the veil is cool for just that reason. Traditionally, the veil has been an object of contempt, it has been looked down upon as an archaic custom linked to poverty and class stigma (Lazreg: 98) or as "a sign of backwardness . . . because it implied the separation of women from 'civilized human beings'" (Göle 2000: 478). In spite of the expansion of hijab fashion described in this chapter as well as in the introduction, polls show that stereotypes of backwardness, oppression, and humiliation of women still cling to the veil in the eyes of most Westerners (Shadid and van Koningsveld 2005: 43, 55). According to French activist Fadela Amara (2004), in the French Arab ghettos the hijab still remains a means of oppression. Faegheh Shirazi has shown how cigarette and perfume advertisers still stress the "backwardness" of the veil in order to hawk their products to Western women (2001: 38). And in Middle Eastern tourist brochures, veils, camels, and tribal people remain "images, which symbolize backwardness, oppression and inferiority [and] are adopted icons of tourism in order to effect tourists' travel decisions and perceptions about those countries" (Al Mahadin and Burns 2007: 138). Above that, for many feminists the veil remains a symbol of colonial sexualization of women: "How can this emblem of sexuality and men's desire possibly serve women?" asks Egyptian feminist Nawal El-Saadawi (Cooke 2000: 133). I would argue that the veil can be cool precisely because of this contradiction.

The "veil as coolness" works in parallel with black cool because the *negative* aspects in both cases have constantly been reintroduced into the social sphere by spitefully using them as signifiers of resistance. Grace Sims Holt has described that

> Blacks gradually developed their own way of conveying resistance using The Man's language against him as a defense against sub-human categorization. The sociocultural context formed the basis for the development of inversion as a positive and valuable adaptive response pattern. (Holt 1972: 153)

The demonstrative introduction of African cultural elements into fashion was supposed to point to an authentic black origin (though this origin was often freely invented). It can indeed be compared with the invention of the woman's Islamic dress known as *al-ziyy al-Islami*, which, according to Egyptian-born feminist Fadwa El Guindi,

> is an innovative construction that was first worn in the mid-1970s by activists. It does not represent a return to any traditional dress form and has no tangible

precedent. There was no industry behind it in Egypt—not one store carried such an outfit. Based on an idealized Islamic vision gradually constructed for the early Islamic community in the seventh century, it was made in their homes by the activists themselves. (El Guindi 1981)

The "veil as resistance" uses "the Man's language against him" or, in Hirschmann's words, these women "subvert the practice by turning its norms against itself" (Hirschmann 1997: 486). Joan Scott believes that "like the adoption of the word 'nigger' by blacks in the United States, wearing a headscarf assumed the stigmatized object as a positive attribute, and might be a variation on the slogan of the American gay-rights group Act-Up: 'We're here, we're from here [*sic*], get used to it!'" (Scott 2007: 139). In extreme cases, the veil can be compared to the "ghetto cool" or vulgar and aggressive coolness flaunted by hip-hop artists who attempt to obtain a recognized place in society by proudly reinforcing—in a more or less ironical way—negative signifiers sticking to black people. "Self-stereotyping" is a common practice among African Americans and it takes place also here in the Islamic context. In order to counter sexism and racism, the veiling woman sexualizes[3] and racializes herself even more; and there exists not even an Islamic precept that could prevent her from doing so. Islam requires that all clothes, as instruments of modesty, conceal the body *and at the same time reflect the sexual dichotomy of the world*. The sexualization of the body is thus in agreement with Islam. Caught between stereotypes with which she refuses to identify, the "re-veiled" woman might deliberately choose to overstate those stereotypes.

The pattern has been recognized by many researchers analyzing veiling and it has been traced to the general insight that "power is not only oppressive but also creative: every relation of subordination and domination also creates a capacity for action and resistance, whereby dominated individuals assert their selfhood through adaptation to, manipulation or subversion of the normative order they are subjected to" (Laborde 2006: 363). The re-veiled woman contests the soundness of the pseudo-liberated woman associated with Westernization and goes for a positive identity sanctioned by Islam. These women use "practices, such as veiling, which have historically underpinned patriarchal oppression to subvert patriarchy and assert themselves as autonomous believers" (Hoodfar 2001: 421, quoted from Laborde, 366). In some way, the pattern is that of the reappropriation of the oppressed condition, paralleling the strategies of Femen and other contemporary feminist groups who support, for example, Gay Pride without being lesbians themselves. It follows that in this transcultural situation, the "cool" aspect of the veil cannot be emphasized enough while "real" values such as social status, authenticity, or identity are still important but remain secondary. Even values such as purity and chastity, which its proponents put forward as stable and absolute, exist only within a social game of coolness, according to Hani Shukrallah: "Our region may be on the brink of disaster, our economy is in shambles, we've never been as maligned and humiliated but hey, we remain as chaste as the driven snow" (from Hammond 2005: 271).

By definition, cool is never merely authentic but always involved in an act of simulation. The "authentic" must be looked for in the game of simulation itself, in its imaginative, fleeting, and fragmented aspects. The assumption brought forward by Karin van Nieuwkerk and many others that the veil helps women "to develop stable identities" and to "return to an original sense of self" (van Nieuwkerk 2008: 445) is thus naïve. This does not mean that the veil establishes merely "fake" identities. The game of "being cool" is illusionist by definition, and identity must be looked for in this illusion, in this false consciousness or, as Nancy Hirschmann writes, in "the lines between agency, choice, and resistance . . . and oppression, domination, and coercion . . . become blurred: Indeed, it is often the case that resistance and agency are simultaneously an expression or illustration of oppression" (Hirschmann 1997: 486).

## "FREE WILL"

The complexity of "free will" in contemporary contexts has already been explained at the beginning of this chapter by showing that Lazreg's idea of veiling or non-veiling as "based on decisions in full knowledge of one's motivations and the consequences of one's acts, after weighing the pros and cons and considering alternatives" (Lazreg 2009: 86) is often shrouded in relativism. Still, for those researchers who see veiling as an act of resistance, it is of utmost importance that women do it on their own will: "They reached this state of religiousness by *iqtina* (conviction). No overt pressure or force was exerted" (El Guindi 1999: 132). Haleh Afshar even believes that it is possible to separate forced veiling from self-veiling, as if this would be two completely different acts:

> To gain an understanding of the problems we need to separate out imposed dress-code regulations, such as those imposed by the Iranian and Saudi governments, from elected ones such as the choice to wear the hijab in the West. We also must separate out the latter from the constructed images of an oppressed, submissive Muslim woman forced, not only by the laws of the land but by the regulation of her community and kin group, to cover to satisfy the honor of ever jealous and vigilant menfolk. (Afshar 2008: 412)

It is certainly possible to detect here a degree of "false consciousness" just as one can detect it in the case of the black people who donned the cool mask. A large part of veiling, just like a large part of black cool, can be considered as "a site of the paradoxical desire for the expression of the freedom to be unfree" (Moallem 1999: 323). For psychoanalysts the fact that victims can "love their hangmen" represents a basic teaching. There is indeed "a resistance towards revolt due to the human fear of giving up the hardship caused by something that is known in favor of an unknown liberty whose dangers are not identified" (Gori 2013: 55).

Coolness as a concept is always ready to bear a part of the burden of "false consciousness" because, by definition, coolness involves any consciousness into paradoxes. Logically, coolness exists only as long as there is some sort of oppression or at least constraint: Absolute freedom is as "uncool" as absolute oppression. Lazreg grasps this standpoint and calls it very aptly the "existential-philosophical" one, which implies "to recognize that the oppressed are not so oppressed after all" (Lazreg 2009: 6). It is certainly no coincidence that a great deal of African American philosophy takes the cue from existentialism. Hirschmann, in her article on veiling, quotes African American cultural sociologist Orlando Patterson who points out that freedom can be of such a central concern only as long as there is oppression (Hirschmann 1997: 462). European Enlightenment discourses on "natural freedom" and the right to happiness embraced by the independent, self-reliant, and self-controlled individual seem to be out of place here because they are purely European and Western concepts. Hirschmann mentions also classical "non-Western" affiliative ideals such as "community, kinship, or nation" as alternatives, but it would be wrong to retrace decisions to veil merely to these motives. It would be equally wrong to list them simply under the heading "false consciousness." It is much more plausible to classify them as attempts at being cool.

Turning submission into style, calling tradition fashion, calling the old the new, can be the manifestation of a "false consciousness" that has become cool because of a particularly ironic attitude with which cultural, religious, or political stances are handled. Social crises like those that Muslim women and black people had to go through can create aggressive and paranoid radicals propagating open violence and conspiracy theories. But it can also create the restrained, cool rebel who pretends to play along with those having power but who insists on putting her own individualistic and creative stamp on everything. Coolness is fractured false consciousness.

The problem is that it is extremely difficult to state if a consciousness is still cool or if it has tipped over into blunt falseness. The "voluntary veiling" described by El Guindi, for example, took place in the Egypt of Sadat—who had encouraged the Muslim Brothers and other radical Islamist groups to expand their activities—in which faith-based literature was actively distributed in order to counterbalance the influence of Nasserist and leftist groups (Lazreg 2009: 10). It also took place during a time when a large part of the Egyptian workforce began to emigrate to the conservative Gulf countries importing more traditionally oriented social patterns into Egypt. El Guindi admits that an "indirect influence of a change in public moral climate in which some men and women became activist symbols of an 'Islamic model' of comportment and dress" (ibid.) did exist.

## THE VEIL IN KUWAIT

As previously mentioned, Kuwait represents an exception. Here the insistence on religion with regard to veiling remains very important. The veil is often prescribed in terms of dogmatic religious imperatives and any implementation of veiling on a *cultural* basis is frowned upon.

I am teaching at a private university in Kuwait and about 65% of our female students wear the hijab, which is perceived here (like in most contemporary Islamic cultures) as a cloth covering hair and neck. At our university, about 18% of those who wear the hijab also wear a black *abaya* and of those who wear the *abaya* about 12% also wear the face covering *niqab* that leaves only the eyes free. This means that more than 80% of those who veil combine the hijab with Western clothes and 0.2% of those who veil wear the *niqab*.[4]

At the time of writing this chapter, no more statistics were available. Having been persuaded in 2012 by the Ethics Committee of my university from refraining from further empirical research on veiling,[5] I had to rely, in this more theoretically-minded chapter, on empirical studies by other people. However, informal conversations with students as well as the "undercover" distribution of twenty-five questionnaires yield some more or less accurate impressions of attitudes towards veiling at my university.[6]

Kuwait is representative of many Muslim countries in which young women subscribe to a complicated network of reasons when veiling because those students are living in complex societies with traditional as well as modern (Western) influences. The veil is not necessarily seen as a traditional item but worn in a modern environment where it becomes not only a politico-religious statement, but also a fashion statement. The Hijabtrendz website is a Kuwaiti production and presents hijab fashion and Islamic swim gear by using hip language and a trendy layout. The site, as well as the visitors' comments, are in English. Many comments are enthusiastic about the fashion potential of the hijab but many also emphasize the importance of "modesty." Islamic values are here marketed in a cool way.

The cultural situation in Kuwait represents certain particularities. On the one hand, there are reasons to see veiling within the conservative Gulf culture as the continuation of a tradition that can more easily be accepted as a sort of habitus based on Bedouin culture and a conservative attitude common to the geographical region. Strong cultural influence from Saudi Arabia after the Iraqi occupation as well as an increasing presence of Muslim Brothersmonitored Egyptian teachers in Kuwait's state schools since 1991[7] account for a further shift towards religious conservatism. On the other hand, a more liberal spirit existed also in Kuwait in the 1970s, which establishes a parallel with Egypt and some other Muslim countries. Furthermore, wealthy Kuwait has developed—after the end of the Iraqi occupation more than ever—into a spectacular consumer society in which young women are often described as fashion victims. My colleagues and I note that whenever girls are asked about their hobbies, "shopping" appears on top of the list in virtually all cases. Student gazettes are full of fashion articles and many female students fly at least once a year to London and Paris to buy clothes, which is amazing given the density of brand-named boutiques that exists in Kuwait itself. The conclusion is that, paradoxically, Kuwait is one of the most Westernized and at the same time traditional countries in the Middle East.

If I compare the comments on "reasons for veiling" I received during my research from students with those published by Arlene MacLeod and by Sherifa Zuhur, who conducted research in the 1980s in Egypt, I find discrepancies that are so total that even my unreliable research sample might be more relevant than expected. As Ahmed has noted (Ahmed 2011: 126), Mac-Leod's and Zuhur's results are antagonistic: Zuhur's women, while not Islamic activists themselves, veiled because they were self-consciously affiliating themselves with the goals of Islamism; while MacLeod's interviewees seemed to be adopting the hijab mostly to resolve personal dilemmas. Mac-Leod as well as earlier researchers (for example, J. Williams 1979) received stock responses affirming that veiling had helped them "to know who they really were."

All of the above options strike my students as utterly outlandish and unfathomable; instead, ready-made answers like "this is our religion" or "my family wants me to wear it" are standard. This is at least partly in keeping with Hoodfar's study undertaken in Quebec where "only four out of fifty-nine veiled women claimed the veil to be part of their Arab or Muslim identity and not an Islamic requirement (Hoodfar 2003: 17). On the other hand, I do not find much correlation between veiling and religious practice, which is in keeping with MacLeod, who found that only a tiny minority of women, veiled or unveiled, prayed daily (cf. Ahmed 2011: 121).

Here are a few portraits of veiled students in Kuwait.

***Nadia*** is one of the few exceptions. A Canadian-born Kuwaiti whose father is Canadian with (largely lost) Arab roots and whose mother is an (unveiled) Kuwaiti, Nadia adopted the veil while still living in Canada, and a search for a stable Muslim identity seems to be a main driving force behind her veiling.

***Sarah,*** a Kuwait-born student of Lebanese origin is telling her story in an almost apologetic way. She was "brainwashed" into veiling at age thirteen in her religious school and took the veil against the advice of her parents. Now she cannot take it off but she plans to take it off once she leaves Kuwait.

*Lulwa's* great uncle, who is the family's "eldest," turned salafist relatively recently. Consequently, he requires all women in the extended family to veil even though the rest of the family, including Lulwa's parents, seems to be against it. Lulwa also tells me of her friends who get "bribed" into veiling by parents who offer them much higher allowances or other material rewards such as luxury cars. Muneera says that her father has offered her large sums of money if she adopts the veil but she said that "the only way to make her wear it is to kill her" (she is driving a luxury car nevertheless).

*Latifa* is one of the few students (three to my knowledge) who went from veiling to not veiling. Coming from a very religious family (though not a Bedouin family, as she insisted several times), she has worn the hijab since she was twelve. Her daily practice of several sports (especially football) as well as the participation in international competitions led her to see Islamic dress code with a slightly critical eye. More decisive were her vacations in non-Islamic countries where she discovered that her self-image and identity is rather hijab-less. "It does not make sense to flirt and to drink alcohol and wear a hijab," she said. Very important was also the fact that she began seeing herself as a less religious person. Her shift towards secularism was very much influenced by reading Richard Dawkins' *The God Delusion*, which she downloaded from the internet. When she took off her hijab at age twenty-three, her family was shocked and hostile but took no measures to stop her. Her hijab-wearing classmates judged her very critically, but since she socializes mainly within her sport community, she does not pay much attention to this. Even months afterwards she receives phone calls (either anonymous calls or calls from distant friends and relatives) urging her to put the hijab back on. Some call simply to insult her. In spite of this, she appears to be serene. She is convinced that the present situation represents a temporary phase and that people will soon get used to her new state.

*Sharifa* appeared one day, to everybody's surprise, hijabless with her hair colored in blue. Being obsessed with Japanese visual key culture, she enjoyed eccentric aesthetic choices. In this aesthetic universe there is no place for the hijab, the more so since Sharifa defines herself as an atheist. In spite of this, her new appearance would last only two weeks. Her cousin took a photo of her and sent it to her parents. A major family drama ensued and Sharifa had to put the black hijab back on. Like Latifa, she quotes her worried parents saying that hijabless women are bound to go to hell.

From many reliable sources I heard that a very large part of our female students who arrive on the campus in the morning (many of them brought by their drivers) wear *abayas* but take them off on arrival to store them in the locker.

Unfortunately I had no access at the time of writing this chapter to the 0.2% of the students who wear the *niqab* but I hear from other students that those are often of Bedouin origin and find it unthinkable to frequent a "frivolous" place such as our university without complete covering.

The lack of reflection on or discussion of the subject, linked to a general fear even to talk about it, is striking. There is not much information available to students apart from ready-made arguments affirming the mandatory character of veiling in Islam that I am constantly invited to "look up on the internet." Almost all students, veiled and unveiled, believe that the Qur'an unequivocally commands women to veil (on the incorrectness of this assumption see note 1 of this chapter). If you are a strict Muslim you veil, if you are moderate you might decide not to veil.

The unreflected and uninformed way of dealing with the matter of veiling that is so striking in Kuwait echoes MacLeod's findings from 1993 in Egypt: "I don't know why everyone wore modern dress before and now we do not, but this is the situation." 56% of the women MacLeod interviewed suggested that veiling is a matter of fashion for which they have no further explanation: "I don't know why fashions change in this way, no-one knows why; one day everyone wears dresses and even pants. I even wore a bathing suit when I went to the beach . . . then suddenly we are all wearing this on our hair!" (from Ahmed 2011: 120).

The conclusion is that veiling in Kuwait is neither a matter of identity search nor primarily due to a rejection of Western values. It seems rather that veiling is "mildly forced" upon the girls and subsequently justified by them as a "sort of free choice" that could not have been eluded anyway because veiling is a religious imperative. It corresponds more or less to Leila Ahmed's "quiet revolution" that the Sunni Islamists were setting in motion in Egypt, which took the form of "implanting in women the will and desire to wear hijab" (Ahmed 2011: 116).

The constraints are not experienced as dramatic; apart from that, the environment does not offer much stimulation for analysis or critique. In this sense veiling *becomes* authentic; it is not authentic in the form of a stable cultural or religious essence but it can be experienced as an authentic way of dressing as it flows out of a "game" played by society. This game has adopted all those imaginative, fleeting, and fragmented aspects with which games are expected to comport. As a matter of fact, Johan Huizinga's classical definition of the game constantly highlights its *indifference* towards real life which, paradoxically, will *not* produce the feeling of the unreal in the player, but rather the feeling that she is acting in an alternative reality (Huizinga 1970: 57–58). This is how games create a second reality: Even games of imitation and doing-as-if get their attractiveness not from their perfect correspondence with reality but rather from a curious inner correspondence with themselves. In this sense, they are not mere imitations, but they are authentic "as games."

The idea of the "authentic" as something imagined and true in its own right has occupied many scholars during the last three decades (cf. Hobsbawm 1990; B. Anderson 1983). It has been found that the authenticity of a nation or a tradition does not preexist in the form of an original quality, but is *produced* by society as it plays a certain game. Jean Baudrillard's (1994) concepts of the hyperreal or of a simulation that simulates only itself are the most radical expressions of such philosophical views. My improvised research in Kuwait confirms the above assumption that, in the case of veiling, it is extremely difficult to state if an individual's consciousness is still cool or if it has already tipped over into blunt falseness. For most veiled Kuwaiti students, veiling seems to be an obligation, but because the amount of "force" by which this obligation has been enforced is usually difficult to spell out, the veil can subsequently be transformed into something "cool" within the consciousness of the wearers. The strong mutual tolerance of veiled and unveiled students (that my research did also reveal) can be explained through this fleeting and unclear status of the veil's underlying "why." I have no evidence for the "secondary cool" effect, which is that of peer pressure ("you are cool when you act like all the others"). In general, veiled students did not admit that such peer pressure exists though non-veiled students claim that it does.

## IS THE VEIL REALLY COOL?

It has been shown that the veil shares some of the principle virtues of coolness: moderation and self-control. At the same time, coolness—in its classical sense—is at odds with Puritan traditions and invents its own virtue code of moderation because it strives to obtain access to a formerly forbidden space. Moderation alone would limit coolness to republican virtues; in order to become cool, there must also be provocation. This creates the clash with Puritanism. Coolness contains a paradox: self-control replaces repression, but it also challenges official power. Submission should be apparent but never real. Does the veil fulfill these conditions? On the one hand, the veil can be seen as a parody of moderation, especially when it grants special liberties that are not obtainable without the cool mask. Here the veil is definitely cool. But where is the provocation? Some Islamic women who veil "on their own" might want to be cooler than Western women (especially when the Islamic women are living in Western countries) whose autonomy they believe to be deceptive. According to some authors, they sport "a positive identity and source of esteem sanctioned by Islam" (Mule and Barthel 1992: 324). Characteristically, Pat Mule and Diane Barthel subtitle their article

"Individual Autonomy vs. Social Esteem" because any coolness depends on the proportional relationship between both. However, if the autonomous identity is absorbed by the authority (be it Islamic or other), the act is *not* cool. The American Muslim woman who wears the veil in Manhattan certainly provokes. To some extent she rejects a part of the Western fashion machine, and this is cool. However, she provokes only the non-Muslim part of the public and not any Islamic authority. Iranian women of the late 1970s challenged the regime, and here the veil did provoke the authorities. Egyptian women in the 1980s made statements against Western and postcolonial cultural influences by inventing the contemporary Islamic dress, but they did not challenge religious authorities. Young French Muslim women wear the veil in their ghetto and stuff it into their purse (in which they also have make up) as soon as they are on the local train heading for the city, and *that* is cool. Everything depends on the context—that is, on *who* is supposed to be provoked.

The cool person is usually in a non-power position and challenges those who have power. The challenge is presented in masked and ironic ways. This is why coolness must always contain just the right amount of flexibility and "fluency." Dictators are uncool and so are all those who oppose power in a *fundamentalist* way because their protest is not subtle or flexible. Moallem insists that "it is a mistake to read fundamentalist encouragement of the wearing of the black *chador* either as a sign of passivity or as a sign of religiosity. It is rather a gendered invitation to participation in political activity and a sign of membership, belonging, and complicity" (Moallem 1999: 333). The problem is that here the *chador* becomes a uniform, which is uncool unless it is worn with ironic implications. As such, the Islamic veil is not flexible because it cannot be taken off in the way in which the wearing of Indian saris or Japanese kimonos or of male traditional costumes (the *dishdasha* in the Gulf region for example) can be selected only for certain occasions. When Iranian Islamic fundamentalist groups encouraged women during and after the Islamic Revolution to wear the veil by saying "My sister, your veil is more assertive than my blood" (Moallem 1999: 329), the matter becomes too straightforward and far too serious to be cool. The veil becomes here a matter of linear symbolism (veil equals blood), which does not leave much room for creative play. The veil has been essentialized as an authentic, traditional, morally correct form of Islamic dress for women.

African Americans who wear sunglasses, speak Ebonics, and overemphasize their black identity through a certain style of clothing might use signifiers that are detrimental to their social development, but they can still see it as a part of the game of coolness, which is beneficial for obtaining their final objective. They create transcultural identities through the principle of coolness. Can the veil function as such a "tool of cool"? Does this piece of cloth maintain the crucial balance between visibility and non-visibility, assimilation and cultural resistance, submission and subversion, control and the inability to control? Or is it not too likely to tip over into either submissive disappearance or monocultural fundamentalist combat? All these questions can only be answered within the context of concrete cases.

Another problem is that the veil can very easily move towards the emotionality of victimhood, a danger haunting black American cool since its inception. Pountain and Robins write in their book on coolness that "victimhood is the moving spirit of our times (in effect occupying the position that we attribute to cool) where growing numbers of people want to feel themselves part of some oppressed minority" (Pountain and Robins 2000: 159). Identity discourses that are too straightforward often become sentimental, fundamentalist, or simply "kitsch" (which is always the contrary of cool); and this happens to the (pseudo-) cool pose as much as to veiling.

Still another problem is that the veil can have an objectifying function. One of the purposes of veiling can be to oppose (especially sexual) objectification and to urge men to recognize women as equal partners. As mentioned, Iranian women who chose the veil rejected Western models of "emphasized femininity with their sexual objectification of women . . . and replaced [them] by a 'combative model of femininity'" (Moallem 1999: 330). To cover the woman's feminine attributes is in line with this project. On the other hand, by covering a woman's head or even face, attributes that are part of a woman's personality and that have no primary sexual function get covered as well. The anti-objectification can easily have a reverse effect of objectification. In my classes, I have more difficulties memorizing the names of my veiled students because to me, many look very much alike. Bob Abdrabboh's phrase that "all women are obliged to don the veil to become indistinguishable and unapproachable" (quoted from Elmusa 1997: 349) can be confirmed, though the juxtaposition of "indistinguishable" and "unapproachable" requires an elucidation.

Some respondents in the improvised Kuwaiti survey described in the preceding section expressed the desire to be unapproachable, and one of them even wrote: "I want to be an unapproachable queen." The veil, howerver, might make one unapproachable, but it also leads to indeterminacy because a part of the woman's natural features, that is, a part of her phenotype, will be hidden by the veil as well. According to Moallem, it is thus not only that "as a system of symbolic and material marking, veiling disciplines and homogenizes all Muslim women into a single category" (Moallem 2005: 114). Also, her distinct identity becomes blurred on a basic phenomenological level. The retrospective personalization of the veil through "veiling fashion" does not contradict this pattern but instead confirms it. Most individuals desire distinctness and personality and they do so especially today, in a world where an increasingly impersonal kind of communication has created the need for special personal devices (profiles) often using pictures of peoples' faces. (I think of Facebook or of the sender's picture that recently began to appear in a corner of most email messages.) The veil diminishes the desired personality though it can be reinstalled through retrospective stylization, at least to some extent.

I should mention that I made the same observations with African American (male and female) students wearing "hoodies" when I was teaching in a Historically Black University in Alabama. I had more difficulties memorizing the names of the hooded students. This means that the parallel with African American cool is also maintained here: The cool black male's stylized way of offering resistance that insists more on *appearance* than on *being* has very often turned him into an untouchable object of desire. The self-produced romantic racialism of many blacks finds a parallel in the self-racialization of veiled women. Apart from that, it is interesting to note that the "veiling" of African American students, who often buy expensive brand-name hoodies, serves the single purpose of inserting them into the world of consumerism. Some people have suggested that "veiling fashion" will go the same way (see chapter 5).

It is not my intention here to establish whether this obtained effect of indistinctness is intentional (i.e. whether it is due to a false consciousness or not). The only point that can be made in this context is that the veil is just another example of how easily the project of "being cool" can go awry. Marlene Connor compares today's cool hip-hop artists with soul singers such as Teddy Pendergrass or Marvin Gaye and finds that the former are "sexually immature" (Connor 1994: 148). The cool black man "can continue to practice being cool and remaining a child, following the rules that have been set up by children" (172). Cool can very easily become uncool and veiling faces similar dangers. The "veil as resistance" uses "the Man's language" against him, but it can also unconsciously adopt the Man's language and engage in self-objectification. Similarly, the woman's objectified sexualized image is hidden under a veil and removed from sight, but underneath the veil her objectified personality can continue to exist. While French writer Gerard de Nerval held "that it is the veil itself and not the woman concealed beneath it that attracts" (Dobie 2001: 127), many authors do not agree with this and insist that the veil leads to the objectification of *what is under the veil*. The list of such authors is indeed long.

For Nawal El-Saadawi, the veil "accentuates rather than conceals the woman's body" (Cooke 2000: 134), and El Guindi points out that "gender markers are not hidden when wearing neutral-gendered or dual-gendered dress items" (1999: 7). Moallem is convinced that "through veiling, the body becomes at the same time desired yet objectified, forbidden and alienated" (1999: 337) and that the veil genderizes and sexualizes women as a sign of femininity. Feminist Margot Badran recognizes the veil as a "double-edged weapon, facilitating their public presence and expanded roles, while reinforcing common perceptions of women as primarily sexual beings" (Badran 2009: 82). And for Lazreg, it is not clear that "if a woman conceals her breasts and legs but leaves her face bare she [is] less desirable to a man" (2009: 28). It is telling that Pamela Taylor, who "donned the hijab to reject the exploitation of women for their sexuality," wonders if "someday I will take it off again in order to reject the suppression of women for their sexuality" (Taylor 2008: 125). As a matter of fact, the term *mutabarrija*, "connot[es] a seductive, showy woman—who, nevertheless, was usually veiled. [It] reemphasized the notion of woman as a sexual being, posing a problem for the feminists and supplying fuel to the conservatives" (Badran 2009: 75).

## CONCLUSION

Given the above interferences between the veil and its coolness, it is difficult to understand why both proponents and opponents are often strikingly "uncool" when talking about it. When French philosopher André Glucksmann classifies the veil as "a terrorist operation" and former French president Jacques Chirac announces that "wearing a veil is a kind of aggression,"[8] they are just as uncool as Islamic fundamentalists and demonstrate, in the words of Joan Scott, "the paucity of their philosophical resources and the weakness of their political capacities" (Scott 2007: 121). In other words, they refuse transcultural approaches which, in their opinion, harm the universal moral and aesthetic values granted by the state. In this debate, only French Green Party leader Alain Lipietz has recognized the transcultural character of the veil when worn in a French context as he confirmed that the message should be understood as merely anti-assimilationist and not as anti-French (Scott 2007: 137).

In theory, any veil, no matter where it appears, is cool as long as it plays with limits, status, and privileges and as long as it does not simply attempt to install purity and moral perfection. According to El Guindi, the latter is precisely the function of the *Christian* veil: "The Christian version was formed to attain a state of purity and moral perfection—a concept linking sex, religion, and moral order in a way that is Christian, not Islamic" (El Guindi 1990: 31). This is why it had become so important during the Vatican II sessions "to get past the idea of a 'good sister' who looked like an adult doll in the dress of another age. It was difficult to discover the real person of the individual sister and take her seriously when she was seen in the mass-produced habit that suggested she was a carbon copy of all her other dressa-likes, leaving her little personal identity beyond 'one of the sisters'" (Lafontaine 2008: 84). Everything depends on how the veil is handled: as a cool and transparent device playing with boundaries or as a purifying machine that insists on seeing the worldly space in terms of religious space. Does the veil produce blunt apartheid or a cool form of separation/non-separation? The problem of spatial separation and transparency will be examined in chapter 5.

If the relative character of boundaries is abused in order to merely transfer rules from one space to the other, the veil is not cool. If anybody is forced to wonder all the time if she is acting in conformity with religious principles, then this is the contrary of cool. Instead, it represents a cynical invasion of one space by the other. It happens, for example, when women do not get a salary raise because their professional status is fused with their (submissive) domestic role or when the veil leads to the exclusion and social impairment of women.

Do Muslim women need saving? It would be preposterous of me to attempt to save them from patriarchy, from their culture, or from their rulers because, in the end, I do not really know what all these items look like from their perspective. In this world there is not only one, but an infinite number of models of femininity (and masculinity) provided by indigenous cultures, religions, and civilizations. However, in spite of those cultural complications it seems to me that many Muslim women want to be cool, and ethico-aesthetic reflections on the veil and coolness are most helpful where any act of liberation is needed.

## NOTES

1. Fatima Mernissi has most forcefully argued that the Prophet had no desire to make the hijab compulsory for women (see Mernissi 1991a part 2). Another clear argument against the compulsory character of the veil has been formulated by Egyptian feminist Nawal El-Saadawi: "Some Muslim women put on the veil as an anti-Western protest, or to assert their authentic, Islamic identity and indigenous culture. They do not know that the authentic identity of a Muslim woman is not to be veiled and that the veil is not an Islamic dress" (El-Saadawi 1997: 96). It impossible to provide here a complete survey of arguments for and against the obligatory character of the veil but it is possible to refer to the principal sources. The most popular passage quoted by defenders of the obligatory character of veiling is the Surah Al-Noor (lines 24–31): "And tell the believing women to reduce [some] of their vision [that is, to lower their gaze] and guard their private parts and not expose their adornment except that which [necessarily] appears thereof and to wrap [a portion of] their headcovers over their chests and not expose their adornment except to their husbands, their fathers." Curiously, this surah shows that the head does *not* need to be covered though proponents of veiling constantly use it for the contrary purpose. The same goes for lines 33–59 of the Surah Al-Ahzab, which is also frequently cited. The Hadith 4092 from Abu Dawud's collection of hadiths is also often quoted, despite the fact that Abu Dawud himself classified the hadith as weak because the narrator who transmitted it from Aisha is not known.

2. See also Thorsten Botz-Bornstein and Noreen Abdullah-Khan's (2014) empirical study of the veil in Kuwait.

3. My use of the word "sexualize" is justified since I define the emancipated women emerging from Western feminism as a woman whose sexual difference from men is less obvious than in earlier generations. The word should be understood only in this sense.

4. Those are numbers according to my own count. The sample (n) was 500 students and the informal "survey" was done by counting students on the campus.

5. The decision has never been formally spelled out but it had been indicated that I would have no chances to get this research authorized because "veiling" is a too personal matter. A colleague who attempted to do research on veiling earlier had received a formal refusal from the committee.

6. The research would be approved much later and has meanwhile been published in Botz-Bornstein and Abdulla-Khan 2014.

7. The more liberally minded Palestinian teachers had to leave Kuwait during the Iraqi occupation (1990–1991) because Yassir Arafat had decided to side with Saddam.

8. In *L'Express* in 1994, number 64. Chirac is quoted from Scott 2007: 84.

# Chapter Four

# Respect and Shame

## Sarah Kofman on Veiling

So far, this book has dealt with mainly one problem: Pro-veiling feminists present women as assertive and powerful but use a visual vocabulary that many feminists would find incompatible with any sort of feminist thinking—the veil. The phenomenon of veiling fashion has made the situation more complex. Instead of becoming a Puritan, the veiled woman establishes her own code of moderation: "Veiling-fashion consumers continuously formulate what constitutes an acceptable ethical action for themselves—and it is often one that diverges from their perceived prescribed moral code of complete covering" (Gökariksel and Secor 2010: 850). This means that, if this system is supposed to function at all, the technique of "self-veiling" depends on a certain amount of ambivalence. To some extent, this ambivalence overlaps with what Banu Gökariksel and Anna Secor describe as a tension between tradition and modernity or between piety and fashion: "Veiling-fashion as an object of consumption does not consent to be wholly captured within the moral discourse of Islam; it is, as Baudrillard would say, morally ambivalent, caught between its function as modest covering according to Islam and its social signification, which can variously be located in terms of fashion, aesthetics, politics, and class status" (848). However, the ambivalence I am interested in here is more fundamental and concentrated in the term "respect." This is why I discuss Sarah Kofman's important text *Respect for Women* (1982). What would Kofman have written had she addressed the subject of the Islamic veil? This chapter shows that social patterns present in the "East" and in the "West" are similar when seen through a historical perspective.

# RESPECT AND AMBIVALENCE

Is veiling not all about respect? A self-veiled Texan woman explains that when you veil, men "don't look at your appearance, they appreciate your intellectual abilities. They respect you" (Read and Barkowski 2000: 405). The American woman Pamela Taylor decided to veil herself because she did not want "to be judged by my body, my beauty, or the lack thereof, but as an individual, for my personality, my character, and my accomplishments" (P. Taylor 2008: 123). And Marnia Lazreg believes that many self-veiled women in France see the "veil as a means of achieving respect by French society" (Lazreg 2008: 94). Some would say that veiling is not mainly about respect but about virtues such as piety, which should be considered an end in itself. However, as any virtue is enacted in society, it is never an end in itself but serves to obtain other values. And one of those values is respect.

It is in this context that I revisit Sarah Kofman's text. Kofman has given much reflection on the kind of respect that men express towards women, and she presents "respect for women" as a highly ambivalent phenomenon. One of her main claims is that the respect that men have towards women cannot be detached from "the two figures of the mother: the virgin and the whore, and the ambivalent approach that men take towards women" (Kofman 1982: 15). In the first place, respect manages to restrain the sexual drive, as is shown by a simple Freudian reading put forward by Kofman in the sense that respect restrains and inhibits the sexual penchant. This appears to be fairly straightforward, but looking closer we discover that this respect is ambiguous. Kofman observes that the male gender tends to "put down and despise certain women while it elevates others on a pedestal by placing them at a distance that makes them untouchable" (15). All this is done because of the needs of the male sexual economy.

Kofman offers similar explanations when it comes to the question why women are cloistered by men. In *L'Énigme de la femme* (1980), Kofman has looked at the problem from a Freudian point of view; and in *Respect for Women,* she extracts similar arguments from Rousseau, especially from Book V of his *Emile: or; On Education.* In this text, Rousseau insists that women fulfill the role as respected mothers, which requires the subordination of women to men. As a consequence, women's lust will be declared a threat to the (male) social order, which justifies the confinement of women within the home. In particular, Kofman finds Rousseau's massive appeals to the respect for women of interest: "If you want to fight against the corruption of ethics there is one remedy: remind the women to be themselves [and] to urge men to respect women" (Kofman 1982: 18).

In order to crystallize the paradoxical constellation created by "respect for women," Kofman decides to submit Kant's concept of moral respect (Achtung) to a feminist analysis. For Kant, respect begins to exist with the respect for women and mothers. The largest part of *Respect for Women* is thus devoted to an analysis of Kant. It needs to be said that overall, Kant has written relatively little on respect. In the *Critique of Practical Reason* he offers a very brief account of respect and explains that it is a subjective feeling and not a judgment (1976: 106). Still, it seems that many commentators have been intrigued by his explanations.[1] They even had a difficult time coming to terms with what Kant understands by the feeling of respect, often concluding that in Kant, respect has a "mysterious status." Kant's idea of respect is indeed complex. William Sokoloff interprets it as a paradoxical quality by linking it to self-affection (Selbstliebe) that he locates in the *Critique of Pure Reason*:[2] "Respect can justifiably be designated as a paradox because it is a feeling that is not received from outside influences but one that is self-generated, that is, self-affected. And self-affection, Kant suggests, is paradoxical" (770).

Kofman offers mainly a reading of Kant's "Anthropology," a text contained in the addendum (or appendix) to Kant's *Doctrine of Virtue*, which is the second part of his *Metaphysics of Morals*. Here, Kant explains in a detailed fashion what virtues humans should acquire.[3] Kant "turns the respect for women into a special case of the feelings that every man must bear a priori for any human being in general" (Kofman 1982: 14). This means that whenever we talk about respect among humans, the woman adopts a particular position, as "it is to the woman in particular that man offers his respect, his homage; and there is no parallel term to signify the deference that women should offer men" (14). Like for Rousseau, "respect for women, far from being for [Kant] one example of respect among others, is a necessary condition for the advent of morality" (17).

What Kant and Rousseau have in common is that they share the project of veiling or of keeping women at distance, always respectfully and under a moral mask. This means that both produce an ambivalent concept of respect, the kind of respect that men have towards women as they are always trying to "repair" women though the women they repair are precisely those whom they have previously destroyed, humiliated, and dirtied earlier and whom they had, in Kofman's words, "transformed into whores" (19). Both Kant's and Rousseau's reflections are relatively nuanced and sophisticated; at least more nuanced than those of John Stuart Mill (born two years after Kant's death), who asserted that "all women are brought up from the very earliest years in the belief that their ideal of character is the very opposite to that of men; not self-will, and government by self-control, but submission and yielding to the control of others" (Mill 1985: 15–16 from Laborde 2006: 369). In Mill's blunt statement, which admits nothing beyond feminine submission and masculine (self-)control, there might be space for "respect for men," but definitely no space for "respect for women."

Kofman's point of departure is that the word "respect" when used with regard to women expresses always a double feeling as it humiliates and elevates at the same time. Even more, the respect for women might merely be "the moral and glorious flipside of men's 'misogyny'" (55). In other words, men's feminism is merely "the reverse side of their 'anti-feminism'" (ibid.). This is where Kant and Rousseau agree. Women should be kept at distance because "their charm, their most powerful effect, is an 'action at distance' which necessitates precisely . . . a distance" (16). All this will be done with the "pretext of moral and respect" (19). The respect that men are ready to pay women is a highly ambivalent quality for the simple reason that women are ambivalent creatures. At the root of all this is the mentioned mother/whore ambivalence that men constantly perceive in women. Women are always attractive/terrifying, fascinating/dangerous, stimulating/petrifying, and men do everything to forget, hide, and cover up these ambivalences. Here, veiling turns out to be very efficient.

Kant himself mentions the veil in a metaphorical fashion by referring to precisely this effect of hiding. Kofman quotes this passage from Kant's *Doctrine of Virtue*:

> In the case of unnatural vice it is as if man in general felt ashamed of being capable of treating his own person in such a way, which debases him beneath the beasts, so that when even the permitted bodily union of the sexes in marriage (a union which is in itself merely an animal union) is to be mentioned in polite society, this occasions and requires much delicacy to throw a veil over it. (Kant 1991: 221; Kofman 1982: 32)

The veil helps men to cope with those unsolvable contradictions because under the veil, the woman can remain the respected mother and at the same time be punished (confined, restricted, hampered) because she is a potential whore.

However, it also follows from Kant's passage that not only women but also men are highly ambivalent creatures, a fact that Kofman is eager to highlight. There is not only the "women's tendency to dominate but men tend to be willingly dominated" (30) while, at the same time, men have "the will to dominate women [which] reinforces their pride and their desire to rule out any inappropriateness on the male side" (31).

This is the male paradox. How do men solve it? By paying respect to women. It is clear that this is not the simple kind of respect but that it flows out of the ambivalent character of both sexes. Kofman has elucidated this ambivalent character in her Freudian writings, where she depicts it more straightforwardly as a fusion of male and female traits or as a deconstruction of the male/female active/passive opposition. However, in these earlier Freudian writings it has mainly been the woman who turns out to be ambivalent. In *The Enigma of Woman* (1980/1985), Kofman insists on Freud's assumption that women are both masculine and feminine whereas man remains simply masculine (1985: 123–126). Man is frightened of woman just because of this undecidablilty of feminine sexuality, which he finds *unheimlich*: "Hidden away and veiled, the strangely familiar woman threatens to appear again. That is the message of 'Das Unheimliche'" (Todd 1986: 528).

## RESPECT AND SHAME

Men can put a veil over women out of respect, but by doing so they also exclude them from the social sphere. There is, however, a view that is classical in Islam, which some believe may have solved this paradox. This point of view considers veiling not in terms of respect, but in terms of modesty and shame. Here the mother/whore ambiguity, which from Kofman's point of view is at the root of the entire project called "veiling out of respect," evaporates within a second.

Shame is not the same as guilt but both are distinct emotional experiences that differ substantially along cognitive, affective, and motivational dimensions. Shame can be defined as "an intensely painful feeling or experience of believing we are flawed and therefore unworthy of acceptance and belonging" (Brown 2006: 47). In a study with 215 American women, Brené Brown found that "participants contrasted shame with guilt, which they defined or described as a feeling that results from behaving in a flawed or bad way rather than a flawed or bad self." Brown concludes that the guilt versus shame distinction is supported by an "I did/said/believed something bad" vs. "I am bad" paradigm (50).

It is interesting to compare Kofman's arguments with those of Egyptian feminist Fadwa El Guindi who criticizes the "modesty model" of Islamic veiling because, in her view, it "represents an ethnocentric imposition on Arabo-Islamic culture" (El Guindi 1999: 83). More precisely, El Guindi identifies the rejected model as the "modesty-shame-seclusion model" and believes that this paradigm, which depends on dichotomies such as "public/ private, and its corollary honor-shame, is the one most commonly imposed upon Arab and Islamic cultural space to describe the division between the sexes" (79). And she believes the modesty-honor gendered opposition to be equally inappropriate (83). Instead, for El Guindi, "veiling in contemporary Arab culture is largely about identity and about privacy" and about how the body can be inserted into space without contradicting the principles of reserve and respect. She points out that "the two qualities, modesty and seclusion, are not adequate characterizations of the phenomenon as it is expressed in the Middle East" (xvii). Therefore, veiling should never be based on what she perceives as purely "western notions," which are those of modesty and shame. According to El Guindi, the modesty-shame-seclusion model "makes more sense in Christian Mediterranean societies and, without shame, the Hindu-based societies of south Asia" (79), while its use in Islamic contexts obscures the nuanced differences of characteristics of Arabo-Islamic culture. Based on some etymological research, El Guindi suggests another, non-ethnocentric concept able to explain the culture of veiling. The words *hurma* (sanctity), *hishma* (reserve), and *haya* (respect) constitute cultural codes on the basis of which she designs a "sanctity-reserve-respect" paradigm that she finds most appropriate for Arab culture. *Hurma* is related to *haram*, "a key concept in the 'sanctity-reserve-respect' code" (84). *Haram* means forbidden, prohibited, unlawful, taboo, and sacred. El Guindi wants the "honor-shame" model to be replaced by this 'sanctity-reserve-respect' code.

El Guindi's approach is problematic for several reasons. First, Kofman's considerations show that "respect for women" is not a typical Islamic theme but that it has been central to Western discussions on the status of women for centuries. It is thus misleading to attribute "modesty-shame-seclusion" to the Christian West and "sanctity-reserve-respect" to the Islamic Middle East. While this seems obvious, there is actually a more interesting question that arises directly from El Guindi's considerations: Is veiling in Islamic societies (and beyond) really *only* a matter of respect and *not* of shame? Kofman, with her Freudian background, would never believe that it is. Her analyses clearly show that the cultural code of "sanctity-reserve-respect" involves the status of women in complexities that are in fact similar to those of veiling. The main reason is that veiling is always linked to sexually charged notions such as shame. Right at the beginning of *Respect for Women*, Kofman declares that "with respect for women, questions that are completely different from those concerning ethics enter the field. There is an entire sexual economy" (15). It is obvious that veiling participates in this economy. Accordingly, Gökariksel and Secor find that for many of the Turkish women they interviewed, "the bikini seems to represent the veil's antipode, entering the body into a forbidden economy of pleasures" (2012: 859). How can veiling not be about shame?

Most specialists cite veiling indeed typically as being "that which covers sexual shame" (Abu-Lughod 1986: 159). It is assumed that women want respect and those who do not want it or who do not deserve respect are shameless and should be *ashamed*. El Guindi's refusal of the shame model is difficult to understand, especially since *awrah* refers in the Islamic *fiqh* (jurisprudence) texts of the *sunna* to the woman's body as a source of *shame* that must be covered during prayers (before God) and in public (before men).

Apart from those religious considerations, a lot has been written from an anthropological point of view about the particular honor code for women in Arab culture. The identification of femininity with shame (and masculinity with honor) in Arab culture revolves around the generic Arab term *'ird*, which is exclusively connected with "female chastity and continence" (Abu-

Zeid 1965: 65). *'Ird* is the Bedouin honor code for women and "was the guiding motive in the acts and deeds of all the Arabs except those of the Yemen. . . . On account of its sacred nature, it was entitled to take the place of religion; the Arab put it in the highest place and defended it arms in hand" (Fares 1938: 96, quoted from Dodd 1973: 40).

Gideon Kressel traces Muslim culture to local Bedouin traditions and believes that "veiling and segregation of women may have had their basis in the code of sexual modesty, which evolved in the region's traditions" (Kressel 1992: 34). It would later be spelled out in precisely those Qur'anic passages that have been quoted in chapter 3 (note 1). *'Ird* is of utmost importance here. Peter Dodd finds that

> among the modern Bedouins we still find *'ird* with all its pre-Islamic force [but] the use of the term *'ird*, in its traditional sense, though less rich in meaning, has continued, keeping its sacred character and its relation with insult. . . . At the present day, the meaning of the word *'ird* has become restricted; in Transjordania it is associated with the virtue of a woman or even with her beauty. . . . In Egypt, the *'ird* of a man depends on his wife's reputation and that of all his female relatives. (51)

The link with shame is provided by the fact that *'ird* is always linked to sexuality and the codes of its repression (cf. Patai 1976). Hassan specifies that "most Muslim men's concept of 'honor' revolves around the orbit of women's sexuality, which is seen as a male possession" (Hassan 1999: 270).

It is exactly here that Kofman's Kantian logic kicks in. If we follow this logic to the end, the "sanctity-reserve-respect" paradigm turns out to be merely the flipside of the "modesty-shame-seclusion" paradigm, just like "respect for women" is always the flipside of misogyny. More clearly this means: respect is always the flipside of shame. Like respect, shame and modesty are socially constructed qualities and both are conceptually linked. Kofman's critique of Rousseau's ideas of modesty and shame as natural phenomena makes this particularly clear as she reproaches him to believe that a "veil of shame" (103) has been created by nature. Freud is criticized for the same reason. In the first part of *The Enigma of Woman*, entitled "The Enigma and the Veil," Kofman points out how ridiculous it is to believe that, as does Freud, "in seeking to veil herself, the woman would only be imitating nature, which has always already covered over her genitals with pubic hair" (Kofman 1980/1985: 4). If El Guindi really believes that veiling of women in Arab Islamic culture is *only* a matter of respect, she is misled by exactly the paradox that Kofman is criticizing in her book.

Reading Kofman's book on respect in the context of a discussion on veiling is particularly interesting since it shows how much any implementation of respect is dependent upon *distance*; and this goes for both Middle Eastern and Western cultures. And in any act of veiling, distance is linked to a sexual economy, that is, to shame. Furthermore, neither Middle Eastern nor Western culture manages to avoid the double standards that are attached to the social strategy of implementing "respect through distance." The problem, according to Kofman, is that an established distance between women and society is supposed to make women more virtuous but this is exactly what does *not* happen. Instead, the result of "respect through distance" is that the woman can now more easily be essentialized and objectified as a sexual being *of which she should actually be ashamed*: "Finally, only the whore can save us from the whore that is, from generalized prostitution" (Kofman 1982: 16). Kofman's logic is radical: Respect leads to seclusion, reserve leads to shame, and sanctity leads to forced modesty. In other words, respect is only a sham; it is a veil behind which one hides the virtues enumerated at the beginning of Book V of Rousseau's *Emile* and which are: timidity, modesty, and shame.

However, even for men, respect and shame are closely linked. Men are asked to respect women, to keep them always at a distance "for not being tempted to lift their veil, to master them" (53). To "master women" is an act that is shameful in the first place. This is why "the lifting of the veil runs the risk to floor man, to crush, to paralyze him" (54), that is, to put him into a shameful position. Veiling is linked to domination which enhances men's pride, and pride is the contrary of shame. As mentioned above, men have the will to dominate women which reinforces their pride.

El Guindi rejects the Rousseauian virtues of timidity, modesty, and shame as irrelevant for Arab Muslim culture and suggests that respect and reserve should be seen as the only virtues that matter when it comes to veiling. It has been shown above that this reasoning is precipitated in any context. Also in Muslim culture, respect for women and modesty/shame are closely linked. The only relevant question to be asked is: Does modesty represent a veil behind which genuine respect is hidden or is respect merely a veil behind which forced modesty is hidden? Kofman believes that the latter is always the case; and I believe that it would be difficult to rule this out offhand for Muslim culture in which, according to some, women "are silenced and distanced from power by having their 'sacred' role defined as to wait in silence at home" (Grace 2004: 161).[4] Respect for women has a price, no matter the culture; and the price is always the flipside of respect, which is chastity, silence, retreat. In the view of Kofman, "the sad share of respectable women" (1982: 19).

## EMPOWERMENT OF WOMEN

Now here is a further paradox, which is linked to the preceding one: Women are empowered just because of this constellation. "True inversion: women's weakness and all typical traits are also levers that serve to govern men" (30). The paradox has perhaps been well expressed in the Middle Eastern context by Ali Mazrui when saying that "Muslim countries are ahead in female empowerment, though still behind in female liberation" (Mazrui 1997: 121). The power of women is non-power, which is one of the secrets of respect. Kofman's book shows that this paradox is not limited to Muslim culture. Neither respect nor modesty is an end in itself. Through respect the woman becomes a mere object; but equally through respect, modesty becomes a means of empowerment. Respected women are not ghosts, they do not necessarily live their lives in a metaphysical beyond but they are empowered: "with a simple sign or a word she sends him to the end of the world." (Kofman 1982: 104). As mentioned, both Kant and Rousseau believed that women "have the tendency to dominate and the tendency to please, and this mainly in public" (30). For the above-mentioned reasons flowing out of the particular deontology of "respect for women," in the war of sexes the weaker sex always has the upper hand. Men have the tendency to be dominated and their readiness to respect women flows out of this constellation. Kofman states that, in general, "men's voices are stifled by women, the mean ones, the degenerated ones" (90) and "wherever women are free we will find bad manners (mœurs)" (ibid.). It is not without reason that French colonial authorities thought, according to Frantz Fanon, that "if we want to destroy the structure of Algerian society, its capacity for resistance, we must first of all conquer the women. In the colonialist program, it was the woman who was given the historic mission of shaking up the Algerian man" (Fanon 1967: 164).

What becomes necessary in this situation is the separation of sexes, as is pointed out by Rousseau who believes that "where manners are policed, it's because women are locked away." Separation is essential and "any familiarity is suspect, any liaison is dangerous!" (90).[5] Women are dangerous and men should "not be as imprudent as being fascinated by them as this fascination is dangerous, paralyzing, petrifying" (15). And men best address this danger "by introducing a separating distance between themselves and women, by forcing themselves to stay clear of women" (15). More precisely, men must place "women on a throne by making them goddesses or queens" (16): "To place them high enough and far enough to avoid the risk of having a close and immediate contact, of being *fascinated* by them" (15). On the one hand, it might seem that women, once they have disappeared beneath the veil, will be respected merely as ghosts who can no longer bother men in real life because they live in the modest and metaphysical beyond to which men's respect has sent them. But beware: They are also empowered through their modesty (which requires respect).

Women are empowered through respect. The cynical conclusion is: Why should men feel guilty in the first place? Given that the pattern of empowerment through respect/modesty contains multiple ambivalences, it can only too easily be hijacked along cynical lines and for the purpose of male intentions: "If only they would want to be just women and mothers, their undeniable power would be immense" (104). According to this logic, *modern* women have lost all their power because they are no longer respected for their silence but rather for the noise they make. The modern women *might appear* powerful because, "bold, cheeky, intriguing, coquettish, she keeps lovers out of mere generosity, makes them obey like valets, but she has no authority and men no longer respect her" (104). In modern life, "the most estimated woman is no longer the one who provokes silence but who makes the maximum of noise, of whom one speaks most, whom one sees most in the world, where one dines most often, who sets the tone most masterfully, who judges, solves, and assigns men merits and virtues and their degrees and places" (104).[6] However, in the eyes of some, this is no real power, at least not compared to the power that women can gain through respect. Women should be respected merely because they are silent and not because they speak.

## CONCLUSION

Sarah Kofman's reflections are clearly linked to the overall topic of this book. In the following chapters it will be shown that female tattoos are one way of breaking the silence and of making noise. Christine Braunberger, for example, finds that tattoos make the body speak in "a culture built on women's silence and bent on maintaining silence as a primary part of the relationship between women's bodies and cultural writing" (Braunberger 2000: 1). Here women no longer want to be passive texts devoid of meaning. Protest nudity serves the same purpose. Again, the result *can* be the loss of respect.

Kofman's analysis of respect for women reveals a series of paradoxes linked to the logic of veiling as well as self-veiling: respect-modesty, sexuality-chastity, power-non-power, existentialization-essentialization. These paradoxes must be of interest for pro-veiling feminists who use a practice that has historically underpinned the patriarchal oppression which they are trying to subvert. One of such paradoxes has appeared in the Turkish reveiling wave (*tesettür*) where women, when they first adopted the overcoat uniformly in the 1980s, "sought to escape from the anxieties of what they perceived to be a lifestyle that is characterized by too much freedom and choice. As they submitted to the boundaries of the overcoat, they chose to be a non-choosing subject" (Sandikci and Ger 2010: 40). The authors conclude that "while wearing the uniform overcoat in the 1980s gets constructed as making a choice, it later becomes reconstructed as being in a mold and, hence, a sign of lack of freewill" (47). As a consequence, the *tesettür* phenomenon began to adhere to more playful, fashion-oriented patterns. However, the inevitable result was that those women lost respect: "While a new wholesome femininity is claimed, *tesettür* women continue to be the object of the male gaze . . . and attempts to regulate the female body, even when it is covered, continue to be as strong as ever" (50). This echoes the opinion of Egyptian film director Oualid Hammad who believes that harassment and the male gaze are "a question of power, not of sex. The more the woman is covered the bigger the challenge. Veiling arouses the men" (Sallon 2013).

Pro-veiling feminists should be aware that veiling practices of any kind are never straightforward but contradictory by definition. The *tesettür* case shows that whenever pro-veiling feminists use those techniques they must be aware that the respect for women is always "the moral and glorious flipside of men's misogyny" (Kofman). If veiling is supposed to bring about a positive identity able to transcend that of the pseudo-liberated woman, these contradictions need to be taken into consideration.

## NOTES

1. Sokoloff mentions Kofman but also Lyotard (1994) and Adorno (1973) as examples (ibid.).

2. In the section entitled "The Application of the Categories to Objects of the Senses in General" (Kant 1965: 165–166).

3. Kofman reads in particular section 7.

4. Grace says this about Indian Muslim culture.

5. Kofman paraphrases here a passage from Rousseau's *La Nouvelle Héloïse*, part 4, letter 10.

6. Kofman paraphrases Rousseau from his *Letter to D'Alambert* (1835: 153).

*Chapter Five*

# "Cool Space"

## *Segregation and Veiling*

In this chapter I examine the spatial function of veiling. I establish the concept of "cool space" by examining the phenomenon of veiling in a concrete and in a metaphorical sense. In particular, I look at two phenomena that have been theorized by many authors: historical *racial* segregation in North America and *gender* segregation practiced in Muslim countries. I explain that in both cases segregation has often been linked to the creation of a "cool space" of playful transgression in which transparency plays a paramount importance. More precisely, I examine in an abstract fashion a philosophical concept of transparency linked to veiling by using examples from certain cultures as a point of departure. The final question will be whether a spatial concept of transparency inspired by coolness and the veil can provide new ideas about space in general and enrich our conceptual vocabulary. It will also be explained when and where veiling does not provide such a "coolness."

Transparent or translucent are items that allow light to pass through so that objects behind them can be seen. The particularity of the veil is indeed that it is transparent: the hijab is a curtain or a permeable membrane and not a wall. Often it is made of translucent muslin. My hypothesis is that through transparency, separation becomes simultaneously non-separation and that this constellation can be a source of coolness. More generally, this last chapter wraps up the multiple points on veiling made in the preceding chapters.

Spatial separation, segregation, and exclusion are not limited to gender and race but have become necessary devices in modern life because they are able to "cool down" tensions. Judit Bodnar writes about the phenomenon of "exclusion" in modern architectural planning:

The genuine desire to escape the alienation of the modern world into a better
familial and collective life and a more "natural" environment was based on
exclusion. The exclusion of work from the household, industry from nature,
women from the danger of the public eye, but most importantly the lower
classes from the bourgeoisie. (Bodnar 2007: 146).

My intention for this chapter is not merely to establish that the veil can be
cool. There is no doubt that for at least twenty years, some amount of "coolness" has been attached to the contemporary use of the hijab because it is, as
has been shown, no longer merely a religious item but also a fashion item,
which has been the topic of some of the preceding chapters. Nor is it my
intention to establish an idealized version of the "veiled woman" in terms of
an "ethnocentric universalism." As pointed out in chapter 3, the veil has
different meanings for different people. Accordingly, the "spatial" experience of wearing a veil will probably differ depending on the cultural contexts. Still, I believe that beyond those cultural experiences, the "veil" signifies something that all those experiences have in common.

The same is true for African American coolness. I do not attempt to
essentialize and ghettoize African American men and women by pretending
that African American culture or the entire African American history with its
reaction to racial oppression can be reduced to mere coolness. Instead, I am
interested in concepts that express certain spatial attitudes. The problem with
concepts is that they always reduce concrete reality, which contains a large
variety of signifiers, to an abstract quantity. However, whenever it is done
correctly, the "reduction" will not flatten the real world but rather enhance its
understanding.

A further purpose of the chapter is to demonstrate that the concept of
"cool space" overcomes certain Western philosophical notions, and that this
transgression is in keeping with some of the most recent Western philosophical developments. I show this by considering the veil as a philosophical
metaphor firmly installed in Western metaphysics but recently deconstructed
by poststructuralism and hermeneutics. I am not saying that negative Western responses to Muslim women's veiling are entirely dependent on those
Western philosophical notions. However, their consideration makes clear
how much the idea of the "veil as a creator of cool space" runs contrary to the
heritage of Western metaphysics.

## THE VEIL IN WESTERN THOUGHT

This is not the right place to provide an exhaustive presentation of veiling
metaphors throughout the history of Western philosophy. However, some
key concepts can clarify in which connotative networks the veil has been
involved, in theoretical contexts, for hundreds of years. In Western thought,

the veil as a separator (even a transparent one) is generally unwelcome because the Western philosophical tradition depends very much on surface/ depth (form/content) dichotomies; and often those dichotomies involve the metaphor of the veil. In the Bible, the possibility of knowledge is described as an act of unveiling: Having eaten from the fruit of knowledge, Adam and Eve do not obtain knowledge about everything that exists in the world; what they do obtain is the *possibility* of knowledge because they can now see things more clearly. Once the veil has been lifted from their eyes they will distinguish good from evil and see their nudity *as nudity* (Genesis 3: 5). Their clear-sightedness is similar to the Greek *a-letheia*, which is often rendered as "truth" but literally signifies a "non-veiled state." *A-letheia* functions as a light making knowledge possible (see Agamben 2011: 81 on this topic).

The most famous Western philosophical surface/depth dichotomy making direct use of the veil metaphor is Arthur Schopenhauer's idea of the Indian "Veil of Maya" in the sense of an illusion shrouding reality. In Indian philosophy, *maya* is the veil of illusion that takes the appearance of concrete "reality" and thereby conceals the true nature of existence. The veiling illusion needs to be overcome, penetrated, and eliminated. Schopenhauer's reference to Indian philosophy was new, but the use of the veil as a metaphor for ignorance was not. As a matter of fact, for centuries, Western theories have reiterated a veil vs. reality system, explaining that the veil either hides or blurs the truth. This strategy was particularly common during the medieval period where "expression" was generally seen as veiling or covering, and "understanding" as an act of uncovering (Weinsheimer 2003: 158). Understanding and interpretation were construed as finding hidden meanings situated underneath a concealing or unclear and blurring veil.

Some modern philosophers accepted the so-called veil of perception doctrine as a valid option. The doctrine going by that name believes that our perception of the world is vitiated by a fundamental flaw and that there is no proof for the existence of that world. René Descartes, John Locke and, in the eyes of many experts, also Immanuel Kant can be included in this category. In a way of speaking, those philosophers reinstate the veil and leave it intact but find sophisticated means of reaching for an understanding that eventually *transcends* the veil.

In contrast, post-war contemporary continental philosophy presents many examples of how the veil/truth dichotomy can be entirely abandoned or deconstructed. Hans-Georg Gadamer's hermeneutics does not attempt to find the text's meanings behind a metaphorical veil but instead offers descriptions for various aspects of interpretation. Gadamer's dialogical notion of understanding is reminiscent of the relational space of understanding which is, according to some, also produced by the veil in Middle Eastern culture. Gadamer's famous thesis that understanding is the fusion of horizons (Gadamer 1989: 306) avoids any hierarchized, surface/depth distinctions and thus parallels precisely those multidirectional and dynamic practices of veiling examined in this chapter. In other words, Gadamer's hermeneutics establishes in philosophical terms what an Iranian sociologist has called a "dialectical relationship between veiling and unveiling" (Naficy 2003: 140). In a similar vein, another hermeneutic philosopher, Paul Ricœur has said that myths or fables throw an "intentional veil" on the truth in order to avoid simplistic interpretations (Ricœur 1969: 295). This, too, needs to be understood as a dialectics of veiling and unveiling that can be contrasted with the metaphysical removal of the veil whose only purpose is to penetrate non-veiled truths.

Jacques Derrida's deconstructive approach is even more radical. In Derrida's philosophy, the veil is no longer seen in a Platonic sense as a covering of truth. For Derrida, truth can be "hidden" though, paradoxically, it remains right on the surface. His notion of the *pharmakon*, which serves as a supplement to the (interior) subject, is not located "deep inside" the subjects examined, but it can also be part of the subject's appearance (of its style, for example). In general, Derrida wants the metaphysical separation between inside and outside, between depth and surface, or reality and appearance to be overcome; and this becomes clearest when he writes about the veil. His "theatrical mask" covers what it represents, which means that the paradoxical role of the veil is both to conceal and reveal (Derrida 1981: 193). In the end, "the un-veiling will still remain a movement of the veil" (Derrida and Cixous 2001: 28). In *Spurs: Nietzsche's Styles*, Derrida analyses Friedrich Nietzsche's interpretation of women as both the signifiers and the "veiling" dissimulators of truth. In *The Gay Science* (Book 2, Aphorism 64), Nietzsche writes:

> I fear that women who have grown old are more skeptical in the secret recesses of their hearts than any of the men; they believe in the superficiality of existence as in its essence, and all virtue and profundity is to them only the disguising (Verhüllung) of this "truth," the very desirable disguising of a pudendum—an affair, therefore, of decency and modesty, and nothing more. (Derrida 1979: 59)

Derrida concludes that Nietzsche's truth "can only be surface" because truth is rather the blushing movement of a truth which "casts a modest veil, which thus falls over such a surface." Finally, only through such a veil, "could 'truth' become truth, profound, decent, desirable. But should that veil be suspended, or even fall a bit differently, there would no longer be any truth" (ibid.). Earlier, in Aphorism 57, Nietzsche had referred to Friedrich Schiller's poem "The Veiled Image of Sais" and made fun of "ye sober beings" who suppress all ornaments and who believe to have discovered a "reality" that "before you alone stands unveiled." Nietzsche asks: Are they not, in their "unveiled condition still extremely passionate and dusky beings?" In the end, even the most sober reality contains "some kind of fantasy, prejudice, irrationality, ignorance, fear." These examples show how the veil/truth dichotomy can be deconstructed by offering different interpretations of the "veiled object," and by avoiding the perception of the veil as a device merely concealing truth. Any analysis of the Islamic veil in a postmodern context should follow this theoretical path.

## THE VEIL, SPACE, AND THE COOL MASK

In order to deconstruct the surface/depth dichotomies on which the above thinking depends and to reestablish the veil metaphor along the lines pointed out, it is necessary to approach the veil as a spatial concept of transparency and ambiguity. The outcome will be a certain conception of "cool space." In general, coolness requires a considerable amount of control. Losing control (of oneself or of a situation) is not cool. As will be shown below, the emergence of African American coolness in particular has to do with segregation, and one of the purposes of cool behavior has been to avoid confrontations between individuals. In reality, things are more complicated since originally (in and before the 1960s) black cool behavior was also linked to African Americans' *inability* to control political and cultural oppression. Mere self-control would rather be associated with Victorian white American coolness. Peter Stearns has shown that a certain type of coolness can be considered a principle of Victorian white American culture determined by asceticism, Puritanism, and self-control cultivated during the Victorian period (1830–1860). The Victorian middle classes of England and America attempted to formulate "recommended norms by which people are supposed to shape their emotional expressions" and opinions about how to obtain "calmness and composure of spirit" (Stearns 1994: 2, 25). However, coolness, as it is conceived in an African American context—which is the context that interests us here—represents rather the paradoxical fusion of *control* and the *inability to control*. Instead of reveling in either total control or total detachment, coolness very often depends on such paradoxical associations.

Can the above patterns be related to the veil? It is useful to look once again at the male veil as it is worn by the Tuareg (chapter 1, Figure 1.3) because here the coolness theme is very obvious (though completely detached from the typically female honor/shame paradigms that have been discussed in the preceding chapters). Robert Murphy has described the space produced by the Tuareg veil as one of semi-commitment, which is a sign of coolness because it simultaneously controls and disrupts control: "Here the actor allows the other enough cues so that the game may go on, but withholds sufficient stimuli so that his further course of action cannot be fully predicted. This not only gives him flexibility, but by decreasing the show of emotional attachment to the means and also the end of action he is not trapped into commitment. More simply, and elegantly, this is what is known as 'playing it cool'" (Murphy 1964: 1259). This means that the veil is transparent: It simultaneously withholds and reveals (it "allows the other enough cues"); and the attitude of coolness depends on this play with transparency. A renewed understanding of the concept of the veil inspired by the hijab togetherer with some thoughts about African American coolness initiated by segregation can thus help us to deconstruct the Western philosophical dichotomies of veiled perception vs. unveiled perception that have been presented in the preceding sections.

Most generally speaking, considering the veil in terms of space is not new. Descriptions of spatial experiences of the veil are numerous. The hijab is not merely a piece of cloth put on the woman's head, but as a social tool it has a spatial function. One of the oldest and most famous of such descriptions is Frantz Fanon's account of the unveiled woman who learns how to walk in the street of Algiers: "When the Algerian woman has to cross a street, for a long time she commits errors of judgment as to the exact distance to be negotiated. The unveiled body seems to escape, to dissolve" (Fanon 1967: 59). Though the description concerns the unveiled body in the first place, indirectly it conveys clear indications about what happens when a woman *does* wear a veil. It shows in which way the wearing of the veil can influence individual spatial perceptions.

The body's relationship with space does obviously change when wearing the veil. This concerns not only geographical space, but also the perception of social space. Banu Gökariksel and Anna Secor have analyzed how a veiled woman in Istanbul is obliged to navigate between what she considers *halal* and *haram* spaces of the city (Gökariksel and Secor 2012: 858). In the Islamic context, desires need to be controlled and space management is essential. When a woman veils, her spatial boundaries become more precise. According to a woman interviewed by Özlem Sandikci and Güliz Ger, "if you are uncovered, your boundaries are blurry, confusing, ambiguous. . . . But when you cover, *tesettür* clarifies your boundaries. That's easier, simpler, more comfortable" (Sandikci and Ger 2010: 18).

## THE TRANSPARENT VEIL

Interestingly, in both cases, that of Fanon's woman and of the Turkish woman, veiling does not produce a blurred perception but, on the contrary, it is the *unveiled* state that lets the world appear fuzzy and unclear. Here the veil is supposed to establish clarity. The question is: Is the border as clear and unambiguously defined as the subjects believe it to be? While the Turkish woman thinks that certain parts of the city are now off limits for her, she is obviously not aware that in other parts of the city she can now walk around more freely.

Sandikci and Ger confirm this as they interpret the veil, on the one hand, as a key marker of the rural–urban division as well as of class identities in Turkey, but insist, on the other hand, on the dynamic produced by this bodily movement. Social developments can lead to constant transgressions of the dividing lines, which is particularly true in cases where the veil has become "modernized"; that is, where it has become involved in the system and structures of modern fashion. Here "women contradicted the prevailing meaning of covering in Turkey. They were visibly religious and yet not rural, poor, or elderly. They had chosen to engage in a practice which was associated with the lower classes" (2010: 18). The deconstructing quality of the veil is emphasized by the paradoxical fact that its *absence* had once been able to *strengthen* social boundaries in Iran. This was the case when the "imposed absence of the veil created a divide between Westernized high classes and the rest of the population" (Balasescu 2007: 132). Also, Fanon's woman who once appreciated the firm corporeal limits provided by the veil, and who felt her unveiled state as that of a diffuse space-body mixture, does not contradict the thesis that, in reality, the veil is transparent and deconstructs borders. Her former state was not one of total confinement but she could take advantage of transparency, an advantage that is now obviously cancelled.

Fadwa El Guindi takes another direction when talking about veiling and space. She argues that in Arab societies veiling "puts its practitioners in a 'permanent sacred space' even as they engage in worldly activities" (El Guindi 1999: 134). Is this supposed to reify the veil as an absolute limit? Probably not, because a dynamic momentum is visible also here: Sacred space and worldly space are not isolated spaces but meet and fuse within social interaction.

Sandikci and Ger's examples show that the "relational" meaning of the veil creates transparency within separation. The word *hijab* translates as "to veil," "to seclude," "to screen," "to conceal," "to form a separation," "to mask," "cover," "wrap," "curtain," "veil," "screen," and "partition" (El Guindi 1999: 157). In spatial terms it means to mark a border, for example, through a curtain or a threshold. The story goes that three tactless guests overstayed their welcome after the Prophet's wedding though the Prophet desired to be alone with his new wife. Therefore Muhammad drew a curtain (hijab) between the nuptial chamber and the inconsiderate companions. The transparency of the veil establishes a link between the veil and coolness because both are matters of spatial experience, which is dynamic. A curtain is not a wall but the typical example of a marker whose limits are ambiguously defined.

How is the spatial experience of separation/non-separation related to coolness? Two definitions of coolness, Marshall McLuhan's and the African

American one, have been explained and used in this book. For McLuhan, coolness signifies "incomplete information" providing, paradoxically, a potential surplus of information because the cool surface is inspiring or mysterious. In an African American context, coolness signifies the control of emotions and to be "emotionally expressive within an artistic frame of restraint" (Dinerstein 1999: 241). Especially in the African American case, coolness did have a spatial function because it modified or subverted the existing spatial ideology of racial segregation. I believe that coolness should be interpreted in the context of such a type of spatial cohabitation.

One of the first proponents of black cool was the jazz saxophonist Lester Young (who has already been mentioned in chapter 3). Joel Dinerstein suggests that his blank facial expression aimed at resisting "the white gaze" (240). Also, here it is obvious that the residential segregation of white and black Americans brought forward behavioral mechanisms similar to veiling. Blacks in America suffered from the sanctions of white society, which they experienced as a social crisis. The moral trademarks of this white society were "republican virtues" established by Victorian culture such as rational thinking, virtuous behavior, but especially *repressed emotion*. As a result, those black people would cover themselves with a veil of emotionless republican virtue, which would be called "coolness." The cool mask enabled them to cope with the realities of their existence, to feel safer, but also to gain power. Being cool made their presence acceptable within white society, helped them to escape manipulation and create space for the autonomous self.[1]

## TWO KINDS OF SEGREGATION

The cool mask is not only about attitude but also about space: It becomes a means of creating and manipulating social space in order to create (ambiguous) instances of proximity and distance. There is an interesting similarity between the African American creation of "cool" behavior and veiling in Muslim contexts: both can be traced to an act of segregation. Also, in the Muslim world, the veil developed out of the ambition to segregate two kinds of human beings: men and women. Like black people in America, women in Muslim societies have often been left out of the larger picture of society and have been defined as mentally and morally inferior. Like the black man in American society, women in Muslim societies were often not recognized as equal human beings. Men usually "define the public world as their own space, [and] women are considered intruders in it. Harassment of women in the street exemplifies men's attempt to reaffirm their own boundaries of space and identity," write Pat Mule and Diane Barthel about Muslim societies in general (1992: 328). With the veil, however, women who had otherwise been confined to their homes can participate in social and professional activities. The veil allows "women to work while they still claim traditional respect" (El Guindi 1999: 163). Like the cool pose for black men, the veil "has helped, in a convoluted way, to carve a new space that Muslim women are using as a means of redefining the terms of their presence in public space," writes Ziba Mir-Hosseini about women in post-revolutionary Iran (2007). Also for El Guindi, a certain power of emancipation remains a characteristic intrinsic to the veil, a fact that she believes to be valid for all Muslim societies: "Veiling also symbolizes an element of power and autonomy and functions as a vehicle of resistance" (El Guindi 1999: xvii). Like the cool mask, the veil can yield empowerment to an oppressed group; and like those American blacks mentioned above, Muslim women could obtain unofficial power within a situation that had officially declared them inferior. Mule and Barthel hold that the veil "reflects women's efforts to gain or maintain esteem within a patriarchal society in which possibilities for autonomy are exceptionally, and increasingly, limited" (1992: 324).

The American racial situation and the practice of veiling show concrete points of connection in many instances. The most obvious instance is the use of the veil by the Nation of Islam, which has been pointed out as a facilitator of cultural identity similar to the cool mask. According to Miriam Cooke, the Nation of Islam's *khimar* (veil) "symbolizes their freedom and social worth in a community that valued its women and rejected their previous sexual objectification under slavery" (Cooke 2000: 132). Jamillah Karim reports of the Nation's practice of protecting women's bodies from the male gaze as an act of honoring one's natural beauty as a black woman, and that it taught the young woman Majorie "to love her blackness" (Karim 2006: 24).

The conclusion is, of course, not that racial segregation and gender segregation are one and the same thing. The veil is only a gender categorization while racial categorizations are not only racial but also intersected with gender. However, in abstract terms, both refer to the same technique: The veil, like the cool mask, is simultaneously an instrument of dissimulation (covering) and of assertion. This paradox is perhaps not equally obvious in all societies where veiling is practiced but still it is present. In certain cultural contexts, the woman will definitely attract attention through her veil, which is a paradox because the act of veiling *could* in the first place lead to disappearance (and in some cases certainly does). As mentioned, for Nawal El-Saadawi, the woman who wears a veil is even explicitly drawing attention to her body as much as the woman who wanders the streets naked. Ahdaf Soueif sees veiling also as "a conscious drawing attention to oneself—not as a sexual being—but as a political one" (Soueif 2003: 132). Of course, everything depends on the context. On a street in Kuwait or Al Ain a veiled woman will not stick out at all. It is interesting to note that El Sadaawi and Soueif attribute the "sticking out" effect to completely different sources; but however we judge the general value of such statements, veiling does not necessarily lead to disappearance. This remains true even when veiling goes through the filter of fashion and other stylistic instances that reduce the straightforward character of a political or religious message without negating it completely. As a matter of fact, the fusion of veiling with fashion can even enforce the "sticking out" effect instead of softening it. Bora Engin finds that the "headscarves [of Turkish *tesettür* women] are more striking, their jackets, pants, and blouses are more elegant. They are much more ostentatious than uncovered women" (Engin 2004, quoted from Sandikci and Ger 2007: 197).

What matters is that veiling embraces simultaneous acts of retraction and assertion; and the resulting effect can be considered cool just because of the paradox contained in this pattern. This is not to say that anything which simultaneously retracts and asserts is automatically cool. However, the playful use of such techniques in terms of stylistics can produce coolness. Furthermore, in contexts in which those techniques are supposed to solve precarious situations or are even methods of survival, the result is definitely coolness. Being cool is much about dignity, which is the reason why it represents a contradictory and complex approach towards assimilation. This is at least what follows from the main lines of African American history. Before World War II, it was generally believed that the Negro "readily takes the tone and color of his social environment, assimilating to the dominant culture with little resistance" (Herskovits 1941: 13). As previously mentioned, according to Cornel West, African Americans first "proceeded in an *assimilation–ist manner*" (West 1993: 17) but would then transcend this level of cultural assimilation. Today most people would agree with W. E. B. Du Bois, who believed that "there is no true American music but the wild sweet melodies of the Negro slave; the American fairy tales and folk-lore are Indian and African" (Du Bois 1997: 43). Or perhaps even with Sheik Anta Diop who held that what distinguishes the white American and his English ancestor "is the Negro laugh, so pleasant, inherited from the household slave who raised his children" (Diop 1991 from Verharen 1997: 480). Black people did not fight alienation through assimilation in order to be *included* instead of being excluded, but they constantly had to reinvent themselves in order to remain dignified individuals. They took pride in their identity, masked their anger, but at the same time they wanted to be visible *as blacks*. This means that coolness plays with opposing paradigms, which is also the reason why it is subversive.[2] In this sense, it is no surprise that those "resisting" women that Soueif and many others speak of would choose as their symbol of resistance an item that, in the past as well as in contemporary Saudi Arabia and Iran, has functioned as the symbol of *oppression*.

# THE VEIL OF TRANSPARENCY

The above sections have shown that any identification of separation with apartheid does not do justice to the initial concept of the veil. More efficient approaches should compare the veil rather to the *mashrabiyya*, the wooden latticework enclosing oriel windows of traditional Arab houses that permit women observing *purdah* to look outside without being seen, or to the Indian *jharokha*, which serves the same purpose (see chapter 1). Transparency as a spatial device is more frequent in non-Western architecture and this not only in Islamic contexts. Japanese *shoji* doors or devices used in the creation of space in Noh plays, for example, establish porous boundaries between inside and outside and are similar to these traditional Arab approaches. The Japanese *aboshigaki* (網干垣), a hanging fence made of bamboo and resembling a fishing net, or the *kabeshiro* curtain (壁代) are supposed to produce an overall harmony among inhabitants of a space that is simultaneous functioning through separation and connection.

Like the *mashrabiyya*, the veil is not supposed to seclude but separate genders in a relative fashion. Veiled women are metaphorically invisible, but they are not literally removed from the space. It has been shown that in some contexts they can even attract attention and stick out. More importantly, they *can* interact with men.

El Guindi says that veiled women carry their privacy and sanctity to public spaces (1999: 95). El Guindi's statement is problematical because, as Secor has shown, her "insight is not, actually, about space at all; it is about the woman's body, which is transfigured by the veil and marked as sanctified" (Secor 2002: 7). Still, since this space cannot be *entirely* sacred, it tells us something about techniques of transgression, fusion, and transparency within space, all of which are enacted through veiling. The same applies to Lila Abu-Lughod's idea of the *burqa* as a "mobile home" in which the woman is "at home though moving in public space" (Abu-Lughod 2002: 785). (It is interesting to note that the word *chador* in Persian means actually "tent" as much as "veil").

The relational character of veiled space is also pointed out by Hamid Naficy who explains that "veiling as a social practice is not fixed or unidirectional; instead it is a dynamic practice in which both men and women are implicated. In addition, there is a dialectical relationship between veiling and unveiling" (Naficy 2003: 140). The view that the order of society rested on separation and that modern, "open" systems expose what should be hidden, thereby creating voyeurism and exhibitionism, is basically wrong. Alexandru Balasescu's description of the flexible use of the headscarf in the life of Iranian members of the upper class (2007: 196) support this assumption. Interestingly, Murphy observed exactly this with regard to Tuareg veiling, which introduces "a form of distance between their selves and their social others. The veil, though providing neither isolation nor anonymity, bestows facelessness and the idiom of privacy upon its wearer and allows him to stand somewhat aloof from the perils of social interaction while remaining a part of it" (Murphy 1964: 1257). In the West, those suggested relational conceptions of space are not often encountered. However, African Americans established similarly porous borders in the segregated South and they did so by means of coolness. The traditional system of veiling in Muslim culture is transparent, which means that it attempts to establish a relative and cool spatial distance between two elements, a distance that entirely open systems cannot produce: neither voyeurism nor exhibitionism are cool (cool is to be understood here both in the technical-philosophical and in the popular sense of the word), and complete retraction is as "uncool" as its contrary. What is "cool" is rather the play with retraction.

Since Muslim segregation is about the separation of men from women, sexual implications are central. The above examples from Muslim culture show that coolness does not create a sexless space at all. El Guindi criticizes in this context the fact that "Christian puritanist belief and a dominant West [have been] constructed as a standard lens through which to project the world of the East" (1999: 45) and reminds us that "unlike other religions, orthodox Islam accepts sexuality as a normative aspect of both ordinary and religious life" (136). This explains why Christian missionaries could interpret the veil (together with the entire Islamic religion) as an institution giving "license to 'lewdness'" (Ahmed 1992: 154) and why "the Puritans of the nineteenth century thought the Muslim woman needed relief from overindulgence in sex" (Haddad 2007: 260). This also proves the claim that—at least originally—this kind of segregation is not at all about simple apartheid and/or Puritanism. Some authors have insisted that in Muslim societies, which traditionally have so much insisted on segregation, the aim has *never* been to encounter existing sexual spaces with total desexualization. This practice had rather been proclaimed by "uncool" Christian missionaries. El Guindi explains that while Christianity chose the path of complete desexualization of the worldly environment, Islam chose to regulate "the social order while accepting its sexualized environment" (1999: 31). The separation produced by the hijab can indeed include a sexual environment. In principle, any Puritan witch hunt exterminating the slightest trace of sexuality is alien to this system. Abdelwahab Bouhdiba confirms that "Islam in no way tries to depreciate, still less to deny the sexual. On the contrary, it attributes a sublime significance to the sexual and invests it with such a transcendental quality that any trace of guilt is removed from it" (Bouhdiba 1974: viii). Sex can be tolerated but it needs to be separated—through a transparent veil—from non-sexual realms. In this sense, the veil is not a mechanism of repression bound to produce its contrary, but it serves as a cool dissimulator.

Also, the African American cool attitude is not supposed to lead to mere asceticism; it gives in only *apparently* to a Puritan claim. Like the transparent veil, African American cool deconstructs the limits between the sexual and the non-sexual realms that Judeo-Christian culture draws so distinctly. Both cool culture and veiling are social expressions inviting interaction and involving the spectator's imagination. In this sense, they transcend both Puritan and anti-Puritan realities. Like Islamic culture which accepts, according to El Guindi, the sexualized environment, African American cool culture has more or less cut the link with the Christian-Freudian scheme of Puritanism as an oppression of nature. Similar to El Guindi's explanations that "the moral standards of Islam are designed to accommodate enjoyment of worldly life, including sexual environment" (1999: 31), black cool culture has been defined as a mixture of American Puritanism and African hedonism (Pountain and Robins 2000: 44). Richard Majors and Janet Billson contrast the African belief systems as "an organic system in harmony with nature," with the Euro-American belief system centering on the mastery over nature (Majors and Billson 1992: 55). Both veiling and cool culture "hold back," but are potentially sexually fecund. Sex is not *re*pressed but it is forced to change its *ex*pression. In other words, both cool and veil engage in a consistent anesthetization of sexuality in which the repressed parts will not necessarily reappear in a sublimated form but rather in a cool and restrained form that enacts an aesthetic surface. In philosophical terms, we are facing here a shift from an ethical to an aesthetical focus (which does not mean that ethical issues would not apply). The veil is part of aesthetic conditions through which sexuality can appear in a "cooler" fashion.

In summary, it can be said that in a paradoxical way, veiling, just like the cool mask, simultaneously cancels and prolongs segregation. The cool or veiled subject is separated from society but at the same time both coolness and the veil allow interaction within the social group from which one would otherwise be excluded. Emotions and expressions remain hidden within a segregated space as well as underneath the mask, but within this confined realm they can develop more autonomously. It is a fact that gender segregation has engendered many disadvantages for women, but according to Fadwa El Guindi (1999), Leila Ahmed (1982), and several other authors, it has also produced advantages. One reason for this is that in segregated societies, almost all activities performed in the world of men by men must be performed in parallel in the world of women by women (cf. Ahmed 1982: 528). Another reason is that segregated society "allows men considerably less control over how women think": "Saudi society would seem to offer men less control than Western society, where women live dispersed and isolated among men" (ibid.). Similar claims have been made about veiling in Western societies. Karim reports about the young, converted black woman Tayyibah who states that "not having to compete with men, not being compared to

men, not having to deal with a male teacher's gender expectations, and not
having the distraction of a sexually-charged atmosphere are all factors that
can positively affect women when segregated" (Karim 2005: 172).

## REVERSE EFFECTS

However, segregation through the veil can also be criticized because in too
many cases it does *not* establish coolness, which means that there is a reverse
effect. Very often the separation of genders and the strong accentuation of
women's otherness lead to a sexualization of situations where normally no
sexual connotation had been intended. I am working at a private university in
Kuwait, and Western teachers here generally agree that the gender separation
(male and female students are taught separately) has the precise counter-
effect of unnecessary sexualization of situations as soon as male and female
students come together *after* class. What has been created is not a cool space
but a "hot space" that is oversexualized and almost lewd. Paradoxically, in
this atmosphere, the wearing of the veil might become more necessary than
ever. The more radical the segregation, the more radical will be the desire for
non-segregation. Enforced coolness is not cool at all but leads to (sexual)
hotness.[3]

Some feminist authors have very much insisted on this latter point. Marnia Lazreg equates veiling and the presentation of nudity in magazines because both reduce women to their sex (Lazreg 2009: 108); and Mervat Hatem
believes that "veiled women were more likely to see themselves as 'sex
objects who tempt men,' and should therefore be veiled and segregated for
the good of society" (Hatem 1988: 417). Here the veil is not a cool separator,
but an enhancer of blunt sexuality. Paradoxically, the overlapping of sexual
repression and sexualization leaves coolness as the only way out of the
dilemma. Being cool (for Muslim women as much as for the black American
males mentioned) means to resist objectification through restraint. The restraint is supposed to prevent any further objectification. For this project, a
playful attitude is essential. However, the project becomes "uncool" when it
fails to engage in the transparency able to create a playful space of coolness,
but becomes a mere sign or marker for femininity instead. Then veiling *can
be* as uncool as pornographic nudity. Unfortunately, in most contemporary
Islamic societies the veil is today established as a non-transparent device,
which does not lead to coolness but rather to its contrary.

## CONCLUSIONS

The preceding examples of veiling have shown how the veil/truth dichotomy
can be deconstructed by admitting an interpretation of the veil as a "surface"

that can be both a signifier and a dissimulator of truth. This veil appears as such a surface within a "cool space" of the woman's autonomous self in which she can escape manipulation. The cool surface represents the woman's personal and living version of femininity (Islamic or not), which helps her to become acceptable in masculine society.

Some African Americans solved those problems through coolness. Being cool made the presence of those blacks acceptable within white society. In no case should the veil produce blunt apartheid but it should rather represent a cool form of separation/non-separation. In this sense the veil will be part of what Eyman Homsi has called "the collective control of bodies in space" (2011: 304) though it does not *have* to serve in the name of a reinforcement of existing (sexual or other) ideologies. Like the cool mask, the veil has, as Homsi confirms with regard to Islamic rituals in general, a "revolutionary potential, a capacity to subvert the sovereignty of Empire." The final question is: Once this coolness has been acquired, can the veil be shed?

The chapter has shown that Nietzsche's metaphor of the veil as a surface and its interpretation are very relevant for the contemporary veiling debate. Are what Nietzsche called "those sober beings," who refuse to consider surfaces, who prefer to go straight towards the "deep truths" that they believe to be hidden under layers of veils, not similar to those who today see the veil as a clear separator of two different kinds of spaces? Are they not similar to those who believe that once they have penetrated and looked under the veil, they can appropriate a space in which "fantasy, prejudice, irrationality, ignorance, and fear" are absent? Such people might indeed have appeared in the recent French veiling debate, which reverberated, often in an uncanny fashion, with echoes of surface/depth dichotomies. Psychoanalyst Élisabeth Roudinesco, for example, called the veil a curtain shrouding "a young girl in silence," making her both blind and deaf; and philosopher Alain Finkielkraut claimed that the veil denies girls access to the great works of culture, "preventing her from developing her rational faculties—literally keeping her in the dark" (Joan Scott 2007: 132). In the end, those misconceptions lead French philosopher André Glucksmann to classifying the veil as "a terrorist operation" and former French President Jacques Chirac to the judgment that "wearing a veil is a kind of aggression."[4] Those "sober beings" interpret the veil as harmful to the universal moral and aesthetic values granted by the state or by civilization at large. It is harmful because it is only remotely related to unveiled scientific clarity. However, in formal terms, such strategies are not much different from Ayatollah Khomeini's dismissal of all philosophy as a mere veil that the true believer needs to overcome when he wrote: "I am afraid that they end up wrapping themselves in the great hijab [of philosophy], become engaged with it, and lose themselves [their senses]" (from Shirazi 2001: 171). In the first case, the veil—together with an entire culture that is believed to be wrong—is said to hide the philosophical truth of enlightenment and emancipation, which can only shine in an unveiled state. In Khomeini's case, those same philosophical enlightenment values represent a veil covering religious truth.

In my view, in both cases, Nietzsche's and Derrida's models of a profound "truth as a surface" appear to be the only remedies. The proponents of "veil penetration" do not understand the important relationships between veiling and the creation of a cool "surface" of understanding pointed out by Nietzsche and Derrida. They do not understand that truth is not necessarily hidden *under* the veil but that it can be contained within the cultural, fashionable, playful veil or surface. Veiling fashion, for example, which attempts to combine veiling with the standards of beauty as well as of marketing methods intrinsic to modern international fashion, takes a playful attitude towards veiling. Its truths (of femininity, emancipation, etc.) must be looked for in the social game of fashion that is played. Those truths cannot be found in the form of firm essences hidden inside the veiled subjects.

The big question that has to remain unanswered is, however, whether the "revolutionary potential" of Islamic rituals that Homsi believes to be able to "subvert the sovereignty of Empire" is used in the right way in contemporary Muslim culture. In the introduction to this book it has been shown that the discourses of conservative websites like Islamwoman.com get involved in playful approaches when it comes to the negotiation of sexuality and femininity. Is the act of concealing not also supposed to highlight something else? By concealing female body parts Islamists highlight at least a more abstract idea of femininity and thus engage in ambiguous approaches.

Do those Muslims who favor, for example, gender segregation in universities really apply moral standards of Islam, which are, in El Guindi's words, "designed to accommodate enjoyment of worldly life, including sexual environment." Or do they not simply declare sexuality to be absolutely evil? Whoever has worked in the cultural environment of the Gulf States will probably confirm that official religious appreciations of sexuality come closer to its demonization and oppression than to anything else. The same is true for religious officials in Egypt when they react to female demonstrators attempting to stage something like a sexual revolution. Guilt and shame are here important parts of the system and the veil is merely used to enforce this system. Recent social development in Egypt have transformed Cairo into a "hot space" that becomes almost unlivable for young women.

Transparency and coolness are theoretical constructs that many authors cherish and highlight because they find evidence of such concepts in scriptures and in the tradition. However, in many Muslim countries the reality looks completely otherwise. This is why the African American experience with Jim Crow segregation can teach us a lesson: Here, the play of assertion and retraction was not bound by absolute imperatives, but the veil of cool could be taken off at any moment. As demonstrated in chapter 2, Third Wave feminism teaches us a similar lesson. In Third Wave feminism, the semantic reversal takes place in a context of irony, humorous reappropriation of traditional symbols, and identities in order to effectuate a structural disempowerment that can lead to empowerment. Humor is the key to success in this procedure.

Whenever the purpose of veiling is not to create a cool space in terms of ethics and aesthetics, but merely to fulfill religious requirements, the result is the contrary of cool space. The spatial concept of transparency inspired by coolness supports this idea. In poststructuralist philosophy, the veil becomes a symbol of the cancellation of the metaphysical separation between inside and outside, depth and surface, reality and appearance. It is thus absurd to retrospectively reify the veil with the help of religious concepts. The same is true for *any* ethical question concerning the veil. The Iranian oppositional politician Zahra Rahnavard has issued multiple anticapitalist warnings about the Western fashion system because it turns women into uncritical beings "wasting nights and days endeavoring multicolor garments, fashion journals, filthy stuff for makeup, scents, and rouges" (*Message of the Hijab*) until the marketing system has transformed them into permanent customers of useless commodities.[5] Those warnings are rationally grounded and would definitely find an echo in Western (and other) leftist circles or any person wondering why in capitalism images of women's bodies are plastered across cars and plasma TVs to attract buyers.

Rahnavard's warnings can also be compared to countercultural protests against standards of commodified beauty by using, for example, tattoos. This book has shown that some women chose tattoos to resist power structures through positive articulations of their agency. However, why do those critical reflections on the cynical character of the capitalist fashion system need to be "topped up" with religious arguments about God's command to wear the hijab? Why must a critical consumer attitude culminate in the adoption of an ancient religious custom? It could as well lead to the shunning of certain commodities, such as the expressionists usage of makeup (an option which is, curiously, chosen by many a veiled woman in the Gulf countries).

When rational criticism is combined with irrationality (as in Rahnavard's case), the result is necessarily non-criticism. This is also the reason why in Rahnavard's writings the assumption that unveiling must be equaled with the worst strains of Western civilization is never critically examined but accepted quasi offhand. It is therefore not surprising that Minoo Moallem decides to beat Rahnavard on her own terrain, suggesting that Rahnavard will end up as a similarly brainwashed victim of the Islamic fashion industry: "Did she know when she picked the veil as a signifier of resistance to consumerism and imperialism, that she would become complicit with the Islamic fashion industry?" (Moallem 2005: 184).

## NOTES

1. It must be acknowledged in this chapter that since the Civil Rights era of the 1940s–1960s racial segregation peaked highest between 1970 and 1980—not in the U.S. South, but in the North, specifically in the Rust Belt and Northeastern metropolitan areas of Chicago, Cleveland, Detroit, and New York. Further, there is the phenomenon of segregation as a choice in places like Atlanta and Washington, DC, which raises new questions about what it means to be cool and black. Those matters are complex and cannot be discussed in this book.

2. I have developed those thoughts in Botz-Bornstein 2011, page 22, from which this paragraph is adopted.

3. Kuwaiti authorities do not see the problem in the same way. Radical gender segregation has is increasingly practiced in Kuwaiti national educational institutions. Kuwait University's new campus has different parts for male and female students with separate gates and a motorway running between them. The bridge uniting the two parts is guarded and can only be used by teachers. At the private Gulf University for Science and Technology where I am working, gender segregation has been practiced since March 2008, but male and female students can come together in all areas outside the classrooms. Still a considerable amount of "self-segregation" can be observed outside the classrooms. Other private universities began to circumvent the segregation law.

4. In *L'Express* in 1994, number 64. Chirac is quoted from Scott 2007: 84.

5. Zahra Rahnavard is the wife of Iranian opposition leader Mir-Hossein Mousavi and a member of The Green Path of Hope. She is also an academic and has written numerous works on Islam.

*Part II*

# Nudity, Tattoos

*Chapter Six*

# Tattoos, Nudity, Veils

The purpose of this book is to reflect the veil against two phenomena that have become important for feminine aesthetics: tattoos and nudity. Before proceeding to the chapters in which contemporary tattoos and nudity will be analyzed more closely, it is necessary to show how complex any comparison of nudity and veiling is on principle. It is complex because one has not only to look at what those social expressions *are* (mechanisms of covering or uncovering), but also at the items they are supposed to cover or uncover. Those items are ambiguous by definition. The hijab covers hair and hair is perceived in many cultures as a religious and as a sexual phenomenon; and it can become political almost automatically through this constellation. According to anthropologist Carol Delaney, "The connection between sex, religion, and hair has wide distribution cross-culturally and has been noted in the anthropological literature since the nineteenth century" (Delaney 1994: 162).

Nudity is just as polysemantic as it uncovers a body that can be perceived as both sexual and non-sexual; and it receives a large part of its political connotations (in nude protests, for example) through this diffuse distribution of meaning.

In cultures determined by Abrahamic religions, nudity is equipped with a permanent "theological signature" (Agamben), which is, again, something that it shares with the veil. Nudity, wherever it appears in cultures determined by those religions, is inseparably connected to the narrative of Adam and Eve's original sin told in Genesis. Abrahamic religions cite Eve as responsible for the fall of man and the origin of sin, and thus associate the covering of the body with the covering of Eve's corrupt nature as well as her shameful body. Through the Old Testament, nudity and veiling become thus inseparably linked. References to veiling appear in Genesis 3: 5, in Genesis

103

24: 65, and in Isaiah 3: 32. The biblical "veil vs. nudity" paradigm has still another function: "In Christianity, women's cover is a symbol of men's power over women because men are regarded as the 'image and glory of God'" (Burns 2007: 147). (It is interesting to note that the old custom of tattooing female bodies on male bodies—often presented as a celebration of women—can be understood as the continuation of this myth: woman is made flesh by man by making her part of his body. See Kang 2012, page 70.)

This means that any sense of shame is never profane but a cultural-religious one, produced in a context in which woman is judged on the basis of her inherent sin (that of Eve), and which she has to accept. Because Eve has sinned woman has to feel shame. Nude protests attempt to negate this shame and to subvert nakedness for other, entirely new purposes.

First of all, the above facts explain a paradox. It is paradoxical that "in the Christian tradition, nudity functions doubly, as metaphor both for innocence and the lack of it" (Barcan 2004: 102). Ruth Barcan's detection of nudity's paradoxical relationship with innocence flows out of the narrative from Genesis that establishes nudity as a sort of metaphorical veil. Before Adam and Eve had obtained knowledge about their nudity, they were never nude but were covered by the divine grace, which surrounded their nude bodies like a veil. The original sin took away their veil of grace and, as a result, the nude body needed to be covered by other means (cf. Agamben 2011: 59).

## Tattoos and Nudity

The link between tattoos and nudity is equally twofold. On the one hand, tattoos are put on the naked skin and the exposure of most tattoos is only possible when taking off at least some clothes and being thus at least partially nude. On the other hand, it can also appear that once the skin is covered with tattoos, it is less naked. Expressions such as the term "sleeve" for a full-length arm tattoo, for example, support analogies of tattoos and clothing; at the same time, European explorers in the nineteenth century found it difficult to accept the tattoos of natives *as clothing* (see Barcan 2004: 23). Barcan writes therefore that "the entire nudity/clothing dialectic is replete with paradoxes" because "nudity . . . can itself be the best form of disguise" (87). Even today both nudity and tattoos can be used by women for one and the same purpose: to reclaim their bodies.

The dialectics of tattoo vs. non-tattoo is submitted to the same paradoxical logic that has been described with regard to nudity: it functions doubly, as metaphor both for innocence and the lack of it. The reason is its twofold relationship with clothes. From a certain point of view, the tattoo resides somewhere in the middle between nudity and clothes. Lewis Henry Morgan wrote in 1877 that "humans [are] entering the first social level of savagery naked, the first level of barbarism in skin garments, and arriving at civilization in woven garments" (from El Guindi 1999: 51). However, for other people and in other contexts, tattoos will appear as even more "barbarian" than nudity. Just like to some, extreme clothing such as full body veils (burqas) appears as more "barbarian" than nudity.

## Tattoos and Veils

Another kind of dialectic can be detected between tattoos and veils. This dialectic is more difficult to guess though it has played an important role in colonial discourse. Daphne Grace explains that "at the heart of Anglo-Indian colonialist discourse was the subaltern women's ornamented but veiled body, a site of colonial rivalry and desire" (Grace 2004: 53). This means that the body's (erotic) signifying power had become unbearably strong through ornamentation (tattoos) and had to be reduced to zero through the veil.

Another point that brings the veil close to the tattoo is the fact that both have radical ways of using and applying symbolisms. What "annoys" some Westerners about the Islamic veil is not so much the fact that women are wearing on their heads pieces of cloth symbolizing a religion or a tradition; what annoys them is rather the radical way in which this symbolism is applied. In practice, "to veil" does not simply signify "to cover one's hair," but *in terms of social appearance* it comes close to a permanent body modification. Though the style of the veil can be changed and the veil can be taken off at home, it can never be entirely taken off in public, which lends it the status of quasi-permanence. Similarly, when some people criticize and reject the use of tattoos, they reject them not simply as "pictures on the skin," but because of the concept of permanence that is linked to tattoos. [1]

The result is that both veils and tattoos provoke incredulousness about "why would someone do something like this voluntarily?" When it comes to tattoos and veils, any—what philosophy calls—"free will" is regularly doubted, most probably by uttering: "No one would do this voluntarily without having been brainwashed beforehand by culture, religion or something worse."

## General Observations

The above descriptions have shown that the standard assumption that nudity as a social phenomenon occurs only in liberal societies while veiling is limited to conservative societies is false. As a matter of fact, all three phenomena are distributed over different kinds of societies though their presence does certainly occur in varying degrees. Officially, tattooing remains a taboo in Muslim cultures because the Qur'an does not approve of permanent body alterations[2]; nor does the Bible.[3] The tradition of facial tattoos, once popular among several Arab tribes (especially in North Africa and the Gulf), has died out under Muslim influence. However, this does not mean that there would be no *interest* in modern tattoos and in getting modern tattoos in those regions. The reactions of the female students of my Kuwaiti university to class presentations on aesthetic questions of tattoos make me actually think that those students' interest in tattoos is very strong. Since tattoos are fashion items, discussions about tattoos in my Philosophy of Art class are always passionate (though *only* in female classes)[4] and, in general, surprisingly relativistic when it comes to Islamic imperatives.

Also, nudity is a taboo in Islam. Some Islamic commentators advise against total nudity even when one is alone. This is because "absolute solitude does not exist in a world in which we share existence with the djinns and angels. 'Never go into water without clothing for water has eyes,'" writes Alusi Zadeh (*Ghaliyyat al-mawa'idh*, volume II, page 6 quoted from Bouhdiba 1974: 36).

These considerations also show that no comparative discourse on tattoos, nudity, and veils can take the concept of modernity for granted and limit itself to ideas of development or Westernization vs. non-Western resistance to modernization. What the present comparative discourse on tattoos, nudity, and veils attempts to deconstruct is: (1) the trope of Western civilization vs. Oriental barbarism, and (2) the trope of the Muslim woman as the ultimate victim of an Islamic patriarchy and ignorance that needs to be liberated by Western regimes of knowledge. However, a new modernity cannot be achieved by merely insisting on tradition and by refusing so-called Western values. The trope of covering as an advancement of (Muslim) civilization needs to be deconstructed as well.

## TEN POINTS THAT TATTOOS, NUDITY, AND VEILS HAVE IN COMMON

It needs to be highlighted that each item—the tattoo, nudity, and the veil—is involved in its own complex historical, psychological, religious, and sexual network. This makes any evaluation of common points a difficult undertaking. Still, there must be a reason why all three emerge simultaneously today, relatively unexpectedly and on such a large scale. So far, in this chapter, I have mainly established parallels between two of the three items. Now it will be necessary to submit a list of what *all three* have in common.

### (1) Sexual Connotations

All three have sexual connotations. One of the first systematic studies of tattoos was undertaken by the sexologist Alfred Kinsey (1894–1956) who was intrigued by sexual motivations and effects underlying the process of tattooing (cf. Kissack 2000). Also, veiling is often viewed in relationship with female sexuality and for nudity the link is evident.

## (2) All Three Concern the Skin

From a phenomenological point of view, all three concern the skin, which is important for several reasons. Nudity is about the skin, but also the veil and tattoos can be perceived as a second skin. Both veil and tattoo juxtapose a person's interiority and exteriority and are fascinating (and controversial) just for this reason. Like the veil, the tattoo is a physical object that seems to be part of the skin without overlapping with the skin; it is therefore a sort of double skin. Charles Taliaferro and Mark Odden explain that "the physical barrier between the ink and the skin draws attention to the exterior of our skin while also sectioning off access to the interior" (Taliaferro and Odden 2012: 11). Physically, the tattoo is thus located under the skin, but visually it is on top of the skin.

The skin reunites the three items in still another fashion. In the field of literature studies, Jay Prosser has found that "with remarkably few exceptions, skin autobiographies associate skin disorder with sin" (Prosser 2001: 58). Through stigmata and shame, the skin is linked to sin. The skin is the immediate point of contact of the sinful subject with the physical world. Prosser mentions Andrew Strathern who, in his anthropological study of shame in the culture of the Hagen people of New Guinea, explains that "on the skin" expresses for those subjects a conjunction of physiological and sociological appropriateness (Strathern 1975: 353). In general, people blush when they are embarrassed or ashamed. In various cultures this shame will be marked with tattoos. Apart from that, shame can be covered with veils or be exposed and sublimated through nudity.

Some general thoughts about the "skin" are necessary here. The skin represents a boundary between an individual and the world, it is "private" and at the same time exposed. This is why the nude skin, the tattooed skin, but also the veil-skin can express a person's intimate individuality while being at the same time dependent on stimulations from the social group in which they are imbedded. In this sense, tattoos, nudity, and veils create an individuality that is not organic or biological but imaginary and dependent on individual or general phantasms that interrelate in various ways with dreams, language, myths, body attitudes, and cultural thought patterns. I am not talking about the merely unclothed body (which is a biological phenomenon), but about the nude body as it appears in various social contexts (nude protests or nude beaches, for example). This body, which is submitted to relational constraints and takes its meaning and significance within a cultural and public domain, is determined by society. It is social and is not more autonomous than the self. While tattoos, nudity, and veils are part of the body, they are not part of the biological body, but rather of the situated body. This situated body is also always imaginary, as Moira Gatens points out: "All healthy people are, or have, in addition to a material body, a body-phantom or an imaginary body" (Gatens 1996: 11). Therefore, all three (tattoos, nudity, and veils) are matters of a body politics constantly creating psychical images of the body by applying models and metaphors. It is through this metaphorical link that all three are related to the skin.

In itself, the skin is one of the most used metaphorical expressions related to the human body ("being well in one's skin," "only skin deep," "getting under one's skin"). This is what the skin has in common with the words "naked" and "veil," which share the fact that their metaphorical use exceeds by far their literal use.[5]

The transfer of the skin metaphor to the veil is thus not unusual because the veil as an imaginary skin has mainly two functions: Just like a skin, it protects human individuality and also serves as a social communicator with others. However, when it comes to women, the envelope metaphor adopts a supplementary dimension. When talking about "envelopes" in relationship with female bodies, the idea of the skin adopts a special meaning. Gatens believes that "the female body, in our culture, is seen and no doubt often 'lived' as an envelope, vessel or receptacle" (Gatens 1996: 41). This means that the female body is seen as "a partial, passive *object*—a castrated body that requires first a man and then a baby to 'complete' it. . . . Women's bodies are not seen to have integrity, they are socially constructed as partial and lacking" (ibid.). This is why female bodies need an additional envelope: the skin is not enough. Does the new skin made of veils or tattoos confer more integrity to women? And can even nudity (as a concept) represent such a kind of envelope? Those are the questions that will be discussed in the following chapters.

One could oppose that the status of the veil in this context is not different from that of *any* clothes. However, the veil is more skin-like because it is often supposed to serve as an absolute identity statement *exceeding* the claim of mere clothes. Unlike other fashion items—but very much like a skin and tattoos—its signifying value is able to approach the absolute. This is also the reason why it can so easily become a fetish. Fetishes are created through an interactive communicative process between the "I" (which sends out signals) and the "other" which projects its own phantasms on the fetish's surface. Like the skin, the veil can serve as a screen on which desires can be projected.

For Baudrillard the fetish is related to the transformation of the female body into a phallus that needs to be *smooth*, that means, that has been rid of all signs (Baudrillard 1993: 102), a fact that is not true for just *any* clothes, since they are normally occupied by a variety of fashion signifiers and other social signifiers. The parallel between the smooth, veiled fetish and the phallus is not far-fetched. Lacan sees the phallus as "a symbol that works only when it is veiled" (Lacan 1982: 82, from Barcan: 184) and the conceptual link between the veil and the phallus is supported by findings of earlier anthropologists like Charles Berg and Edmund Leach. In the 1950s, Berg submitted the idea that the cultural treatment of hair is linked to sexual instincts (in *The Unconscious Significance of Hair*), a thesis that would later be accepted by Leach when he wrote: "When head hair becomes the focus of ritual attention this is very commonly because the head is being used as a symbol for the phallus and head hair as a symbol for semen" (Leach 1958: 157).

In this sense, the naked skin and the veil are similar, while the tattoo might be able to prevent the fetishization of the body. However, the tattoo can become a fetish in its own right. The concept of "phallocentrism," sometimes seen as one of the main causes of veiling, adopts here an entirely new meaning. It will be explained in chapter 7 where Baudrillard's ideas about the transformation of the female body into a fetish will be discussed at length.

In any case, the veil-skin—just like the tattooed skin and the nude skin—is more than a surface hiding an interior essence. It is an essence appearing in the form of an envelope. As mentioned, we are today far removed from Plato's conception of body as a covering of the soul. Anne Anlin Cheng's defense of the skin as "a semi-transparent envelope" invites indeed "profound reimaginings of the relationship between interiority and exteriority, between essence and covering" (Cheng 2009: 99). The surface is not a mere cover, but "sometimes it is not a question of what the visible hides but how it is that we have failed to see certain things on its surface" (102). The body (with its various skins) is neither a truth nor is it hiding a truth but it is a means of expressing values. I agree with Sara Ahmed and Jackie Stacey, who point out in their book on the skin that our aim should be to address the "question of embodiment without fetishizing the body" and that instead we should "think the body through the skin" (Ahmed and Stacey 2001: 3). I understand Ahmed and Stacy's suggestions in the following way: Instead of fetishizing the body by *merely seeing it as a skin*, we should attempt to locate the particular logic of the skin. In this book I show that this logic overlaps with the logic of tattoos, nudity, and veils in a contemporary context.

## (3) Magic of the Body

Tattoos, nudity, and veils can be interpreted as attempts to reinstall the magic of the body which, according to Robert Muchembled (1983), has been persistently devalued by church and state since the sixteenth century (cf. Linke 1999: 4). As a matter of fact, all three phenomena are in search of a mystique rooted in older—perhaps primitive—attitudes towards spirit and body.

"Magic of the body" can also be defined as a surplus quality of the body. It is able to frame the body as a self-sufficient phenomenon resisting utilitarian visions of objectification of all kinds by referring to anything from religion to counterculture. This does not mean that tattoos, nudity, and veils always reinstall this "magic" in an appropriate fashion, but at least they have this potential. In this sense, all three raise questions about the nature of personal autonomy and the relationship of the self with the body. In spite of this, many people (including feminists, as will be shown) can find body-conscious issues revolving around tattoos, nudity, and veils detrimental to women's self-esteem.

## (4) Truth Effects

Though—or just because—they are envelopes, nudity, tattoos, and veils have an exceptionally powerful visual "truth effect." While the values expressed by the body are never absolute but mediated through social interaction, it seems that they are often perceived as close to absolute when they are expressed through tattoos, nudity, or veils. Nudity can indeed be very "revealing"; it is linked to truth in a straightforward metaphorical way, as evidenced by the expression "the naked truth." On German theatre stages since the 1970s, nudity occurs frequently because it is believed to pay tribute to the "'seriousness' expected of the theatre" (Toepfer 2003: 167). Along with nudity, veils also have such a truth effect. This is the reason why both nudity and veils are preferred cover images for books, as has been noted by Marilyn Booth: "The publisher's flap copy and imagery thus privilege a politics of personality wherein the hijab encircling the author's face (invariably young and attractive to a Western audience) creates a truth effect" (Booth 2010: 160).

A similar truth effect applies to tattoos. To some extent, the truth effect of tattoos, nudity, and veils follows from their fetishistic power as well as from the fact that all three have a strong symbolical signification. The symbolism of tattoos is particularly strong and has been linked to that of a dream image: "Like the dreaming process, tattoos condense, symbolize, and displace psychic energy to a meaningful image," writes Gerald Grumet (1983, quoted from Sanders 1989: 39). Michael Bakaty holds that tattoos are "the only form of human expression we have left that has magic to it" (from Fleming 1997: 35). In the same way, anti-Islamic militant Ayaan Hirsi uses the tattoo metaphor to express the concept of total religious devotion: "Muslim women who shift from total submission to God to a dialogue with their deity . . . pray, but instead of casting down their eyes, these women look up, at Allah, with the words of the Quran tattooed on their skin" (Hirsi 2007: 1).

## (5) Identity

Tattoos, nudity, and veils can be seen as a means of establishing identity. Classical nudists would occasionally affirm "that nudism can give its practitioners an unprecedented sense of control over their identities and capabilities," and in the 1930s German nudism was supposed to redefine the identity of the German nation (Toepfer 2003: 151). The link between identity and nudism has been persevered until today though on a completely different territory. According to a photographer publishing nude photos of ordinary people interviewed by Barcan,

> such practices are a form of identity work. For many clients, even the decision itself to be photographed nude (regardless of the actual photos) helps build self-esteem, since it represents a triumph over fear. "[For most clients] it's almost like a baptism of fire, [something] they've got to do; they've always wanted to do it." Mostly, this occurs when identity and/or body image have become self-conscious or precarious in some way. (Barcan 2004: 249)

The parallels with veils are obvious. Fadma El Guindi holds that "veiling in contemporary Arab culture is largely about identity, largely about privacy" (El Guindi 1999: xvii), and Karin van Nieuwkerk finds that veiling has helped women "to develop a stable identity, [to] return to the original sense of self" (van Nieuwkerk 2008: 445). Also, Pat Mule and Diane Barthel believe that the veil provides "a positive identity and source of esteem sanctioned by Islam" (Mule and Barthel 1992: 324).

Tattoos have traditionally had a strong identitarian function and were once even believed to be symptoms of an "underdeveloped ego" and "a mechanism by which the tattooed person copes with this inadequacy" (Hamburger 1966, quoted from Sanders 1989: 38). For Donald Richie, when analyzing traditional Japanese tattoos, the tattooed person had "solidified his own skin and become that solid object, that permanent identity that all men in fear of the amorphous become" (Richie 1980: 68). Jean-Chris Miller also insists that tattoos are "symbolic of life experiences and identity" (Miller 1996, quoted from Velliquette, Murray, and Creyer 1998: 465). It is true that more recently, the identitarian factor of tattoos has become more relative and blurred be it only for the reason that tattoos are no longer a stigmatic mark. The postmodern tattoo often avoids establishing identity through ontological simplification and codification but attempts to create more complex webs of meanings. It is also true that tattoos can *destroy* certain female identities such as "neatness, diligence, appliance, femininity, [and] passivity" (DeMello 2000: 173). In spite of this it remains true that—at least in some way— tattoos still "recast the means to express one's identity and spirituality" (Frenske 2007: 56). The latter point establishes a clear link with veils. Still today, the tattoo can be associated with the quasi-dreamlike or almost religious experience of finding one's identity through the confrontation with a higher form of reality: "It's almost like a tattoo pulls you back to a certain kind of reality about who you are as an individual. Either that or it transfers you to the next step in your life, the next plateau" (tattooed person interviewed by Sanders 1989: 43).

It is important to note that identity does not equate to individuality. While many people try to cultivate their individuality in order to develop an identity, the converse is also possible. Individuality can be sublimated in order to fit into a group, which helps creating an identity. This is valid also for tattoos, nudity, and veils.

## (6) Public vs. Private

On the one hand, tattoos, nudity, and veils are able to refer to privacy and to the most intimate sphere of human beings; on the other hand, they can also easily be redesigned as public and marketable objects. Like few other aesthetic expressions of humanness, tattoos, nudity, and veils have a public–private character, which has created much confusion. When women in France and in Turkey claimed, for example, that their adoption of the veil is merely an expression of their personal faith and not the public endorsement of state-censured Islamist politics, the public has been skeptical and held that the veil *is* a public politico-religious statement.

## (7) Fashion

Tattoos, nudity, and veils operate in the realm of fashion though the status that society attributes to their signifiers is normally much too "serious" for the realm of fashion. This means that they explore the limits of fashion because they operate with concepts that are, to a considerable extent, more absolute than the intrinsically playful phenomenon of fashion will allow. A particularly tricky question arises here with regard to the veil: Does the "increasingly common blurring of boundaries between fashion and religion" (Moors and Tarlo 2007: 5) make religion more fashionable-playful or does it make fashion more religious? Most authors working on the subject seem to think that the latter is the case. There are, however, also cases demonstrating the contrary. The fashion doll Barbie, which has been converted in some Islamic countries into a veiled "Muslim Barbie" has been seen as such a case. Faegheh Shirazi comments that "these entrepreneurs are transforming an innocent, fanciful plaything into a powerful symbol for religious correctness and piety" (Shirazi 2010: 11; see also Botz-Bornstein 2012).

An important question is whether the veil can be a part of the "game of fashion" playing with signifiers. Normally it can't. Playing or being playful means to be submitted to the constraints of the game but to be also able to step out of the game (that is, to take off the veil) at any moment. Otherwise it's not a game but work. Anthropological and philosophical definitions of games from Johan Huizinga to Mary Midgley highlight this voluntary and liberal stance as one of the fundamentals of the definition of games (Huizinga's idea of games have been explained in chapter 3). The other problem is that "play" in a fashion context can never be, as Özlem Sandikci and Güliz Ger say about *tesettür* women, a matter of entirely "asexual femininity" freed "from the predatory gaze" (2010: 40) though many of those women seem to believe that this is the case. Banu Gökariksel and Anna Secor interviewed a woman "who was dressed conservatively in a buttoned-up black overcoat and a large headscarf that covered her shoulders and bosom in a style that is no longer in fashion, [and she] asserted a strict interpretation of the moral code of Islam. Her response to Esin's confession stresses the necessity of taming the *nefis* [sexual desire] to such a degree that there is no longer the desire for things and places considered illicit" (Gökariksel and Secor 2012: 853). However, in reality, fashion (any fashion) cannot be reduced to the simple suppression of desire but it is rather the play with desire.

In veiling fashion or even in conservative discourses on veiling, this problem has never been solved. Strangely, even conservative Islamic websites like *islamwomen.com* insist on a relatively ambiguous approach towards the "concealing" of the body when writing: "A woman who covers herself is concealing her sexuality but allowing her femininity to be brought out." The curious juxtaposition of female sexuality and femininity signifies that the act of concealing is not supposed to merely conceal but also to highlight something else. It conceals body parts (which are called "sexual"), but by doing so it highlights a more abstract idea of femininity. However, is it really possible to think a highly connoted concept like "femininity" as *completely* detached from any notion of sexuality?

What is the feminine without the sexual? It is interesting to learn about such ambiguous approaches towards veiling from the website of the Institute of Islamic Information, whose text on veiling has been copied and reposted an infinite number of times. Is this website really introducing a playful potential towards the veil? At the same time the authors sternly affirm that the only reason why woman should veil is "that Allah wants them to veil."

## (8) Overcoming of Taboos

All three are linked to certain taboos that used to exist in the past but have been partially lifted. Tattoos were once seen as social stigmata and "because of its association with shame, nakedness can readily be used both metaphorically and in practice as a form of punishment, humiliation or degradation" (Barcan 2004: 134). Even nudity as practiced in nudist camps could in the quite recent past be labeled by sociologists as "deviant."[6] However, also the wearing of veils has represented a taboo in various contexts. Veiling once challenged the social order in modernizing Muslim countries and it is still today seen with a critical eye when worn in Western countries. Sandikci and Ger go as far as defining veiling as "a deviant practice stigmatized in the secular and urban mindset" (Sandikci and Ger 2010: 3), which implies an explicit reference to Erving Goffman's notion of the stigma "as an attribute that is deeply discrediting" (7). While those authors compare veiling with the once stigmatized jeans and tattoos (ibid.), Reina Lewis takes the countercultural legitimization of stigmata a step further by comparing the establishment of Muslim magazines in Western countries with that of lesbian/gay/queer magazines (Lewis 2010: 60). In chapter 1 it has been shown that it is even possible to compare the veil to sunglasses, which have once been "the badge of the afflicted, and are now compatible with youth, smartness and sex appeal" (Huxley 1974: 29).

## (9) Ambivalence

Looking at the history and classical anthropological interpretations of tattoos, veils, and nudity, we can state that all three share a considerable amount of ambivalence: All three have been interpreted as signs of backwardness, subordination, oppression, and ugliness (and are still seen as such by many people, cf. Afshar 2008: 420; El Guindi 1999: 3). And at the same time they have been evaluated as progressive, emancipated, beautiful, and sexy. This is the reason why tattoos, nudity, and veils possess not only an impressive fetishistic power, but also a great amount of innovative power. In the way they occur today, all three use aesthetic expressions that have been used in the past but foist different connotations on old signifiers. This innovative element is particularly important with regard to the veil because the idea of re-veiling had from the beginning not been to refer back to a tradition. John Williams pointed out in 1980 that "this costume is not traditional, but in its specific form it is new" (Williams 1980: 75). It has been shown above that veiling, which has traditionally been seen as a symbol of feminine submission, is engaged in a new play of signifiers when it becomes a fashion item. Of course, this play can only be considered innovative as long as the act of veiling has been freely chosen and not been forced upon the woman. "Re-veiled" women usually insist on this: "Participants in our year-long conversation with Muslim women said 'I choose to wear the hijab, I'm not forced. My dad would ideally like me to wear Western clothes to avoid all the hassle, but I choose to wear the hijab!'" ("She Who Disputes" *National Commission Report 2006*, page 5, quoted from Afshar 2008: 421). However, like any choice, the "choice" to veil is not entirely free; the freedom of choice is itself determined by social conditions. Moroccan sociologist and feminist Fatima Mernissi reminds us in this context that confusion has always existed between Islam as a belief, as a personal choice, and Islam as law or as state religion (Mernissi 1991: 23), which makes it impossible to speak of veiling as if it were an entirely freely chosen act. Beliefs (religion) and laws are normally incompatible with choice, which means that the veil is answerable to more than only the playful demands of fashion. Paradoxically, this complication saves women, in the eyes of some Western interpreters, from being regarded as blunt terrorists. Women who "chose" are no longer victims but "the very act of veiling [that] may imply some element of choosing to be publicly labeled as Muslims [could be seen] not only as threatening to the very fabric of society but also an act of desperation and thus a dangerous deed" (Afshar 2008: 420).[7]

Also, tattooing has overcome earlier "bad" connotations and has reinvented itself in the form of a modern mainstream aesthetics; and nudity, in the way in which it appears today, steers away from older political discourses of nudism as a utopian vision (and even older ideas of nudity as "primitiveness") and has very much reorganized its outlook. Looking at how nudity appears in contemporary environments today it is difficult to maintain the initial radical association of nudity with innocence, an association that had once been so dear to classical nudists. One of the reasons is that we live in a virtualized and sexualized universe where pornography and pedophilia are much more present than thirty years ago. This means for example, that today more than ever, women engaging in nude protests have to negotiate the perception of nudity as an expression of purity, innocence, and strength and nudity as an expression of submission, (moral) deficiency, and even commercialization. Still, in the case of nude protests the shock value seems to be real: In spite of its omnipresence in modern societies, nudity can still be used for the purpose of protest.

## (10) Humiliation vs. Empowerment

The last point which tattoos, nudity, and veils have in common follows from the preceding one. They can be interpreted as *both* humiliating *and* empowering depending on the context and the intentions to which they connect. The veil emancipates but can also be merely a mock emancipation. The same is true for nudity and tattoos, which can both elevate and humiliate women: "Early efforts to keep women away from tattoos—and then perversely to draw women in—both involved degradation of the female body as a desirable object and desiring subject" (Braunberger 2000: 4). Of course, everything depends on whether the tattoo, the nudity, or the veil has been chosen voluntarily or whether it has been forced upon the woman. It has been said above that it is difficult to establish whether the veil has been chosen freely or not. However, once this ambiguity has been recognized, it is possible to establish various transversal links between the three phenomena.

# THE NEW WOMAN

Like the naked women in Vanessa Beecroft's performances, the new woman who emerges from nude protests is confident and courageous but also—to some extent—unapproachable. While Aliaa El Mahdy deconstructs the opposition between clothes and nudity, between fully covered bodies and nude bodies and everything in between, she reverts to a radical non-dress (neither nude nor clothed), which is similar to the tattoo. The reason is that covering cannot be rejected in terms of nudity and nudity cannot be rejected on the grounds of a "better" covering. The conundrum is well known in discourses on clothing in general. According to Barcan, "In philosophical and moral discourses, clothing has been imagined as both covering up obscenity and as constituting a form of corruption in itself" (9). The main point is that El Mahdy's picture can become a gendered image only if El Mahdy agrees with her supposed position as an object of male desire. Only as the recipient of male desire can her position be constructed around her own objectification. However, since she does not agree with this position, the picture's sense shifts towards something more indefinite.

All this is in agreement with what has been said about the veil and about tattoos, or simply with everything concerning the contemporary perception of the human body. The contemporary body is no longer political or religious but marketed, and it finds its identity within a complex network of fashion, privacy, and commercialization. This does not mean that the body has become less egocentric. On the contrary, very often the contemporary body attempts to resist various influences, which can lead the body to its transformation into an "egobody." French philosopher Robert Redeker, for example, defines the egobody as a "body without soul" and a "body without self." Paradoxically, the egobody is a de-egotized body in the sense that here the body replaces the ego. It is an unspirited body impossible to separate from soul/self or psyche/ego because this body has absorbed both the soul and the self.[8] At the same time, it is clear that no pure, one-dimensional identity of the body can be obtained. In this sense, the body—no matter whether nude, tattooed, or veiled—is subversive by definition.

## NOTES

1. Of course, I am talking here only about traditional tattoos that are (almost) permanent. There are new tattoos on the market that can be removed relatively easily through laser surgery. See http://infinitink.com.

2. I am dealing in this book only with permanent tattoos and not with temporary *henna* tattoos that are current in the Middle East. In Islamic scriptures, there are four hadiths speaking out against tattoos, one of them putting forward the argument that the body should not be permanently changed. The hadiths are: Sahih Bukhari Vol. 7, Book 72, Numbers 815 and 823; Sahih Muslim, Book 24, Number 5300; and Abu Dawud, Book 28, Number 4157.

3. The ethical command from the Old Testament, binding for Christians and Jews alike, goes: "You shall not make any cuttings in your flesh on account of the dead or tattoo any marks upon yourself: I am YHWH" (Leviticus 19: 28). For the history and reasons of this command see Adam Barkman 2012. Among other things, Barkman explains that the main reason for the command in the Old Testament was to establish a visible difference between the Jewish people and neighboring peoples who *did* tattoo themselves. He holds that the Bible says nothing intrinsically bad about tattoos, which is why Christians and non-orthodox Jews will usually not attach much importance to this passage from Leviticus. A reference to the inchangeability of the body exists in the New Testament (Corinthians 6, 19–20) but it does not refer to tattoos.

4. Classes are segregated in Kuwait.

5. Barcan finds that "any search in a library catalogue under the words 'naked' or 'bare' provides rapid and startling evidence that the metaphorical uses of nakedness far outweigh any literal studies" (136). El Guindi notes a similar phenomenon with regard to the veil (1999: 10).

6. See this quotation from an article on nudism: "Social nudists (i.e., those who practice nudism in a nudist camp) are thus defined as 'deviants' by their disregard for body covering. . . . The remainder of the paper will discuss an empirical study of this group of systematic deviants" (Weinberg 1965: 313).

7. Afshar refers to Moore (2006) and Barry (2006: 26).

8. Redeker says this with regard to the "Viagra-body," which is the topic of his article (Redeker 2011: 72).

# Chapter Seven

# From the Stigmatized Tattoo to the Graffitied Body

## *Femininity in the Tattoo Renaissance*

While chapter 5 has analyzed the spatial function of veils, in this chapter I analyze the spatial function of tattoos. Since ancient times, tattoos have been utilized to signal religious affiliations, strength, or social status. In Western countries, from the beginning of the twentieth century onwards, the practice of tattooing was predominant among sailors and other working-class members and, a little later, also among bikers and inmates. Subcultures such as punk and the gay movement picked up elements from tattoo culture in the 1980s. Today, tattoos are not just for bikers and sailors but have become acceptable for the educated and professional middle class. Worn by celebrities and role models (e.g. Angelina Jolie, Melanie Griffith, Victoria Beckham, and Johnny Depp), they have become mainstream. Though in clinical studies the tendency to link tattoos to certain pathologies such as juvenile malaise or to criminality and drug abuse still persists (cf. MacCormack 2006: 67), cultural commercialism has altered the appearance of tattoos in a way that they are no longer necessarily identified as items linked to subcultures. Pop-rapper Wiz Khalifa is wearing a full-body tattoo suit, but is accepted by a broad mainstream public.

Tattoos have also entered the art world. An art exposition of tattoos in a Parisian gallery organized in 2011 by the French magazine *Hey!* attracted 60,000 visitors. The tattoos were exposed mostly on leather supports and dummies.

Arnold Rubin (1988) has coined the term Tattoo Renaissance, which refers to a movement beginning in the 1950s and leading, in the late 1980s, to a popular interest in tattoos. This chapter analyses the spectacularly rising popularity of tattoos by showing that tattoos have become a *spatial* project in the largest sense: The way tattoos participate in the creation of social space today is different from the way tattoos did so before the Tattoo Renaissance.

I use "spatial" in the way it is defined through the Platonic *chora* as a self-determining space that can be opposed to the Cartesian concept of space as a preestablished, geometrical, "empty" extension filled with objects.[1] The *choraic* space is a creative matrix in which things arise, it is a personal *place* able to transcend geometrical limits and this condition concerns also all objects developed within this space. Along these lines, I describe the creation of a "tattoo space" as a shift from traditional tattoos to body graffiti.

## FEMININITY IN THE TATTOO RENAISSANCE

In the past, tattoo-spheres could be located within the margins of society. Once an identity had been assumed through the adoption of a tattoo, the person could be assigned a particular geographical position within an urban sphere. Contemporary tattoos have this one-dimensional identifying function to a much lesser extent, which influences the way in which these tattoos create space. Within the new tattoo space, the skin does not wear the stigmatic *mark*, nor does it function as a screen of male desire, but it becomes a wall on which multiple desires are projected. In this sense, tattoos have become graffiti. This pattern concerns female tattoos in particular. The principal difference between graffiti and tattoos here is *not* that in the former bodies circulate around an immobile inscription while in the latter the inscription is on the circulating bodies. The decisive point is rather that the graffiti is *received* by a wall and that the wall has to "cope" with it. Instead of identifying its bearer through the tattoo (postulating that all tattoo bearers are criminals, savages, etc.), the postmodern tattoo involves the bearer in a more social game thus creating *choraic* places.

First, I will establish the particularity of the female tattoo as opposed to the male tattoo by focusing on an important element of the pro/contra discussion of female tattoos: the purity and "blankness" of the female skin. Jean Baudrillard's concept of the blank female skin as a "void" that men rush to fill with their own desires (Baudrillard 1979: 81) is central to this discussion and will be elucidated in the context of his thoughts on fetishism. Looking at theoretical material as well as some literature in which tattoos appear, it will become clear why tattoos transition into graffiti when a woman decides to draw the mark in her own fashion. Finally, I will show that the spatial function of narcissistically oriented female tattoos is at least partly established within the Suicide Girls interactive website, which, according to Tao of Tattoos, "really kick started the whole thing [female tattoos] off." I use statements retrieved from the Suicide Girls website as well as those of Tao of Tattoos and Rank My Tattoos, all of which have blogging facilities. I analyze posted texts and comments of models and members using the method of discourse analysis.

The last decade or so has seen the publication of many works on female tattoos among which are Amy Krakow (1994), Victoria Lautman (1994), Margot Mifflin (1997), Myrna Armstrong (1991), Christine Braunberger (2000), Margo DeMello (2000), Silja Talvi (2000), Karin Beeler (2006), Patricia MacCormack (2006), and Mindy Frenske (2007).[2] These works delve into the history of female tattoos or into contemporary culture in order to explore the feminist significance of tattoos. However, none of these studies attempt to consistently explain how female tattoos create a particular kind of space that can be used for the creation of new identities. This chapter contributes to the body of work of feminist geography as it attempts to rethink the relationships between space, place, and body. The "tattoo space" I examine challenges conceptual geographical constructs *in a bodily way*, which is one of the most original premises of feminist geography. Feminist geography often challenges constructions of space determined by gender inequality and ideologies of identity because it believes that these categories do not match with a fractured and discursive reality. It examines, for example, how gender is lived in and across spaces by focusing on sexualities and embodiment. Feminist geographer Gillian Rose combined geography with feminist accounts of space by claiming to analyze "space of everyday and the maps that women's movements chart" (Rose 1993: 17). For Rose, time-space geography is supposed to recover the everyday ordinary (22).

On the interactive tattoo-related blogs, women suggest that their motivation for getting tattooed is the will to "claim back the body," which also signifies "claiming back space," the more so since, according to MacCormack, "skin itself marks the body as both taking up space and existing within a particular space" (2006: 60). In this sense, this chapter works along the lines of the feminist project, pointed out by Anne Witz (2000), of retrieving the body from the clutches of biological determinism and instating it in the realm of the social without succumbing to social determinism. Looking at tattoos in a "spatial" way means to reconstruct female sociality not through biological or sociological determinism, but as a dynamic body-space.

The present analysis has been limited to the significance of tattoos within heterosexual relationships. Most probably, also in homosexual relationships the skin (tattooed or not) can function as a recipient for the other's projected desires in the way it has been defined by Baudrillard. Braunberger (2000: 4) reports that "the connection between tattooing and sex, in which tattooing is deemed a sexual act, is staunchly refuted by [heterosexual] men when they tattoo each other." A proper analysis of this phenomenon would transcend the limits of this chapter.

# MALE AND FEMALE TATTOOS:
## THE QUESTION OF SMOOTHNESS

When, during the present "Tattoo Renaissance" or New Tattoo Subculture, members of the counterculture began "to wear tattoos as a sign of resistance to heterosexual, white, middle-class values" (DeMello 2000: 71), both the masculine and the feminine tattoo could be defined as a playful transgression of a common notion of "the good." However, in the case of men, the aesthetic play with stigmas or the voluntary forfeiting of a great deal of social approval is much more acceptable. Were this fashion to concern only men, it could easily be explained as a renewed search for masculine "coolness." Tattoos have always been dominated by masculinist aesthetics and the concept of male "coolness" has most often included the playful refusal of social recognition, while for women there is "nothing ladylike about being tattooed" (Talvi 2000: 212). Shoshana Magnet affirms that large tattoos "are symbols of hypermasculinity" as they "disrupt traditional notions of demure female beauty and sexuality" and can be read as unfeminine (Magnet 2007: 592). According to Braunberger, female tattooed bodies could even be read as

> criminal trespasses into the masculine, their inky digressions a secret language stolen from men. Censured by neglect, women have been erased from the history of Western tattooing which remains almost exclusively about male bodies, growing out of the homosociality of sailing and military communities (Braunberger 2000: 4).

However, in reality, female tattoos are much more than an imitation of male tattoos as they challenge conventional body standards in a different fashion.

First of all, male and female tattoos do not look the same. The Rank My Tattoos website specializing in male tattoos states that

> a large portion of men with tattoos will choose images involving animals—some believing that the animal's characteristics are, in part, given to the bearer of the animal's tattoo. Therefore, the strength, courage, and power that many animals hold, may also be bestowed onto the one wearing the tattoo of the lion, tiger, dragon, or snake. This concept certainly enhances the masculinity of the tattoo as well. (Rank My Tattoos website)

Clinton Sanders mentions "bloody daggers, skulls, dragons, grim reapers, black panthers, and birds of prey" as dominant images in the conventional repertoire of tattoo designs chosen by men. He also notes that "the designs chosen by men are usually larger than those favored by women" (Sanders 1989: 50). For women the most popular tattoos remain, according to Tao of Tattoos, "floral [and] tribal designs across the lower back, fairies, unicorns, butterflies, and sunflowers. . . . Dolphins were the most popular tattoos for women in around the 1990s but are a bit clichéd now."

However, it is not the choice of motives but the tampering with a certain aesthetic category that establishes the most important difference. According to Talvi, the "standards of acceptable beauty for women still dictate unblemished skin" (Talvi 2000: 212), which means that smoothness can be seen as a feminine privilege. MacCormack (2006: 68) confirms that "the male body seems more readily a canvas able to be written on in its entirety" and Baudrillard goes as far as suggesting that smoothness is on par with castration because the male body "can never really become a smooth, closed and perfect object since it is stamped with the 'true' mark." (1993: 104). In European societies, women have been using makeup and jewelry for centuries, but only tattoos contradicted the standard of smoothness. For a long time, women have even been allowed to undergo aesthetic surgery and receive silicone implants without the slightest public outcry. However, only men were allowed to transform their bodies through the application of tattoos.

The subject of tattoos is also clearly distinct from that of modern primitivism as a parallel subcultural movement employing other means of body modifications such as piercing and flesh hanging. These movements refer to "indigenous practices as alternatives to Western culture, which is perceived as alienated from the body's spiritual, sexual, and communal potential" (Pitts 2003: 8). However, the less extreme forms of such body modifications have been found much more acceptable by mainstream society than female tattoos. The reason is that piercing does not corrupt the imperative of purity and the symbolizing quality of female skin. Most piercings are similar to a sort of jewelry affixed to the skin. Tattoos, on the other hand, are similar to writings and their inscribing power can be conceived as much more polluting.

Purity is a central notion because tattoos are all about the skin. Diets and plastic surgery might destabilize the metaphorical power of the body more than tattoos, but they do not interfere with the body's purity. In the first place, female tattoos are not a matter of decoration or body transformation, but instead they concern the symbolic purity that is important for the economy of male desire. Baudrillard states that "there is something incredibly powerful about the blank, perfectly made-up face of the living doll. She is the void we rush to fill with our own dreams and desires" (Baudrillard 1979: 81). This means that the female body-screen is supposed to *reflect* male desire; that is, to desire *because* she (or her skin) is desired.

Baudrillard developed the concept of fetishism mainly in order to analyze the subjective sentiments of the consumer towards consumer products. Before Baudrillard, the concept of commodity fetishism played a crucial role in Marx's critique of capitalism as well as in Freud, for whom the fetish is a substitute of the woman's lacking phallus discovered by the boy who begins desiring it and finally depends on it for sexual satisfaction. Combining the

Marxist understanding of the fetish with the Freudian one, Baudrillard shows that the "cultural mystique" surrounding a product creates not only illusions about the product's virtues but can even develop a life of its own.

For Freud, as for Baudrillard, fetishism is mainly a male penchant. More precisely, for Baudrillard it is related to the transformation of the female body into a phallus that needs to be *smooth*: "The naked thigh and, metonymically, the entire body has become a *phallic effigy* by means of this caesura, a fetishistic object to be contemplated and manipulated, deprived of all its menace" (1993: 102). Anthropologist Max von Boehn, in his classic *Dolls and Puppets* (1932), pointed out that "the doll, among ancient and among modern peoples, plays an important part in magical practice." For von Boehn, "almost anything can become a fetish, but generally human forms are preferred." Also, MacCormack notes that "tattooed women are frequently described as disrespecting the sanctity of their female bodies," which has been linked to a "disrespect for the symbolic power of the phallus" (MacCormack 2006: 67). One proof is that "men do not get their penises tattooed on the whole because, within a phallocentric system, this is the symbolic signifier of their subjectification, the point where the flesh is already not marked but subsumed entirely as a symbol" (MacCormack 2006: 70).

## The Veil as a Fetish

It is impossible to discuss the subject of female smoothness without referring also to veiling. In many contexts, smoothness bears an immediate link with veiling, which creates—apart from a link with nudity—another important link: the one between veiling and tattoos. In architectural theory, metaphorical "veiling" is equated with "smoothness"; that is, with the contrary of the tactile expression, as Kenneth Frampton explains: "The tactile opposes itself to the scenographic and the drawing of veils over the surface of reality" (Frampton 1983: 25).

Does veiling fetishize women or does it *prevent* fetishization? Historically, veiling has often been seen in terms of fetishization, which is not limited to the East but occurs also in the West. According to Sarah Kofman, "The reasons women would have for veiling themselves and for wanting to be enigmatic would all link up with man's need for a certain fetishism, in which woman, her interests being at stake, would become an accomplice" (Kofman 1980: 59/1985: 4). Kofman does not speak about Muslim culture here.

On the other hand, to see the veil as a fetish can appear as counterintuitive to the extent that—at least in Islamic culture—veils are most commonly understood as devices *preventing* the fetishization of another item: female hair. Hair seems to represent—even more than the skin—a common female fetish that the veil is supposed to cover. Westerners often find the Islamic obsession with woman's hair peculiar though (as mentioned in the introduction) it has been current in many cultures including Western culture. Very often women's hair has been considered dangerous. Ashraf Zahedi explains that "though there is nothing inherently sexual about female hair, most societies throughout history have assigned sexual symbolism to it, letting it determine a woman's attractiveness and power over men" (Zahedi 2008: 251). Because dangerous and powerful hair should not become a fetish, Islamic culture decided to convert it into a smooth and phallic surface through veiling. However, the fact that a smooth cloth covers dangerous hair does not exclude the fetishization of the veil itself.

Baudrillard believes that "eroticization always consists in the erectility of a fragment of the barred body"; and if women are not fetishists they might decide to "perform this labor of continual fetishization on themselves" (Baudrillard 1993: 102, already quoted in chapter 1). Through the process of fetishization, women can become "sexualized dolls"; that is, smooth effigies on which male desire can be projected (Baudrillard 1990: 235). According to this scheme, the woman's sexual pleasure will be constructed only around her own objectification by a male because she is not more than the recipient of male desire.

As mentioned above, man's overwhelming urge is to conceal and to obscure woman because she signifies an essential lack. According to this theory, the veiling of women by men can be interpreted as a compensation of the above-mentioned castration complex. In the patriarchal subconscious, the woman, because of her lack, symbolizes a threat of castration. Since man is the owner of both language and any symbolic order and, therefore, the provider of meaning, the transformation of the woman into a phallus can appear as the logical consequence of this compensating act. More clearly, this means: Woman is not only hidden because she symbolizes a lack and because nothing can be seen, but also because woman is actively reified as the smooth object that man would like to see.

## The Tattoo as a Fetish

Though Baudrillard has not written much about tattoos in particular, on the grounds of his thoughts about fetishism it is possible to interpret female tattoos as anti-fetishist devices. This pattern changes, of course, when men put tattoos on the woman's skin. A man might tattoo a woman and subsequently turn her into an object of *his* desires, a theme dealt with in several films,[3] in which case it is not the woman who becomes a fetish but the tattoo. The symbolic power of "man tattooing woman" is reinforced by the penetration parallelism that reconfigures tattooing as a sexual act, and which has been a popular theme in early anthropological accounts of tattooing (see Perry 1933). It is clear that within this logic, the woman cannot be permitted to express a male symbol of desire on her own, and especially not on her skin. Her body is rather cast as "virtually uninhabited, a shell of skin desiring only to be desirable, to be raped, to have permanent beauty mysteriously drawn upon it" (Braunberger 2005: 5). For men, female skin must be blank and smooth. How important this is becomes clear when we consider that the skin is a memory accumulating various marks during a lifetime. Very often those marks remind us of what we would rather like to repress. In this sense, blank skin symbolizes innocence. The FEMEN activist Marie de Cenival confirms precisely this argument when she describes "the body of women [as] a luminous screen, a blackboard on which one should be able to write anything, if, otherwise, the female body does not speak on its own, and it speaks even very loudly" (de Cenival 2013).

It can be concluded that tattooed female skin disrupts the process of the creation of male desire as it "control[s] and subvert[s] the ever-present 'male gaze' by forcing men . . . to look at their bodies in a manner that exerts control" (DeMello 2000: 173). In the worst case, this male loss of control equals impotence caused by a female tattoo.

Further, the mechanism of fetish-prevention through tattoos extends into the domain of colonialism. In *Voyage en Orient*, a famous novel by the French nineteenth-century writer Gerard de Nerval, the narrator discovers a tattoo on his newly wed Zeynab which submits him to a state of confusion because he recognizes that the tattoos and burn marks embossed on her skin are signs of a personal and cultural history. Madeleine Dobie explains that "the recognition that Zeynab is not simply a blank text that awaits his creative imprint immediately becomes a barrier to the imposition of his fantasy of exotic difference" (Dobie 2001: 142).

All these are reasons why societies have made so many efforts to keep women away from tattoos. When women decide to get tattooed, eroticism shifts from sex sustained by pure female skin ready to receive male erotic projections, to lascivious, immoral, and impure forms of sex. Consequently, across all cultures tattoo artists used to be exclusively male. Apart from that, there are also fictional accounts of how a man tattooing a woman turns the woman—almost magically—into a desiring subject whose focus he controls. The male-made tattoo on the woman's skin will *empower* the woman as it stimulates the desire of *other* men who read the tattoo as the erotic projection of another male. In Jun'ichirō Tanizaki's (1962, 99) short story *The Tattooer*, for example, the tattoo artist Seikichi says to the young woman he has tattooed: "To give you beauty I have poured my whole soul into this tattoo. From now on there is not a woman in Japan to rival you! Never again will you fear. All men, all men will be your victims." Apparently, *this* lasciviousness fascinates men: "Despite her youth she had the mien of a woman who had spent years in the teahouses and acquired the art of mastering men's hearts" (Tanizaki 1962: 100).

## TATTOOS AND SPACE

The contemporary Tattoo Renaissance implies that women empower themselves, which, in return implies that women have the right to decide *themselves* what is erotic and what is not. This represents a very distinct anti-fetishistic pattern. Third Wave–era feminism, as it has been defined by Mary Kearney (1998) and Jennifer Baumgardener and Amy Richards (2000), is essential to these developments. Women who choose to have tattoos do not reject the male gaze (they might even encourage it), but they refuse to receive an erotic mark from the hands of male fantasy. The tattooed feminist says: "If you want to look at me please do; but look at my tattoos."

In other words, the tattooed woman draws the mark in her own fashion, thus potentially alienating male desire. Or, as says Emilie Zaslow about Third Generation Girl Power feminism, "the male gaze is now internalized" (Zaslow 2009: 58). The result of such post-feminist behavior is the paradoxical combination of "both radical and conservative, real and unreal, feminist and feminine" values that can let the woman appear as both "slave and master, victim and perpetrator" (Hopkins 2002: 6, 44). This is why the Tattoo Renaissance is immediately linked to the Girl Power–era feminism because both evolve "around a neoliberal discourse of individual choice and agency, which elides the collective strategies of second-wave-feminism" (Zaslow 2009, 135).

However, the current feminine tattoo has also changed the idea of the tattoo itself. For centuries, tattoos have served "to make the amorphous self into something certain, strong, unchanging" (Richie 1980: 65). Girl Power feminism, on the other hand, puts forward the lack of a "core self" and the affirmation of "shifting identities" (Zaslow 2009: 35). For Donald Richie, "tattoos are able to reduce the world to a firmly opposed series of rights and wrongs" and "a man who is fully tattooed is stable, unchanging (65). The tattooed man has "solidified his own skin and become that solid object; that permanent identity that all men in fear of the amorphous become" (68). The postmodern female tattoo, on the other hand, does not establish identities, but destroys conventional female identities such as "neatness, diligence, appliance, femininity, [and] passivity" (DeMello 2000: 173) without replacing them with something more precise than "more feminine, sexual" ideologies (ibid.). The new feminine tattoos transgress merely symbolizing functions as they allow for the emergence of an alternative space in which not only right and wrong, but also purity, desire, and the self adopt a new, ambiguous status. In other words, what is in question is no longer the provocative or demarcating affirmation of a position *within* a given social space, but the *choraic* creation of a space dependent on more female priorities. Within space, bodies are constantly moving, and meanings and identities change accordingly. Fixed symbolizing functions are not possible within this dynamic logic of space.

Some analysts have recognized this particular spatial function. DeMello claims that the task of tattoos is "to revitalize modern North American society—to change the world by changing its body" (DeMello 2000: 3). Tattoos reclaim a feminist, but also a more erotic space in a world where sexuality is rationalized and commercialized. According to Florence Boodakian, "Eroticism is close to and almost extinct in certain Western cultures, and especially in the United States of America. The current political and social climate can't sustain it" (Boodakian 2008: 49). The new erotic space cannot be established through mere resistance (which could be the reestablishment of a resisting, pure, and modernist nude), but instead it depends on the creation of a new feminine tattoo space. As mentioned in the introduction, in the past, (predominantly male) tattoo-spheres could be located within the margins of society and once an identity had been assumed through the adoption of a tattoo, the person could be assigned a particular geographical position within an urban sphere. Tattoos had their "place" in society just like in pre-capitalist societies consumer goods used to reflect an unambiguous social order. Through the democratization of signs within the urban space in the modern era, bodies have become more mobile and social roles and signs have become dynamic and multiple. As a result, also the tattooed body as a carrier of signs has become part of a complex communication network and tattoos can no longer be read as vertically determined symbols.

In the past, when women received tattoos (mostly from men), they would usually be *identified* as belonging to the same space. Contemporary female tattoos no longer have this one-dimensional identifying function, which influences the way in which these tattoos create space. Within the new tattoo space, the skin does not wear the stigmatic *mark*, nor does it function as a screen of male desire, but it becomes a wall on which multiple desires are projected. In this sense, tattoos have become graffiti. The tattoo is no longer an inscription functioning as an intimate label but a message written on a wall that can be interpreted in various fashions. Tattooed woman Tina Marie, for example, develops a leisurely attitude towards interactions between her tattoos and the social space within which she is moving: "I don't mind if people are interested in my tattoos and want to talk to me, but some people can ask the dumbest questions!" (Tao of Tattoos interview). By getting tattooed, Tina Marie has the impression of reclaiming a space for herself within society:

> I guess I did this as a way of protecting myself from any further hurt, I kind of just wanted to fade into the background so no one would notice me and as a result I wouldn't get picked on anymore. You can only deny the real you for so

long, and when I got into my early 20's I decided enough was enough, and I wanted to claim back the real me.

Having been enclosed in an oppressive social space before getting tattooed, she will avoid getting enclosed in a new, symbolical, socially restricted tattoo space of stigmatization. For her, the tattoos create a new dynamic, interactive space.

This is in agreement with the observations of Mindy Frenske. According to her, tattoos have not simply shifted "from the practice of desecration to one of decoration" (Frenske 2007: 56), but they have evolved from an interested mark into a body decoration that remains "indifferent" in the sense that it does not establish a clearly demarcated symbolical space. This does not mean that postmodern tattooing does not include the use of strong symbols; on the contrary, the symbols can be very strong. The Tao of Tattoos website claims that

> one of the most frequently repeated reasons a tattoo artist gets from female clientele when they go to get a tattoo is that they just broke up with their boyfriend. Women very often visit a tattooist when their divorce papers are signed.

However, the assumption seems exaggerated since a look at corresponding websites reveals that the concept of the tattoo as an art form prevails. Most tattoos seem to have a merely aesthetic and not a symbolic function. In any case, most tattoos are no longer perceived by society as a spectacle or a show disclosing a vertically determined symbolic meaning. They are as far as possible removed from nineteenth-century tattoo shows presenting tattooed people in circuses. It is true that sometimes the "subversive and mystical power" (Beeler 2006: 18) of contemporary female tattoos creates complex symbolisms of existential self-definition. However, first of all, the tattoos are simply *looked at* in passing, establishing a half-abstract and half-concrete space. Because the symbolizing power and the expression of desire of these tattoos are complex, their spatial economy has shifted to a horizontal level. While conventional (predominantly male) tattoos tended to create a social sect or a caste, female body graffiti creates an environment.

## BODY GRAFFITI

Like tattoos, graffiti inscriptions are narratives of the self, but they are inscribed in a spatial dimension, which makes their identity more abstract. Both tattoos and graffiti are "savage" writings that establish identity in a world of anonymity, but in the case of graffiti, a partial conservation of anonymity is part of the concept. While the conventional tattoos tend to establish a ghetto-space (among bikers, sailors, etc.) providing feelings of community and belonging, graffiti tends to be expansive as it screams, "I don't respect your boundaries—textual or spatial" (Carrington 2009: 418). Graffiti permits communication through specific use of jargon and symbols not only among members of a community but also within urban space in general. According to Victoria Carrington, all graffiti pose the "interesting philosophical question, where private property begins and where it ends and where the public area begins" (417). This means that graffiti are not merely tattoos drawn on walls attempting to draw attention to the materiality of the body they occupy. It is, instead, more that the being of graffiti is involved with the spatiality of the city.

Most of the time, graffiti is put where it is not supposed to be. The wall does not change its being *because* it has received graffiti but it has to "cope" with it. This is what signifies the shift from tattoo to graffiti. Instead of identifying its bearer through the tattoo, the postmodern tattoo involves the bearer in complex social games through which she has to define her identity within a social space. This is why both graffiti and postmodern female tattoos "can be read as an important textual practice that ties individual and communities in a complex dance around identity, power and belonging" (Carrington 2009: 419).

Most analyses of tattoos still cling to the symbolic order of the tattoo, just like classical psychoanalytical interpretations of dreams used to insist that dreams must be seen as a consecution of symbolical expressions. Jean-Chris Miller insists in his article "But What Does It Mean?" (1996) on the choice of design, size, and location of the tattoo on the body because they are "symbolic of life experiences and identity." Miller lists all sorts of symbols:

> For instance, angels may symbolize divine inspiration and protection, clouds may represent the intermediary between heaven and earth, crosses signify the relationship between the spiritual and earthly worlds, devils may personify earthly desire, skeletons may represent death, and fairies symbolize supernatural forces or magic in nature. (Quoted from Velliquette et al. 1998: 465)

However, these symbols get subsequently involved in an interactive game that does not only *take place* within social space but that also *creates* social space. Those symbols are active and not passive containers of meaning.

For analysts clinging to the symbolic order of the tattoo, the space of the tattoo is represented by a tattoo-covered skin area whose symbolic power needs to be traced. The tattoo "invests the incised region in tactile and sensory terms, marking it as a special, significant bodily site, eroticizing the region," writes Elizabeth Grosz (1994: 218). What is lacking in these interpretations is the depiction of a tattooscape (just like psychoanalysis rarely talks about a dreamscape) that sees tattoos as aesthetic expressions able to create

space. The mere decoding of symbols has been useful for conventional tattoos; however, the shift to the spatial dimension brought about by the new
type of graffiti-like tattoos implies that any commitment found in tattoos
needs to be seen through perspective. In space, perspectives are constantly
changing; there is no absolute signifying message. Grosz believes that tattoos
"create not a map of the body but the body precisely as a map" (1994: 139).
These maps extend the limits of the mere body surface because body graffiti
creates a body-space. According to Henri Bergson, "To the extent in which
my body moves in space all the other images vary" (Bergson 1988: 44). For
Bergson the body is not an object used by individual consciousness, but is
always actively involved in the world, it is a "center of action," which means
that it is neither a material object nor a center of perception but a "center of
habits." Like Plato, Bergson criticizes the geometrical character of space in
which time plays a subordinate role and pushes space from (timeless) ab-
straction towards the (timely) concrete, suggesting, once again, the idea of a
*chora* settling between being and non-being, between the sensible and the
intelligible (cf. also Derrida 1993: 15).

The tattooed body (just like any body) creates human space because it is
able to resume both space and time in itself. When the body wears tattoos
that are more complex than simple symbols, it becomes a *choraic* phenomenon linked to the history of the place by creating the place in a hermeneuti-
cally circular fashion. Those tattoos do not create a geometrical, Cartesian
*space* of stigmata but a dynamic *place*. On the one hand, the tattoo suggests
boundaries, and on the other hand, the sense of every tattoo depends on those
boundaries.

This is one of the reasons why words like "skinscape" (Mark C. Taylor)
could become more prominent. DeMello insists that for tattooed women the
body is "a temple to be decorated" (2000: 93). Architectural metaphors like
this are telling because they demonstrate how the skin has adopted the spatial
function of a wall. They also explain the ambiguous creation of place through
tattoos. Compared to skin, walls are indifferent and disperse symbolizing
meanings in a spatial fashion. The effect of graffiti is very different from that
of branding. Tattoos corrupt the smoothness of the skin while graffiti leaves
the walls as smooth as ever. Skin desires, while walls do not desire anything.
Contrary to the tattooed body, the graffiti-invested body is neither a material
object nor a center of perception, but becomes, in a very Bergsonian sense, a
spatial "center of action." Everything works towards spatial dispersion rather
than towards symbolic concentration.

Tattoos' involvement in the creation of a place makes them more playful
and less serious. Walls containing graffiti are neither decorated nor branded.
They instead undergo a process of spatial reanimation through inscriptions.
Graffiti involves walls in an urbanistic game where persisting architectural
symbolisms are destroyed by creating new spatial environments. Baudrillard

says that "by tattooing walls, SUPERSEX and SUPERCOOL free [those walls] from architecture and turn them once again into living, social matter, into the moving body of the city before it has been branded with functions and institutions" (Baudrillard 1993: 82). The city shifts from official geography to the organically urban. Likewise, the body shifts from a merely biological function to that of a historical being.

Women who decide themselves what is erotic and who "are not afraid of what guys think" (Hopkins 2002: 44) manifest a playful indifference towards men. They become walls. Men might feel like talking against walls when trying to convince them of the value of certain symbolisms. Impeccably smooth bodies receive graffiti as if they were walls. The possession of tattoos by women envelops them in a shroud of the untouchable.

## SUICIDE GIRLS AND THE EROTICISM OF SOCIAL CORPSES

The spatial function of narcissistically oriented female tattoos seems to be established in the California based Suicide Girls (SG) interactive website (founded in 2001), which receives about five million visits per month and is said to attract a predominantly female audience (there is no way of checking if the audience is really predominantly female). SG call themselves as such because they are considered to have committed social suicide by getting tattooed. Formerly, the site also featured a picture of a female Palestinian suicide bomber, which made the metaphorical link with rebellious suicide very strong. The website is interesting because here, feminine eroticism has created a space for itself through feminine tattoos without the use of marks, stigmata, or symbols; and female tattoos follow this pattern of spatial construction. Such spaces might have existed first in Japan, where hyperfeminized images of women have been current in so-called young girls' *manga* (*shojo manga*); that is, in *manga* exclusively read by women.[4] Though numerous *shojo manga* have created scandals because of sexist presentations of women, in general, neither authorities nor feminists frown upon these *manga* simply because as women's *manga* they escape patriarchal categories (cf. Kotani 2006: 167; Ogi 2001: 180).

More than twelve hundred women are said to function as models for the Suicide Girls (SG) website. Apart from the anti-standardization of female beauty that this site claims to produce, SG seems to subvert the "traditionally gendered consumption of pornographic images" (Earle and Sharp 2007: 13) that sociologists have observed with regard to the use of the internet. The moral ambiguity of this institution is most obvious as it functions as a soft-porn website (attracting nerds and hipsters alike) and at the same time as a woman-oriented interactive platform designed to inspire confidence and help women build personality.

The title page of the website announces that SG are unique, strong, sexy, and confident women. If this is true, then classical capitalist terms like that of self-exploitation no longer seem to be appropriate. Officially, the real and direct style of the site, which shows mostly nude tattooed women of the "girls next door" type, claims to help women express themselves. In the models' profiles presented in the book (2004) *Suicide Girls: Beauty Redefined* edited by cofounder Missy Suicide, quotes like "I feel more confident, more secure" are central.

Tattoos play a prominent role in the SG aesthetics because they are said to "give you attitude." The owners of SG never call their website "feminist" but hints towards feminist topics are frequent on blogs and group discussions. In a special group called "Feminist Topics," both men and women discuss women's issues.

The Goth, post-punk, emo, and indie style of most models could suggest the spatial model of ghettoization; however, looking closer, stylistic identities are relatively fluent and not narrowly defined. Many women have no tattoos at all but are perceived as fitting into the general "empowerment" context. "Attitude" is defined in a complex fashion: Punk aesthetics is combined with old fashioned pin-up looks, classic burlesque, Sesame Street-like cuteness, or Japanese *kawaii*. The only continuity in terms of identity is racial: among the hundreds of profiles I viewed there was only one black woman and four or five Asian women. The overwhelming majority of models as well as members are white American.

The site features not only pictures but also a large number (around eighteen thousand) of interviews and articles of general interest. Interestingly, there are no interviews with participating models explaining their tattoos. Since 2011, SG has also become a comic series (Figure 7.1) following a visual aesthetics reminiscent of *manga*; some bloggers actually indicate parallels with the Japanese classic *Akira*.[5] Apart from that, the comic abounds with naked women, cyborgs, and robots and the blurb of issue Number 4 reads like this: "The six member Suicide Girl team has been reduced to four free members. The rest are imprisoned by the crazy Orwell style cult. The team is going to get their sisters back." There is also a "reality horror movie" called *Suicide Girls Must Die* (2010).

The site's roughly two thousand members have the option of creating a profile, keeping journals, and uploading their own photos and videos. Altogether, there appear to be almost 300,000 uploaded photos on the site. SG models have their own blog (so-called online journals). The topics discussed on those blogs are most of the time completely unrelated to the photos or any other erotic themes. The number of comments reached 30,000,000 by 2012. Models *must* participate regularly on bulletin boards and online journals. Here they can also talk about their tattoos.

**Figure 7.1.    Suicide Girls comic. Courtesy: Suicide Girls**

SG is eager to maintain local features: Members are asked to indicate their location, and within geographically organized boards members can post their favorite local haunts, tattoo shops, and other businesses. The boards and groups meet outside the website's activities. SG highlights regional groups and provides calendars of events as well as maps. A link with "real" localities is also provided by SG Burlesque Shows that are regularly touring through North America. Further facilities present on the website are message boards, public and private networking groups, and a chat room. There are special "boards" for hook-ups, events, sex talk, and discussions of pictures. The boards are relatively public but more intimate discussions are possible in "groups" dealing with Arts and Entertainment, Technology, Culture and Community, Eating, Drinking and Drugs, and Fashion and Beauty.

The ambiguity through which the website works is not obvious to everybody. Female anonymous blogger Milva V, for example, has posted on her blog Ink-ography a lengthy analysis of SG in which she maintains that

> the website only reinforces negative stereotypes surrounding the availability of the tattooed female body, and it in fact prescribes to the status quo more readily than the creators might want to admit. The site's design and content fetishizes these tattooed bodies, fragmenting and decontextualizing them, aestheticizing them to titillate the spectator. (Ink-ography blog)

This blogger goes as far as stating that "the Suicide Girls enact a sort of parody of early exposure to tattooed bodies in North America at Freak Shows and Carnivals." Interestingly, she perceives these tattoos as "voids," which the male gaze can fill with its own male desires. This would mean that *in spite of their tattoos,* these bodies have become dolls or hyper masculine phallic objects and are fetishized for the consumption of the (male) spectator. This is possible because the website excludes, in Milva V's opinion, explicit references to the personal relationships that the women have with their tattoos. The framing remains too conventional and the potential threat of a woman's active attempt at reclaiming her body is violently disciplined. Finally, "the viewer is left to fill in the gaps with his or her own sadistic desire."

Milva V's reading contradicts that of sociologist Shoshana Magnet who finds that SG "interrupt[s] the male gaze through the subversion of the standard photographic practices helping the site to meet Kaplan's (1983) call for women to 'own the gaze' in taking the cameras back into their own hands through staging their photo shoots" (Magnet 2007: 580). Models have indeed considerable influence on the staging and dramaturgy of their photo session. Magnet also notes that "an overwhelming number of the photographs are of women's faces. Focusing on the face rather than the body is a highly unusual practice in pornography" (580). Lengthy series of facial shots inaugurate indeed all photo sessions (Figure 7.2).

Milva V's reading of the site also contrasts with the equally feminist account of Megan Jean Harlow, for whom tattooing represents "a form of

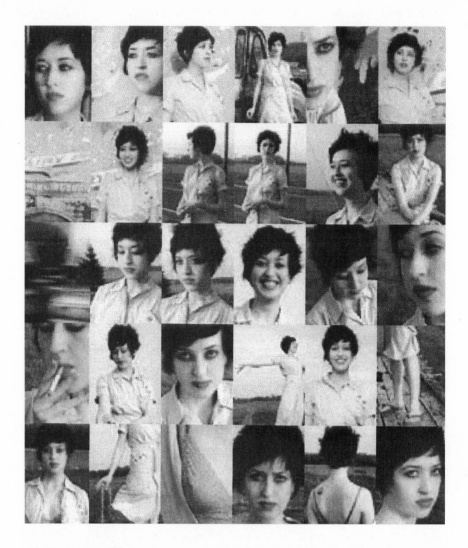

**Figure 7.2.  Lengthy series of facial shots inaugurate all photo sessions. Courtesy: Suicide Girls**

radical feminist identification" able to "upset beauty's hegemonic control on women's bodies." For Harlow, SG clearly subvert imposed subjectivities as well as beauty as a system of control. The tattoos help those women to "resist power structures through positive articulations of one's agency" (Harlow 2009).

Milva V suggests that the symbolical meaning of tattoos that has become so complex and diversified during the Tattoo Renaissance has once again become simplified and commodified through the SG website. On the one hand, this is what has happened to many subcultures—to punk, for example, or to hip-hop cool. In the worst case one could conclude that SG, overwhelmed by its success, is on the brink of becoming blandly commercial. Catherine Redfern and Kristin Aune provide what is so far probably the most negative comment on SG: "A passive, faux-naive, peek-a-boo sexuality that has little to do with real female pleasure and everything to do with mimicking whatever we are told is 'sexy.'" Former collaborators of Suicide Girls whom Redfern and Aune interviewed explain thus: "Suicide Girls is like the middle-class version of a reader's wives feature, which I find sad—the concept of a perceived middle-class, seemingly 'better,' less sleazy way to be objectified by men." Penny agrees: "Burlesque serves up misogyny in a tasteful package of feathers." (Redfern and Aune 2010: 54).

On the other hand, it is not obvious that the SG concept is really such a paramount example of the commodification of the new tattoo culture because the website makes a big effort to view female tattoos in a "spatial," that is, more complex fashion, escaping at least the worst tendencies of commodification. This means that the "object" is not as *unified* as it appears to Milva V and Redfern/Aune but it is constantly subjectified through the blogs, images, and posts whose content is almost throughout non-sexual. This clearly subverts a reading of the site as a mere spectacle. Tao of Tattoos therefore points out as a very positive feature that "Suicide Girls are not completely up themselves and actually respond to comments made on their blogs." Most commonly, SG offer comments to other girls' pictures where relaxed loyalty is reminiscent of non-erotic nudism: "Thanks for sharing." Apart from that, it is true that most comments rarely go beyond "sexy," "gorgeous," and "loved it." However, even here the relative indifference with which these comments are uttered pushes the entire project towards the creation of a nudist space rather than towards fetishist contemplation of symbols.

Magnet notes the complexity of SG and concedes that "some of Suicide Girls' unique online practices do open up feminist possibilities" (578–579). However, in the end she seems to concur with Milva V's views though she bases her observation to a large extent on the quasi-absence of non-Caucasian models: "Rather than a location of liberation or of feminist sexuality, cybersex on Suicide Girls significantly reproduces the commodification of women and reinforces racialized hierarchies of sexual subordination."

In any case it can be retained that the body aesthetics of SG is representative of many reconceptualizations of the female body in current contemporary society. Officially, SG practices resistance as a part of an erotic aesthetic, which represents a consistent attempt at freeing democratic society of the barrier to the nude body that has been erected through Puritan, hypocritical, and oppressive-patriarchal devices. In spite of the certainly relevant skepticism voiced by blogger Milva V, Magnet, and others, in principle, SG attempts to function beyond both virtualizing body negation and materializing

body cult. For SG, the ontological grounding of the body has become architectural and spatial, and tattoos help the body to shift towards a complexity
that can be found neither in conventional pornography nor in the body aesthetics of classical non-erotic nudist movements. After having committed
social suicide, the body becomes a wall covered with graffiti whose eroticism
spectators are asked to appreciate.

## RECUPERATING THE POLITICAL BODY

The spatialization of the body through tattoos has unexpected consequences.
Like graffiti, the contemporary tattooed body "challenges notions of con-
sumption-driven public space" (Carrington 2009: 420) and forms a "counter-
point to commercialization of the city and its public space via the use of
particular forms of text" (417). Like graffiti, the tattooed body is "shouting to
be recognized against the dehumanizing forces of modern city life" (ibid.).
Jill Fisher points out that "the socially diseased body is suffering from a loss
of agency due to the complex power of the state over the functioning of the
body. In other words, the body has been infected by the state" and "in
conditions of general repression and strict control of the body, these groups
[of people who get tattoos] need to re-exert ownership of their own bodies"
(Fisher 2002: 103). While all forms of body transformation position "the
body as a site of exploration as well as a space needing to be reclaimed from
culture" (Pitts 2003: 7), body graffiti does not merely attempt to "rescue the
body and the self from the problems of the modern world" (3), but it also
attempts to modify urban space.

Through this mechanism the female body becomes again a political body.
The female tattooed body does not accept the moral imperatives derived from
the sphere of advertisements and athletics, which increasingly transforms
bodies into non-political, self-sufficient egos. It becomes political in the way
in which bodies have been political in the past. Examples include the naked
body of the 1920s, which had been submitted to an ideology of modernism;
the totalitarian athletic body of the Nazis, which was submitted to racial
politics; or the absolutely clothed body that had once been submitted to the
imperatives of the Christian Church (and continues to be so in some countries submitted to Islamic imperatives).

Like the nude body in the context of protests as well as the veiled body,
the female tattooed body sticks out in the postmodern body landscape, which
almost exclusively employs neutral and post-political bodies. The realms
where both the male and the female body are featured most of the time are
those of advertisements and of athletics. Here the body is post-political because it is predominantly commercial and its politically symbolic meaning
has been reduced to almost nothing. This goes hand-in-hand with the general

tendency of commercials and athletics, which have reduced the world to *images* depriving the body of its spatial dimension by reducing it to an object whose aesthetic aspect can be freely fashioned. The tattooed female body, on the other hand, creates its own space which depends neither on universal laws nor on rules valid only within a presumed tattoo-ghetto. Like this, the tattooed female body escapes the post-political replacement of the body with the symbolizing ego (or the projection of another symbolizing ego), by re-thinking the body as a spatial phenomenon.

## CONCLUSION

Female tattoos, in the way they are present, for example, in the Suicide Girls project, are prone to create an open "tattoo sphere." A sphere because, at least officially, SG is a site by women *for* women meant to escape patriarchal categories. Female tattoos seem to support this mechanism. Generally speaking, while male tattoos are macho, female tattoos are narcissistic; that is, they do not refer to a firm signifying substance but simply to *themselves*. At the same time, the sphere is not closed but encourages exchanges with the outside (male) world. All this taken together creates the tattoo space as a self-determining space in the sense of a *chora* that can be opposed to the Cartesian concept of space as a preestablished, geometrical, "empty" *extensio* filled with objects. Within this dynamic place, the symbolizing process of the female tattoo can work in the service of women's own economy of desire. This does not mean that the tattoos will leave men indifferent; but unlike the traditional Tanizaki-style "male-made" mark performed on female skin, contemporary women's tattoos are very much made for women. Mark C. Taylor writes that "when reality becomes virtual, the body disappears. *Tattooing represents the effort to mark the body at the very moment it is disappearing*" (Taylor 1995: 41) However, all this is only true for the conventional tattoo while the graffiti-tattoo represents a form of *indirect* opposition. It integrates the body into space, but at the same time, it challenges the space by trying to redefine it. Instead of establishing identity through ontological simplification and codification, it creates a complex spatial web of contradictory meanings.

## NOTES

1. The term *chora* is discussed in Plato's *Timaeus* (52d) and has been important for Heidegger (1976) and Derrida (1993). It is a "space containing space" thus sparking an infinite series of containments. It is neither being nor nonbeing but a time/space interval.

2. The field of academic literature covering tattoos and their historical, socioanthropological, technical, clinical, and aesthetic aspects is extremely vast. I mention here only those works explicitly dealing with female tattoos. Of more general importance are: M. Atkinson: *Tattooed: The Sociogenesis of a Body Art* (University of Toronto Press, 2003) and K. Hewitt: *Mutilating*

*the Body: Identity in Blood and Ink* (Bowling Green, OH: Bowling Green State University Popular Press, 1997).

3. For example: *Tattoo* (1981) dir. Bob Brooks; *The Tattooed Woman [Irezumi]* (1981) dir. Yoichi Takabayashi; *Eastern Promises* (2007) dir. David Cronenberg.

4. *Manga* is the Japanese word for "comics." Though being similar to Western comics in general, *manga* follow some different aesthetic and dramatic requirements.

5. *Akira* is a famous *manga* series by Katsuhiro Otomo that exists also as *anime* (animated cartoon).

*Chapter Eight*

# Nudity and Tattoos

*From Naturism to Suicide Girls*

## NATURE, "PRIMITIVISM," AND CIVILIZATION

Tattooing has been practiced for centuries and has been widespread from Polynesia to South America. Traditional tattoos do still exist in indigenous cultures of, for example, the Maori in New Zealand or the Hausa of Niger and Nigeria. Traditional tattoos (like body painting) can mark tribal identities but can also be used for the mere enhancement of attractiveness. Clinton Sanders explains that "the Nuba of the Sudan, for example, have developed body painting as a major form of personal decoration" (Sanders 1989: 4). In Western societies as well as in industrialized Asian countries, tattoos were most of the time limited to certain social groups. As mentioned in the preceding chapter, despite some taboos, tattooing has become more popular than ever, first of all in North America in the late 1980s when members of the counterculture began to wear tattoos as a sign of resistance to heterosexual, white, middle-class values. The Tattoo Renaissance, or New Tattoo Subculture, has led to the ultimate mainstreaming of tattoos as icons of popular culture.

Does this development represent a shift of social or moral values? In order to answer this question it is necessary to first disentangle two notions: the "savage" and the "civilized," both of which are closely linked to the cultural discourse on tattoos. Next, the discussion of tattoos in a "civilizational" context leads to further comparisons of tattoos and nudity. Some tattoo-nudity arguments were touched upon in the last part of the preceding chapter when introducing the aesthetics of the Suicide Girls. However, while the latter discussion revolved mainly around tattoos and their new spatial economy, the present chapter attempts to crystallize the conceptual link that tattoos maintain with nudity in a postmodern context.

By examining positions that see tattoos and nudity through the perspective of the savage as opposed to civilization, it will become possible to answer the following questions: Is nudity itself "primitive," and do tattoos effectuate a shift from the primitive to civilization? If not, does this mean that the untattooed, pure skin still represents a supreme civilizational value?

In the end, this chapter will show that the link between tattoos and nudity is twofold: On the one hand, tattoos are put on the naked skin and the exposure of many tattoos is only possible when taking off at least some clothes (that is, while being at least partially nude); on the other hand it appears that once the skin is covered with tattoos, it can be perceived as less naked. I show that a new, contemporary approach towards tattoos has abandoned all essentialized notions of nature that were still common during modernity. I also show that the naked is no longer seen as pure, which means that it can no longer function as an ideal of civilization in the classical sense. Contrary to what had happened about seven decades earlier, tattoos are now used in order to reinstall the body as a civilized entity. In other words, the tattooed body is never entirely naked and can never be entirely savage.

Historically, in many cultures tattoos have been read through a paradoxical scheme that opposes "the primitive" to civilization, and simultaneously—but for reverse reasons—nature to culture. Very often, the tattooed body has been called "primitive" because it has been held to be incompatible with intrinsic standards of civilization. In Jewish religion tattoos were forbidden, most probably because the surrounding polytheistic peoples who had tattoos were considered savages and culturally inferior (see chapter 6, note 3). A similar strategy could lead to the ban of tattoos in the New World once settlers became aware of the Native Americans' habit of tattooing. In those cases, tattoos were taken, in the words of Jane Caplan, "to mark off entire 'civilizations' from their 'barbarian' or 'savage' neighbors" (Caplan 2000: xiv). It is thus consistent to view contemporary tattoos as symbols of the "postmodern primitive" brought about by a cultural abandonment of the centuries of resistance to primitive desires and savage impulses (cf. M. Taylor 1997: 97, 129). The piercing movement is indeed often referred to as "neo-primitivism," too. This primitivism can even be seen as representative of an "infantile state of humanity" (M. Taylor 1995: 31). Also, Jean Baudrillard mentions tattoos as typically "savage" outfits that he groups together with "negritude, bronzed skin, [and] nudity" (1993: 104).

However, curiously, when tattoos are dismissed because they contradict the standards of civilization, very often these standards of civilization are defended by referring to nature. This is a paradox: Tattoos are criticized because they alter the *natural* state of the body and at the same time *this quality* is seen as being against civilization. This pattern becomes very obvious when it comes to female tattoos. Christine Braunberger summarizes the situation with regard to female tattoos as they are seen in contemporary industrialized countries like this: "When a woman's body is nature, a tattooed woman's body is primitive" (Braunberger 2000: 1). It follows that if the tattoo is primitive it must be against civilization. However, this begs the question whether "the primitive," just because it is removed from civilization, is not closer to nature instead of being against it.

"When a woman's body is nature, a tattooed woman's body is primitive." The sentence remains paradoxical to the core. However often we turn it around, the opposition of nature (which is presented here as compatible with civilization) to "the primitive" remains puzzling. The untattooed body is praised for its naturalness held to be highly compatible with civilization while tattoos are said to refer to a non-natural sort of primitive pre-civilization or non-civilization. Why will this civilization not accept tattoos as a part of itself but declare them to be inappropriate on the grounds of their "unnaturalness"? And why would "civilization" put forward *nature* as the main reason why tattoos should be rejected?

Mark Taylor correctly states that "for those who believe in the rationality and morality of modernity, history represents a steady march from uncivilized barbarism to cultivated refinement" (1995: 31). Still, this does not explain why those who believe in rationality and morality cannot accept tattoos as signifiers of cultivated refinement. A priori there are many ethical and aesthetic reasons to interpret tattoos as being part of a civilizing process. Tattoos alter nature, tattoos resist time as they create lasting marks on the body that defy aging. Tattoos signify commitment. In contemporary civilization, the body is more and more "caught in the expectation that it should constantly be modified and reformed through diets, aerobics, plastic surgery and fashion" (James and Carkeek 1997: 117). Here tattoos can reestablish the body as a concrete, stable, and reassuring human condition and provide authenticity where identities become increasingly disposable. Tattoos fulfill many functions that *could* make them eligible as catalysts of civilization. Still, tattoos are so often said to be "against civilization," paradoxically *because* they alter nature. Even their search for permanence and commitment is interpreted as a "lack of discipline and self-control, of an inability to consider the future" (DeMello 2000: 140).

One way to solve the paradox is to say that the rejection of tattoos is not so much due to a fear of pre-civilizationary primitivism but that the "primitive" represents the mystifying substitute for a fear that is typical for upward striving classes. For these classes the tattooed body is not necessarily primitive, but intrinsically linked to the culture of the lower classes. As mentioned, historically, in Western (but also most Asian) societies, tattoos used to be linked to the culture of the working class and to that of bikers, sailors, and the underworld. Originally, having a tattoo meant to be stigmatized. Erving

Goffman reminds us that the word *stigma* originated with the ancient Greeks who used it to refer to bodily marks or brands that were designated to expose infamy or disgrace in order to identify slaves or criminals (Goffman 1963: 196). In Japan, tattoos were first used to keep track of people belonging to the despised *hinin* and *eta* castes (Richie 1980: 12). Later, postclassical Japanese literature ascribed tattoos to courtesans, catamites, gamblers, and hoodlums (18). Neo-Confucians believed the body to be sacred since it was bequeathed by one's parents and had to be respected and remain unaltered (de Bary, Chan, and Watson 1960: 469). In this context, the recuperation of tattoos by members of higher classes can be interpreted as an attempt to imitate lower-class culture indicative of a general decline of society. Donald Richie explains that "in an emerging civilization, the lower and idle classes ape the upper classes [and] it is often just the opposite when that civilization begins to decline" (Richie 1980: 28). Richie names—apart from tattoos—blue jeans as examples for such a decline.

## TATTOOS AND NUDITY

All this might explain why society speaks out against tattoos, but it still does not explain why it can do so by contrasting them with an ill-identified concept of nature and by declaring tattoos to be contemptible because they are "unnatural." The real reason is the presence of a body-ideology built around an essentialized, simplified, and eternalized notion of nature that is typically modern. This concept likens absolute—that is, tattoo-less—nudity to nature. Here arises the "tattoo vs. nudity" paradigm. The refusal of tattoos needs to be explained by first analyzing the position of nudity in modern, or simply "civilized," society. The idealization of nudity as a natural state is a typical attribute of the European civilizing process and it culminates at the peak of modernity at the beginning of the twentieth century when German nudists claim that "civilization has stolen the purity of nakedness" (Ross 2004: 5) and suggest that nature can restore the soul.

In Western society and especially in the context of typically modern values, nudity can indeed be conceived as a part of a civilizing program that interprets the shameful hiding of the body under clothes as the most primitive behavior. The nude savage can be civilized and the civilized can be savage, which represents a string of thoughts initiated by Rousseau. It is Sarah Kofman who has extracted the following attitude from Rousseau's *Emile*: "The closer women are to the state of nature, the more they are modest (*pudique*). Don't believe that the savage women's nudity denies this because this nudity provides no sign of the absence of modesty. It is rather the clothing that stimulates the senses by exciting the imagination and nudity is a sign of innocence" (Kofman 1982: 87).

Interestingly, this modern ideology rejected tattoos for the same reasons for which it rejected clothes. The idealization of nudity, and not the idea that Western societies value civilized clothes more than tattoos, explains the hostility towards tattoos. For this view, the most important human qualities are supposed to be inscribed *in* the body: they should not be written or worn on its surface. Human qualities are supposed to be contained in the body in the form of habits, as Henri Bergson would point out in the early twentieth century by explaining that the body preserves habits through a *mémoire* that becomes *matière* (Bergson 1938: 267). Habits or "character" become part of the body, but they are supposed to be "inside" and not merely written on the body's surface. For this body-philosophy, not only tattoos, but also clothes and other exterior attributes must be neglected when it comes to the evaluation of a human being because the most valuable attributes are "interior" qualities while the rest is superficial.

The German naturalist or nudist movement of the 1920s was no counter-cultural hippy movement but the result of the middle classes' intention to redefine the "modern relations between desire, the body, and the gaze" (Toepfer 1997: 22). In principle, its objective has been the rationalization of desire by freeing it from "mystification, ignorance, and irrationality" (J. Williams 2007: 25). Here, any decoration of the body, even the one involving only makeup, jewelry, or clothes, was seen as a reflex determined by pre-modern behavior. In a genuinely modern world "no one shall be able to hide weaknesses behind clothes" would proclaim the Koch School of naturalism (Alfred Koch later joined the fascist NSPAP) announcing that "only in pure nakedness can the pure truth be seen" (Williams: 64). By following this new body ideology, "people [will] rise above their primitive urges [and] liberate themselves from bourgeois morality" (ibid.). German nude culture before the Nazi era went even further by expanding this body ethics to the identitarian discourse of nationalism. It sought "to show how nudity, even if it could not unify German society, could nevertheless exert a transformative, emancipatory influence upon the nation" (Toepfer 2003: 173). For the naturalist anti-bourgeois (who would, paradoxically, most likely belong to the bourgeois class), "nudity symbolically equated modernity with the assertion of a more naked identity" (Toepfer 1997: 22). The naked body was supposed to be a stable metaphor able to symbolize moral and intellectual purity. Any idealization of nature and of the natural state of the body was considered an expression of an ideology firmly linked to typically modern ideas.

Sometimes the concept of nature would be idealized and exalted. Evocations of "light" (in the word *Lichtbund*, for example) might indeed relate not only to the natural light of the sun but also include theological connotations going back to the idea of the grace that covered Adam and Eve's naked bodies in paradise. Giorgio Agamben insists on this nudists "dress of light" (Lichtkleid) as an unconscious evocation of "the ancient theological conception of innocent nudity as clothing of grace" employed by the German nudist movement (Agamben 2011: 66). In this sense, nudity is not really nature but divine grace, which confirms the complexity of the "nudity equals nature" equation.

Though nudism was presented as the opposite of "rational" industrialized society, "body culture, especially gymnastics and dance, was hardly lacking in enthusiasm for system, for rationalistic, technocratic, and mechanistic constructions of identity" (Toepfer 1997: 12). All this shows that while nudists fought the malaise of civilization by claiming to go back to nature, their intention had never been to become savages; on the contrary, they wanted to attain a *higher state of civilization* inspired by nature.

In this context, the untattooed nude body represented a rationality that could be diametrically opposed to the irrationality of the tattooed body. The foundations of this ideology are indeed deep: Chad Ross explains that many modern "nudists considered skin to be the only way humans experienced the world. Nudism posited itself as the primary means to cultivate and to care for a healthy skin, guaranteeing the body full benefit from its encounters with the outside world" (Ross 2004: 84). More generally, blankness would often be associated with whiteness, which can lead to another set of reflections inspired by racist ideology. According to Uli Linke, iconographic representation of the body, taking form just before World War I, "entailed the propagation of two interrelated signifiers: white skin and nudity" (Linke 1999: 29). Linke believes that "in the Western scholarly imaginary, white skin is designated a discursive construct: Unmarked, unseen, and protected from public scrutiny, whiteness is said to be deeply implicated in the politics of domination" (Linke: 27). When nudism lays bare this white skin it can become a symbol for a whole range of Western bourgeois values.

## CLOTHES, CIVILIZATION, AND PURITY

Against this background, it needs to be concluded that Jean Baudrillard commits a mistake when grouping together tattoos and nudity suggesting that these primitive phenomena should be opposed to the more civilized clothing. Alphonso Lingis commits the same fallacy when coining the compound and mystifying concept of "tattooed nakedness" as puerile and shallow (Lingis 1984: 43). More or less reissuing Bergson's claim about the necessary interiorization of cultural habits, Lingis claims that "identity is inward" and not outward (ibid.). Furthermore, for Lingis, the coded and fixed character of tattoos as an indicator of identity remains incompatible with the more sophisticated, "civilized" way of signifying identity and values through clothes or other cultural objects.[1] For him, tattoos as cultural signifiers are primitive because they are too simple. However, would a society that despises tattoos because of their all too straightforward way of signifying find "complicated" cultural tattoos more acceptable? In fact, such tattoos do exist: The "subversive and mystical power" of contemporary female tattoos creates contradictory images of violence, desire, memories, love, pain, and cultural otherness (cf. Beeler 2006: 13 and 18) as well as complex symbolisms of existential self-definition. Arguably, tattoos can "help women to reclaim their bodies in the aftermath of sexual abuse or trauma" (Talvi 2000: 215) and can have therapeutic functions (Miori 2012).[2] Research suggests that body modification can enable traumatized individuals to handle personal experiences (Atkinson and Young 2001; Carroll and Anderson 2002). All this transcends the reading of tattoos as one-dimensional identitarian labels.

However, a society that despises tattoos will still despise them even when those "complex" features are acknowledged. Especially in the case of women, the ideology that superposes the scheme "civilization vs. nature" with the scheme "civilization vs. the primitive" brings forth a very specific claim concerning the meaning of "the natural": in a modern, bourgeois context, "naturalness" equates to *purity*. The "advantage" of purity as a concept is that it can function as an attribute of both nature and civilization, which becomes clear in Margo DeMello's statement that the female body is "inviolate, too pure to be disfigured" (DeMello 2000: 140). A concept of purity intrinsic to non-civilized nature is here silently transferred to the realm of the *civilized* female body, thus turning purity into an attribute of civilization. This is how "smoothness" could become a feminine privilege—a smoothness that Baudrillard suggests is on par with castration. Baudrillard points out that the male body "can never really become a smooth, closed and perfect object since it is stamped with the 'true' mark" (1993: 104). Both the natural male and the natural female body have been idealized, but male shifts towards the "non-natural" as well as towards the "primitive" do not have to face charges of purity.

Modernity, with its attack of bodily decoration that constantly rhymes with the Loosian "ornament is crime" has not weakened this system but reinforced it. The proverbial war cry issued by the Austrian architect Adolf Loos at the beginning of the twentieth century against premodern ornamentalists was based on the assumption that cultural evolution is synonymous with removing decoration from utilitarian objects. This attitude communicates with the same essentialized concept of nature that is used when it comes to the rejection of tattoos. Loos himself explicitly linked the architectural crime to the subject of tattoos by insisting that "if someone who is tattooed dies in freedom, then he does so a few years before he would have committed murder" (Loos 1962: 276).

The tendency to identify crimes with ornament was common during Loos' times and cultivated "in natural history, medicine, criminal anthropology and architectural and aesthetic theory" (Canales and Herscher 2005:

251). The "ornament and crime" theme went hand-in-hand with Charles Darwin's theory of the savages' passion for tattoos[3] followed by the generally accepted conclusion that ornaments will most probably follow evolutionary patterns of development (cf. 245). Loos' concept that "one can measure the culture of a country by the degree to which its lavatory walls are daubed" (277) is not original, but was almost commonplace at the peak of modernity. More original is Loos' inference from the primitive state of tattoos to the particularly vicious connotation of *female* tattoos. He states that "in the final analysis women's ornament goes back to the savage, it has erotic significance."[4] For Loos, "all art is erotic" (276) and women's tattoos transport the civilization/primitive controversy into the realm of sexuality.

The conclusion is that, for the modernist architect, pure surfaces should not be *raped* by ornaments, but look uninhabited like skin desiring to be desirable. In this sense, the typically modern fascination with simplicity, whiteness, and undecorated surfaces is linked to an eroticism based on an unconscious idealization of nature. Pure nature *is* civilization. The subsequent curious fascination with modern Scandinavian architecture in the 1950s, especially with the works of Alvar Aalto, is only thinkable against this cultural background. Aalto and other Scandinavian architects designed "natural" and organic spaces that were perceived as ultra-modern because of their "purity."

## FROM NAKED TO NUDE

When the nudist movements of the 1920s declared that "only in pure nakedness can the pure truth be seen," in reality they were not referring to nakedness, but to a well-defined idea of the *nude*. What matters for classical nudists is not nature as something natural, but rather as a pure, ideal space. Much of early twentieth century nudist photography is not set in nature, but "in an uncontextualized 'ideal space' without any motivating or situation-determined connection to a recognizable environment" (Toepfer 1997: 54). This makes necessary certain distinctions between the naked and the nude.

The classical distinction between the naked and the nude goes back to Kenneth Clark's book *The Nude: A Study in Ideal Form* (1956). Clark explains that the nude is a "body reformed" (23) whose negative other is the "naked" as the non-aesthetic manifestation of the unclothed body. The shift from the naked to the nude signifies thus a shift from the actual to the ideal, as well as from matter to form and, certainly, also *from nature to civilization* as the *nude* body is produced and regulated by culture.

Of course, this also has theological connotations (which Clark does not mention): Adam and Eve were naked in paradise but only in the sense that they had no clothes. In other words, they were not aware of being "nude."

Nudity and the awareness of being nude are possible only in a state of civilization. This is why some Christian scholars accept—contrary to what could be expected—the "naked" state of the body but clearly refuse "nudity." "Naked" is the paradisiacal naturalness which is followed by civilized nudity that is intrinsically evil. Recently a religious scholar on a Christian blog has argued that there is a distinction between tasteful nakedness in art and an objectifying nudity. She then referenced several examples of classical and Renaissance art in relation to the former, and pornography to the latter (Vandoodewaard 2011). Surprisingly, for her, Renaissance nudity is naked while pornographic nudity is nude.

When thinking about the "unifying" effect of this shift from nature to civilization that pushes the naked towards the nude, it is impossible not to mention Derrida's concept of the frame as a site of meaning, which sees all art as "inside" a frame, clearly distinguished from all outside matter and events. Contrary to the naked, the nude is framed. For Derrida the frame designates "a formal and general predicative structure, which one can transport intact or deformed and reformed according to certain rules, into other fields, to submit new contents to it" (Derrida 1987: 55). In other words, the frame unifies the object by applying the device of spatial limitation. Consequently, also Clark perceives nakedness as the mere "unframed" occupation of space by the unclothed body.

The French philosopher François Jullien has provided his own analysis of the difference between the nude and the naked, which is worth mentioning in this context. Jullien points out that the nude leaves "nothing to expect, no possibility of onward progress. Everything is there, definitive" (Jullien 2007: 2). While nakedness is not more than the diminished, shameful, savage and pitiful state of being stripped or laid bare, the nude provides a sense of civilized plenitude and total presence. The purpose of Jullien's study is to show that the nude as opposed to nakedness in aesthetics is purely Western and does not exist in Chinese or Japanese art. Only in Western aesthetics we find the "dizzying effect of the nude" providing a "fixity of essences" (2). In Western civilization, the nude body is "absolute" and does not permit any further decoding because it is permanent and lifted out of any spatial context: "All other subjects, whether real or invented—streets, clothes, hairstyles, and even landscapes and 'nature'—show as much evolution over time as variety among themselves. Whereas the nude does not and cannot change: it is invariable—it is still essence" (4).

Furthermore, Jullien concludes that the nude can only be hostile to symbolic body marks because the nude body is supposed to symbolize nothing but itself:

> In [non-nude] photographs, an intention can be discerned, or at least, effects can be identified, the meaning can be investigated, symbols developed, narra-

tives woven. They can be read, they are open to appreciation in an infinite
variety of ways. Each has its caption: they are signs. The nude, on the other
hand, always has the impact of an immutable revelation. (3)

What does all this tell us about the state of nudity in modern culture? It is
obvious that the "nakedness" practiced by modern nudism is not naked at all
but nude because here nakedness is highly informed, constrained, unified,
and regulated (it is interesting to note that in German there is only one word
for both naked and nude). What takes place especially in early twentieth
century nudism is an idealization of *nakedness as nudity*, which becomes
particularly obvious in nudist photography of that era. In spite of its insistence on its *natural* aspect, the nakedness of nudist camps is not natural but
civilized in exactly the way in which Clark sees the nude. Nudists are not
naked but nude because their lifestyle functions for them like a "frame"; it
equips their unclothed bodies with the coherence typical of a "unified" work
of art, clearly framed by a social ideology based on well-defined presupposi-
tions about subjects such as environmentalism, simplicity, modesty, temper-
ance, education reform, food reform, sexual mores, etc.

Any tattoo (or even jewelry) must be perceived here as a work of art
within a work of art bound to compromise the frame supposed to separate
civilized nudist "inside" space from the savage outside space. The concept of
the nude supports the ideology of modern nudism with all its preconceptions
of the purity as an attribute of civilization. This is why Jullien insists, similar
to Baudrillard, on the importance of smoothness; that is, on the contrast
between the infinitely smooth skin texture and the hirsute which "makes the
female nude more unadulteratedly nude than that of the male, a kind of
superlative nude" (Jullien 2007: 7). This smoothness is purely modern because it reinforces, like all modern aesthetics, the abstractness of form. And it
is this unique concept of the nude that has contributed to the development of
modern nudism. The shift from nakedness to nudism overlaps thus with
Jullien's postulations of the nude as an absolute present:

> The modern body is, one might say, the context, the determining power of the
> space it chooses to inhabit: perception of the body determines the identity of
> the world, the reality external to the self. This decontextualization of the body
> implies that the more naked the body becomes, the more the body dominates
> perception, the more the body assumes an abstract identity. (Toepfer 1997: 1)

All this is true for modernist body aesthetics as much as for modernist architecture. Traces of this "modernism" might be found in the most recent "body
fashion" that makes the shaving of pubic hair and other body hair commonplace (for females but increasingly also for males) also outside the context of
pornography.

By July 1910, the main façade of what is today called the "Loos House" in Vienna was smooth, white, and bereft of adornment, and Loos predicted that "soon the city streets will shine like white walls!" Loos wanted walls to be essentially nude but not naked. Nude architecture tends to be monumental while naked architecture simply "lacks clothes." This confirms all above observations—derived from Clark's distinction between the naked and the nude—about the incompatibility of modern nudism and tattoos.

## FROM NUDE BACK TO NAKED

The nude body is supposed to be not a bearer of signs but a "fixity of essences," a radiant total presence expressing civilized plenitude. For nudists in the 1920s it was a stable metaphor symbolizing moral and intellectual purity. It was "a sign for a modern, liberated identity in the age of mechanical reproduction" (Toepfer 1997: 22) as well as a sign of health, strength, and beauty. A certain political, social, and cultural consciousness was meant to be inscribed in the blank, nude body and the message was straightforward.

Through the tattoo the body becomes a mere *bearer* of signs: now messages are inscribed not in the idealized body but in tattoos. In principle, any tattoo applied on the nude body is a stigma transforming nudity once again into nakedness. While tattoos were taboo within the realm of nudism, today tattoos as well as piercings abound on nude beaches.

One reason is that the unclothed body is no longer seen as pure, which means that it can no longer function as an ideal of civilization. As a consequence, the naked cannot be transformed into the nude. What remains once the civilized, radiant nude has become impossible is only embarrassing nakedness that needs to be covered—with tattoos. As paradoxical as it sounds, tattoos are helpful in such a situation: a tattooed body is never entirely naked. Consequently, it will also always be closer to civilization. Of course all this is entirely contrary to what has been thought about tattoos, nakedness, and civilization by Western culture from Rousseau to classical German nudism. For them, any sign covering the skin was uncivilized because it was unnatural. The removal of clothes and the baring of untattooed skin could lead to a superior and more "natural" state of civilization. Today it seems to be increasingly difficult to sustain "naked" (i.e. untattooed) nudity. The untattooed nude, that is, the unclothed body which is not simply savagely naked but civilized nude, is practically impossible. One reason is that civilization no longer manages to think itself as a basically "pure" enterprise. We remain in the realm of paradoxes but the paradox has been inverted. *Today it is no longer nature but the savage that can be seen as civilized.*

This is why tattoos can be integrated into civilization. Postmodern tattoos refuse to accept the *nude* body as an idealized and fixed essence able to shine merely through its civilized plenitude and total presence. Instead, tattoos are put on the *naked* body as if it were a graffiti-covered wall (see chapter 7). And walls cannot be categorized in terms of social stigma. For Loos, ornament was a crime because it was not organically linked to modern civilization and could not be seen as a living expression of that civilization. Today tattoos *can* be seen as an expression of postmodern civilization. The state of tattoo-civilization can be experienced as the dropping of rigid standards, as the establishment of a "conception of the body that is open" (DeMello 2000: 141) or as a liberation, as states Rebecca Walker: "The body, the blank page waiting for words, and beauty, a subjective idea looking for a location have been liberated to meet up in a variety of unique and often surprising ways" (Walker 1998: xvi).

It has been said above that pure nudity needs a frame in order to exist, either in the form of a physical boundary or of an abstract framework constructed with the help of ideologies. In the contemporary world, such "frames of nakedness" have become increasingly difficult to establish. Rob Cover speaks of the "destabilization of the contexts" in which non-sexual nakedness and gazing have been legitimated in modernity (2003: 55). One reason is the sexualization of the public sphere that has already been mentioned in the introduction. Cover examines "the encroaching prohibition against nakedness in school showers, on film, [and] in family photo albums" (66) that have made nakedness impossible. Why? Because this nakedness cannot be "framed" as civilized nudity. A family picture of a child eating a sausage in the bathtub can evoke images of pornography.[5] Why? Because the frame supposed to distinguish civilized nudity from savage nakedness has become blurred in a culture that is so much permeated by erotic images through media and the internet. It is not, as says Mark Taylor, that "when reality becomes virtual, the body disappears" (1995: 41). The problem is rather that through the virtualization of reality the body can too often appear out of context and can bear too many inappropriate connotations.

Early nudists had to tackle a similar problem because very soon nudist photos began being published in pornographic magazines, which gave nudism a bad reputation. These early ideologists of nudism declared that "the real danger to social mores and to youth came from the publications that utilized naked photos to sell copies" and concluded that "the naked movement assumes a new face entirely as soon as it becomes literary" (Ross 2004: 44). However, at that time, the overlaps of "natural" nudism and pornography could be more easily distinguished and "frames" could be restored. Today, it is much more difficult to separate real reality from mediated reality. Cover notes that even "the 'protected' sites of nakedness—children bathing, locker-room showers—are likewise 'crashed through' and sexualized" (67). Cover also observes that the instability or inefficacy of context has given way to "a certain hysterical conservatism" (65).

## SUICIDE GIRLS AND "URBAN NUDISM"

In this context it is interesting to look again at the Suicide Girls interactive website which can also be understood as an interesting attempt at coping with the particular crisis of postmodern culture characterized by slippage across contexts (or frames). As mentioned in chapter 7, SG functions simultaneously as a soft-porn website and as a woman-oriented interactive platform designed to help women build personality. Can any frame be more blurred than that?

What the tattooed nudism of Suicide Girls shares with classical nudism is that both position the body as a site of exploration as well as space that needs to be reclaimed from civilization. One difference is that with SG nudism has shifted from a natural (though civilized) nudist environment towards an "urban" complexity in which signs abound, overlap, and become ironic and often difficult to grasp. It is the exact contrary of an idealized space. In this sense, SG's concept of nudity is diametrically opposed to that of the modern nudist movement that was looking for "natural, rural settings as an educational method for moral strictness" (Williams 2007: 28). It is also working against the dualistic reconstruction of the unclothed body once announced by Kenneth Clark. Pre–World War II nudist movements saw nudism as a social *rebirth* while for Suicide Girls it is one of ironic social *death*. Formerly, nudist middle-class Westerners undertook a revision of the relationships with their bodies, the earth, and their spirituality. Now, Suicide Girls reflect nudity against a complex flood of virtual and real images within which any "framed" reality is difficult to establish. Already any post-1945 German nudism "is notable for its lack of ideology" (Ross 2004: 16), which joins Ruth Barcan's argument (discussed in the introduction) that nudism has become a mere lifestyle and nothing more.

In the twenty-first century, the ideological frame of nudism has been undermined in the most radical fashion by questioning the status of the real and the unreal. As announces their macabre name, Suicide Girls have died but not for real. This new attitude has nothing to do with the morbid theme of "real" death prominent, for example, in the Japanese conventional tattoo ideology where "tattooed [*yakuza*] men think and talk much about death" (Richie 1980: 68) because of their dangerous professions. SG nudism can only exist once the simplified, essentialist, coherent, unified, and eternalized concept of nature that has been present in modernism is abandoned.

SG also destroys Clark's binary oppositions of naked and nude, passion and reason, mind and body. What disappears together with this is the binary opposition of the civilized non-tattooed subject to the tattooed savage. It becomes untenable to assume that a non-tattooed subject whose cultural value is too complex, significant, and intimate to be announced on the skin, is superior to the subject wearing all relevant information about her person on her skin in the form of a mark. Other aesthetic categories become obsolete as well. While nudist photography, when revealing the essence of bodily movement (for example that of Willi Warstat) did everything to avoid kitsch effects (cf. Toepfer 1997: 54), tattooed nudism is not afraid of kitsch and often pushes its aesthetics, through the use of numerous ironic twists, towards camp.

## CONCLUSION

Loos wanted walls to be smooth and white so they can shine. Graffiti turns not only naked walls but also dead and nude architecture into a more complex kind of urban experience. Similarly, the shift from tattooless nudity for which clothes are criminal to the postmodern form of tattoo-covered nakedness is revolutionary in terms of body aesthetics. Nudity is militant for modern nudists just as conventional tattoos were once militant. In classical nudism the objective is the bright, radiant nude that is symbolic. This is not different from conventional tattoos: Men especially used to become more concrete through tattoos because their tattoos were seen as symbols highlighting a "real" kernel. The monumental nude is shining and the resisting nude is fighting against its own indefiniteness. Modernist nudity engaged in such a political fight and tattoos followed this scheme. Also, tattoos have been said to work against the disappearance of the body by making the body more present and essential.

The postmodern tattoo, on the other hand, represents a form of indirect opposition. It integrates the body into space, but at the same time, it challenges this space by trying to redefine it. Nude beaches in the 1970s presented unerotic nudity. Not that it has become erotic nowadays, but contemporary nude beaches can be experienced as a graffiti-splattered nude city, which would have been unthinkable for the founders of the nudist movement. The SG project in particular shows that nudism can acquire a more "urban" dimension. While modern nudism sealed itself off geographically by being restricted to camps and aesthetically through abstract stylizations of photos, on interactive websites such as SG, nudism is able to enter the real life of people. As mentioned in chapter 7, on the website, other Suicide Girls offer comments to other girls' pictures where relaxed loyalty is strangely reminiscent of non-erotic nudism. The modern, essentialized, simplified, and eternalized notion of nature has here clearly been abandoned. Nudity is still seen as "civilized" but the standards of civilization have changed: Civilization is no longer seen as compatible with purity and as inspired by nature but it is inspired by a postmodern world of abounding images and slippages of contexts.

# NOTES

1. The fallacy of Lingis' reasonings about the savage and the applications of tattoos has very well been analyzed by Grosz (1994, chapter 6).

2. Some research does actually suggest different conclusions (see Holland 2004 and Rubin 1988).

3. Charles Darwin in his *The Descent of Man*, page 606, quoted from Canales and Herscher 2005: 239.

4. "Ornament und Erziehung" in *Wohnungskultur*, 2–3 (1924), page 81, quoted from Canales and Herscher: 237.

5. "In a case in California, police were called in by a photo developer when he discovered 'family snaps' of an eight-year-old boy and a six-year-old girl together in the bath eating sausages. What alerted the developer and caused the police to consider the photographs as 'indecent' and 'degenerate' were the sausages" (Cover: 64).

## Chapter Nine

# "Veils and Viagra"

## *A Double Victory?*

The book has shown that tattoos, nudity, and veils can be traced to similar social and psychological patterns. The veil has become part and parcel of a new script of body culture that also implies nudity and tattoos. Throughout this book the focus has been on a paradox, which has been called in the introduction the "protection-imprisonment paradox" or the "liberty-oppression paradox." The roots of this paradox have been crystallized as a sort of circular thinking. While veiling and covering apparently (though not undoubtedly) remove women from being perceived as erotic objects, it remains also a fact that the intention to see almost every part of the female body as erotic is what has created the problem in the first place. When the Islamic party of Algeria (Front Islamique du Salut/FIS) insists on women wearing the veil in order to stop "looking like cheap merchandise that can be bought and sold," one has to ask whether the idea that women *could* look like that in the first place is not a mere product of the fantasy of the individuals who require such strict veiling. The same is true for Murtaza Mutahhari's (ideologue of the Islamic revolution) suggestion that "a woman who leaves her home with only her face and two hands shows that she does not invite men to herself." Why should we suppose that the woman who does show more than her face and two hands *does* invite men to herself?

If female bodies could be perceived in a more "natural" or—perhaps as Aliaa El Mahdy or classical nudists have suggested—in a less obsessively sexual way, the problems surrounding Islamic veiling would probably not even appear. "Natural" in this case does not necessarily mean that nudity will be entirely removed from the realm of the sexual, but rather that the sexual will be seen as a natural quality acceptable, to some extent, in civilization. In other words, the *erotic* will be handled in a more "natural" fashion. The first step to achieve this would be to dis-eroticize the female body and to see it, in a classical nudist fashion, as more natural, though not necessarily as asexual. True, as this book has shown, it has become very difficult today to refer, in relationship with nudity, to the concept of nature as a fundamental ethical or aesthetic quality. Even nudists are struggling with this; and the concept of nature is even more difficult to handle when it comes to veils and tattoos.

Still, it must be possible to define a more "natural" way of dealing with nudity, a way which is more civilized and which can also be described as a way of seeing the body in a context that avoids any fetishism. It is important to insist that all this has nothing to do with "Western" or "Eastern" ways of seeing the female body or with "colonial" or "anti-colonial" points of view. The "Western" point can be just as fetishistic as the "Eastern" one. The forced unveiling of Arab women by the French colonial powers, for example, manifested an erotic voyeurism based on conceptions similar to the fetishistic Algerian or Iranian approaches mentioned above.

The non-fetishistic way of seeing the human body does not necessarily imply that it is to be viewed in a non-erotic way; it simply suggests that the erotic subject will not be fetishized and not be seen as an object. Baudrillard points out that "in a non-fetishistic culture (one that does not fetishize nudity as objective truth) the body is not, as in our own, opposed to the face, conceived as alone rich in expression and endowed with 'eyes': it is itself a face, and looks at you" (Baudrillard 1990b: 33). In other words, nudity will be *potentially* erotic but never *explicitly* erotic; that is, it will never be ob-scene. It will have acquired the state of unclothedness similar to that of the face, which we do not normally perceive as objectively nude. While the face can be erotic, it is not a fetish. The "natural" quality of the body should be established along such non-fetishistic lines.

It has been shown that in today's civilizations, in which even nature represents a complex, polysemic, and paradoxical referent, the "natural" state is not given by nature at all but needs to be achieved in the form of a certain state of civilization. This means that "natural nudity" is also a state that needs to be achieved by civilization. The problem of nudity in relationship with civilization has appeared in chapter 8, where the Iranian Islamicists' slogan that "if unveiling is a sign of civilization, then animals must be the most civilized" (Shirazi 2001: 107) has been shown to be missing the point. The "no-veil position" that will be defined in this conclusion is opposed to this "the veil equates civilization" position. However, it is opposed to it not because it would be against civilization, but rather because it aims to obtain a sort of non-fetishistic nudist innocence towards the unveiled body. Animals, which do not have to overcome any shame, do not need to learn this civilized attitude, which is the reason why the above Iranian slogan does not make sense. Equating clothes with civilization is a simplification, which is in many cases based on the idea of clothing as presented in the Old Testament: Clothing would arrive only once the paradisiac state of natural nudity had been lost. The same "clothing equates civilization" paradigm is still present in Freud, who believed civilization to be based upon the shame produced by the visibility of the genitalia. However, this logic, just like that of the ayatollahs, will lead to the absurd conclusion that the maximum of clothes signifies the maximum of civilization.

## NUDITY DESEXUALIZES

This book, in which veils and nudity have been compared on a concrete as well as an abstract level, has shown that a certain type of nudity is a more efficient device of desexualization than veils. In most cases, the veil stood for the artificial creation of signs of femininity; and the concept of nudity could be crystallized as an attempt to overcome this type of consolidated femininity. However, in spite of this logic, in everyday life, veil and nudity continue to be seen as antagonistic, especially when it comes to the sexualization/ desexualization of the body. The main reason for this is the economy of fetishism that underlies most modes of thinking about the body.

### Arab Men

What can be done to improve the situation? I think that the ball is now in the camp of the men. If men decide, for example, that female hair is a highly charged symbol of female sexuality and of female power that needs to be covered and controlled, *they* have to deal with the consequences. One of the consequences is that some people will never agree with this, despite the huge cultural and religious machine that has been employed for centuries in order to defend it. Some people will always refer to alternative ideas of the "natural" character of hair and put forward, for example, non-fetishistic visions of the human body.

The remaining question is: Why are men doing this? Tradition and culture are among the main reasons and, in general, nobody can or should be accused of following and reproducing one's own tradition and culture. In Arab culture, women are seen as the principal vehicles for transmitting values to the next generation. However, once again it needs to be asked: *By whom* are they seen as such? Some feminists insist that *men* want women to play the role of this cultural transmitter (cf. Enloe 1990: 52; Grace 2004: 26). This means that men do not seem to think that women are playing this role "naturally." Many Arab men find women most susceptible to assimilation to outside values from which they (women, men, as well as society at large) need to be protected. In this view, just like in many other contexts, women are seen as passive vehicles for male-imposed meaning.

It is time, in this book on women, to make some important statements about men. First, while a good deal of the present analysis has focused on ways of wrenching women from stereotyped discourses and to establish a more complex image of the contemporary woman, it must be recognized that *men* also suffer from various stereotypes, especially in a Muslim context. Arab men's images as machos or terrorists that circulate in the West might be even more problematic than those of the "oriental woman." Judith Lorber is right in insisting that "feminists have looked at the Middle East and its problems through women's eyes, vis-à-vis oppressive husbands and fathers. Perhaps it is time we studied the social construction and political uses of Middle Eastern masculinities" (Lorber 2002: 388). An analysis of masculine pride, identity, and identity-crisis is just as essential as an analysis of the symbolizing power of the feminine aesthetics.

A closer look at the situation shows that the cliché of the Arab man is incorrect, be it simply because in Middle Eastern countries—probably more than anywhere else—masculinity underwent an important crisis due to modernization and Westernization, which some have classified as a "cultural emasculation" (Moallem 2005: 72). Hamideh Sedghi points to power struggles among men (over the control of women's sexuality) brought about by the modernization efforts of the Shah in Iran who "used unveiling to emasculate the clergy and to promote modernization and Westernization" (Sedghi 2007: 7). She points out that "on a deep emotional level, unveiling must have produced a sense of personal fearfulness and powerlessness on the part of many men: fearfulness over losing control over women; and powerlessness for being unable to neutralize the power of the state" (89). The loss of premodern (rural, tribal, religious) masculinities in those countries could partly be compensated by new "civil" male power obtained within the context of modern citizenship. However, this process is far from being straightforward. In Iran for example, decades after the Shah's Westernization efforts, the Islamic Revolution "mobilized a premodern male homoerotic and homosocial world of meaning, throwing into crisis the heteronormative world of modernity" (Moallem 2005: 115).

What is the "real" image of Muslim men? Some accounts are apparently incompatible with the cliché of the Arab man as a hero or macho. An example is journalist Wajeha Al-Huwaider's article "A Call to Arab Women: A Single Life Is a Thousand Good News for the Unmarried Women," which addresses the situation of Arab men. The article has been published on the British-Arabic website Elaf. Strangely echoing Moallem's and Sedghi's above statements, Al-Huwaider attributes to the Arab man an "impotence complex":

> Most Arab men have been emasculated since they were young, they have no power to give, and therefore they are incapable of granting a respectable life to

anyone." According to Al-Huwaider, Saudi men are afflicted by an "impotence complex," spending more on impotence drugs than men anywhere else in the world in a desperate effort to regain their masculinity. These "pathetic" men need to lord it over women in order to feel complete or intact. "They are afflicted by a chronic germ that has determined that guardianship (of a woman) is a sign of masculinity, and that without it their limbs will not be in balance. (Quoted from Bradley 2005: 167)

How does this go together with the image of the fiercely strong Arab man who loses control of his libido at the mere sight of a female hair lurking from beneath the hijab? Of the man who must be protected from his own hormonal drive, so powerful that no woman should even think of titillating it outside the confines of the conjugal bedchamber?

As a matter of fact, men's anxiety and worries about their sexual power have surfaced at some places in this book, for example in the sections on the "women are dangerous" theme. Abolhassan Banisadr's statement that "concealing female hair says more about men's sexual anxiety than about the seductive power of women" (Zahedi 2008: 259) supports Al-Huwaider's idea. It was suggested in chapter 7 that the male loss of control when confronted with a female tattoo can perhaps even cause impotence. And male anxiety has been depicted most graphically in the same chapter by suggesting that the veiling of women by men can be interpreted as a compensatory act striving to overcome a castration complex because in the patriarchal subconscious the woman symbolizes the threat of castration. Through an act of veiling-fetishization, man bestows meaning to woman by transforming her into a phallus.

Anthropologist Gideon Kressel provides another depiction of Arab male anxiety through a detailed account of observations of three Arab men in search of prostitutes in Israel. One of them, named Awad, approaches a prostitute whom he engages in a conversation. Though he seems to be enthusiastic about her at first, he suddenly loses interest, turns his back and leaves her astounded. The others, as well as Kressel, are surprised and enquire what has happened. They want to know "what she had said, how she could destroy his desire [and] 'break' his male organ" (Kressel 1992: 43). After some hesitation, the man confesses. It turns out that he had said to her "I will enter you up to here" (reaching a hand to his chin) and that she had replied "yum yum." Awad had perceived this answer as a total "turn down" making him instantly impotent. Upon further questioning, Awad explains to Kressel that

such a woman is "the most dangerous," having the courage even to stab a man the minute he ejaculates. Elaborating on this idea made Awad's expectation clear; a whore "should give for money," but she should be miserable, she is supposed to look down, to be [act] worried while being threatened [subjected to stabbing] by a huge penis. Total "indifference" to coitus, the traditional

ideal for a female, leaves a man the dream of finding, perhaps in non-tradition-
al circles, a more responsive counterpart, who will be moved by his abilities.
But how should this other woman approve gratification, being impressed by
him? How should she react when excited? Since bawdiness is masculine, and a
sexually desired woman can stab like a man, the anticipated leeway she has for
reflecting agitation includes bashfulness, helplessness, and, favorably, horror.
(ibid.)

We find in those observations a paradoxical combination of veneration of
women and misogyny, a combination that is not untypical for Arab culture,
and which might account for many other paradoxes. One such paradox was
pointed out by Joseph Massad, that while Islam is often identified as "feminist," Arab society is often identified as "misogynistic" (Massad 2007: 155).
Ali Mazrui refers to a similar paradox, which has already been mentioned in
chapter 4: "Muslim countries are ahead in female empowerment, though still
behind in female liberation" (Mazrui 1997: 121).

Of course, the phenomenon is not just an Arab one. The fear of the "dark
continent of the feminine" has also dominated Western culture probably ever
since. The fear became particularly strong during the Victorian era (can it be
a coincidence that the Victorian era is also the period in which veils, which
were often described in literature as a symbol of secrecy and deceit, were
worn in England for the last time?). And we find strong echoes of the same
fear also in Freudian psychoanalysis. Baudrillard has picked up those
psychoanalytic threads by drawing links between male weakness and the
"panic men feel when faced with the 'liberated' female subject" concluding
that when "a woman demands sexual satisfaction by becoming conscious of
the rationality of her desire," the liberated female subject represents a "de-
vouring, a gaping voracity" (Baudrillard 1990b: 26). This is in agreement
with the example from Kressel. Also, the success of FEMEN, who have been
a paramount topic of interest in this book, is very precisely based on this
cultural phenomenon. Wherever FEMEN stage their protests, they create
chaos in liberal societies (quite similar to the Muslim *fitna*) not because their
nudity would break the norms of good taste (those societies are much too
liberal and open-minded to be shocked by nudity) but because their nudity
provokes a certain kind of violence. FEMEN's protests bother people in
liberal countries because here the female body, which could so far be controlled as an erotic *object* of male desire (and perhaps of possession and
exploitation), suddenly becomes a demonstrating *subject* that is not merely
seducing but capable of free political will. The problem is not that men in
those societies would (at least consciously) reject the idea that women can
have a free political will; they just want those women's bodies to be clothed
at the moment they are engaging in this activity. The alienating ("verfrem-
dend" in the sense of Bertolt Brecht's and the Russian Formalists' theories)
juxtaposition of female nudity and political protest reveals certain subcon-

scious patterns in societies. This strategy is also typical for Third Wave feminism, which insists on combining "masculine" physical and social formidability like independence, power, and strength with conventional feminine appearance and sex appeal.

Still, it seems that the resentment of strong women is more pronounced in Arab culture. In 1960, the nationalist Lebanese philosopher Abd al-Latif Shararah described in his *Philosophy of Love of the Arabs* (Falsafat al-Hub 'ind al-'arab) a certain male "'resentment' [*maqt*] of women that represented an obscure psychological state—very obscure—of rebellion against women's authority during the pre-Islamic age of ignorance (jahiliyyah)." Shararah argues that during that age, "powerful ruling women were so tyrannical, 'violent and strict,' due to women's 'closeness to daily living, and their intimacy with sadness and pain, on account of their suffering in love, in marriage or lack thereof, in pregnancy or lack thereof . . . that once they ruled over society or within the family, or the State, they would use violence often against their subjects and cause them suffering'" (quoted from Massad 2007: 123). Shararah's findings refer to the early history of Arab society, but it is certainly no coincidence that he observes such psychological patterns in the present in societies where many people have found a good deal of male "resentment" towards women.

Against this background, we must ask again how the image of male sexual ferocity that prefers women to be veiled in order to avoid woman-initiated chaos (*fitna*), goes together with Al-Huwaider's image of the pathetic Arab man. For Al-Huwaider the answer is clear. Arab men "need to lord it over women in order to feel complete or intact." Guardianship of a woman is a sign of masculinity that compensates precisely for the lack of masculinity. Traditionally, men's honor has been associated with their hold on women. To control and seclude women, to restrict them on their physical appearance, their sexuality and labor has been a source of male power and masculinity, and in many cases it still is. Al-Huwaider continues her account of Arab masculinity by suggesting that Arab men are "spending more on impotence drugs than men anywhere else in the world." Her allusion to impotence drugs can easily lead to the cynical conclusion that, at the end of the day, a re-veiled Middle East means that Muslim men have obtained a double victory in the form of "Veils and Viagra." However, are things really that simple?

There is still another way of linking both items, that is, the strong over-protective man to the weak man. The Arab man needs to be protected from his own sexuality but by whom? Of course, always by women! Here we join Al-Huwaider's theme of defenseless and helpless masculinity from the other side. One of my female Kuwaiti students has put the parallel, when responding to a survey, like this: "Men are like children and women have to control men's sexuality in the same way in which they put a pair of scissors out of reach for children because they don't want them to get hurt. If they hurt themselves, the adult is responsible." Faegheh Shirazi (quoted in Chapter 3) confirms this pattern by writing that "by focusing on the proper hijab for female protagonists, the government censors reveal their concern for the purity of the male spectator" (Shirazi 2001: 69). The same point is summarized by the veiled punk character Rabeya, in Michael Muhammad Knight's novel *The Taqwacores*, who explains: "The more you accept man's intrinsic weakness, the easier it is to hate girls. Suddenly all your bad thoughts are their fault since they should have known how weak you are" (Knight 2004: 55). There is a certain "paradox of protection" in Muslim culture suggesting that the protecting male subject needs to be protected from himself by the subject that he is supposed to protect.

In this book this became clear through the strong link between the protection and the nudity theme. The analysis of the concept of *awrah* that has been the subject of chapter 2 was supposed to highlight this. *Awrah* refers to the woman's body as a source of shame that must be covered. However, this is not the only meaning. Ziba Mir-Hosseini (2007) explains that *awrah* can also mean "defenseless house" and concludes that a woman without hijab must be seen as defenseless and unprotected. On the one hand, this confirms the claim that weak women need to be protected by strong men, which has been identified in chapter 2 as the PWM (Protect Women from Men) position. On the other hand, it can also be read in the sense that women *are supposed to be* innocent and defenseless because that's how men prefer them to be. Since man wants to be strong, woman has to be weak.

## Tattoos, Nudity, Veils, and Freedom

Is all this limited to Muslim culture? Certainly not. One is reminded of the contemporary infantilization of women in Japan (and other East Asian countries), which becomes most graphic through women's excessive and mannerist use of *kawaii* (cute) behavior, and which often leads to women's self-infantilization (see Botz-Bornstein 2011). In the present book, a similar phenomenon has been dealt with in Chapter 2 when "the cute but powerful girl-woman" was described as an emanation of Third Wave feminism. In Japan, by adopting the aesthetics of *kawaii*, women pose as weak: They are *kawaii* because they speak the language Japanese *men* want to hear. However, also with regard to this topic, it has been said that *kawaii* is not just mere submission, but that it can also lead to women's empowerment, which is the reason why it could be linked to Third Wave feminism. Just like the veil, *kawaii* is a double-edged sword: It can be understood as a form of female empowerment similar to that provided by fashion, nudity, eroticism, or tattoos; and it can be understood as a form of female dis-empowerment for precisely the same reasons. In a Japanese context this means, in the words of Rebecca Johnson (2007), that "cute meekness and empowered sexuality" complement each other. Sometimes, according to another specialist of Japan, it can even appear that "the cuter the girl, the more powerful and dangerous she is" (Lent 1999: 7). The reverse side of the coin is that very often the freedom that women obtain through *kawaii* is only the freedom of women who have decided not to grow up. The aesthetics of cool is not far removed from this pattern, as demonstrated in chapter 3 where Marlene Connor compared today's cool hip-hop artists with soul singers from the 1970s and found that the former are "sexually immature" (Connor 1994: 148). Also here it turned out that the cool black man "can continue to practice being cool and remaining a child, following the rules that have been set up by children" (172).

Is the freedom that can be obtained through veils, nudity, tattoos, and *kawaii* really the freedom worthy of autonomous ethical beings or is it not rather the freedom of children? Is it not rather an artificial freedom projecting us into the realm of the virtual where "real" power has been replaced with metaphorical, symbolical, hoped-for, and imagined power? In other words, are tattoos, nudity, veils, and *kawaii* not merely feminine versions of Viagra and aphrodisiacs that are not meant to *repair* the lack of political power but rather to dope her into power? Tattoos have indeed been called "politically empowering aphrodisiacs" (Lee 2012: 158). On the other hand, since we are talking about the "virtual," it needs to be said that the virtual is not just an illusion or a dream, but rather a Matrix-like reality supported by an almost absolute consensus (which is actually why it is called "reality").

# Conclusion

In this book, the veil has been compared with tattoos, high heels, makeup, nudity, Slut Walks, and male chastity belts—which is unusual even in post-modern settings. In addition, a whole series of paradoxes have been discovered: respect, modesty, sexuality, female power, female non-power. It has been found that what tattoos, veiling, and nudity have in common is that they are playing with fire by using and distorting heavily loaded signifiers; and they are successful only because their new engagement with those signifiers is to a large extent determined by mere play. This means that the signifiers are charged with a large amount of ambivalence. However, this ambivalence does not only depend on the amount of ambiguity that has been enclosed to them by the sender, but also on the environment within which this new aesthetic play of signifiers is enacted. And this environment is equally ambivalent, which is the reason why those movements hit the nerve of the time. For example, in our highly complex mediatized and virtualized environments, one and the same expression of nudity can appear as innocent and as lewd. The ambivalence is reinforced by the tension existing between personal moral values and the values of marketing—tensions that can blur such otherwise basic distinctions like that between nature and commodity. When the distinction between nature and civilization is deconstructed, nudity can very easily be commodified, as revealed by a caption from a cosmetic commercial cited by Ruth Barcan: "The less you wear the more you need new Palmer's Aloe Vera Formula." Barcan concludes that this signifies that "the more 'natural' your body, the more it needs a commodity" (Barcan 2004: 207). The use of tattoos and veils needs to be understood in the context of the same dynamics.

What tattoos, nudity, and veils have in common is that they can be used in order to contradict objectification, but can also become a subject of objectification; and even as symbols of liberation they remain entangled in conventional patterns of domination. Some might say that those patterns need to be changed. Yes, they should change, but it is certain that they cannot change if men do not do so first. No matter what women believe the veil signifies *for women*—what matters in the end is what the veil signifies *for men*. History has shown that both veiling and unveiling can be inscribed in patriarchal structures. In Reza Pahlavi's Iran, women were discouraged from publicly unveiling *themselves,* but always had to be unveiled *by men*: "Men became the moral subjects of this ritual while women were objectified through domestication and denial of their free will" (Moallem 2005: 70). Feminists can issue tons of treatises on female empowerment through the veil, nudity, tattoos, and *kawaii*: All this remains useless as long as men do not believe in the empowerment part and decide to hijack the feminine signifiers for their own purposes.

Any discrepancies between the three phenomena and the environment into which they are imbedded should thus not surprise us. The increasingly liberal use of nudity in advertising, for example, *could* be seen as symptomatic of nudity's increased acceptance. However, the contrary is the case. Rob Cover (as well as many others) reports of "the encroaching prohibition against nakedness in school showers, on film, in family photo albums" (Cover 2003: 66). This concerns certainly America more than other parts of the non-Muslim world. Among the reasons is also, as Barcan points out, "an increasing uneasiness about children's exposure to the nudity of adults. This concern is in part prompted by increasing knowledge of and publicity about the operations of pedophiles" (91) as well as the fact that "consumer culture has made young people increasingly aware of body image and increasingly unhappy with their bodies" (130). However, this behavior is not at all determined by the intention to contradict the classical nudist war cry that "nudity is *not* obscene" by saying that it *is* obscene per se. I concur with Cover who holds that this behavior is due to the increasing ambivalization of our environment in which not only the local and the global, but also the real and the virtual, or the pure and the impure, tend to get confused:

> The more productive understanding of this phenomenon is to consider the slippage across contexts as an element in a crisis of postmodern culture. The loss of "easy" definitions between contexts which allows a reading of nakedness as, ostensibly, sexuality, combined with the increased liberality of sexual depiction throughout late 20th-century culture, is a more predominant reason. (Cover 2003: 66)

The same is true for pro-nudity choices like female celebrity nudity, which has gone through a curious postfeminist twist as it "has come to be seen by some as a sign of liberation. What was once imagined as the exploitation of women can now be repackaged as a victory for feminism, with economic freedom seen to coincide with both sexual liberation and freedom of choice" (Barcan 2004: 242). We find here a clear parallel with the veil, whose signifier can relatively easily be shifted from oppression to liberation.

The result is that nudity (just like tattoos and veils) cannot be defined in terms of an ideology of, for example, the Puritan, the hedonist, the religious, or the rebellious. Even moral or aesthetic categories like identity and beauty escape all attempts of being forced into an ideology. Even protest nudity like El Mahdy's is affected by this. Otherwise, why does she wear stockings and ballet shoes colored in red? Does this accentuate or conceal/play down eroticism? If, as writes Anne Anlin Cheng, the critical approach towards nudity has deconstructed the concept of nakedness as animality and rawness in order to construe it as a socialized and juridicized concept of nudity,[1] we must conclude that nudity has once again been deconstructed.

We can make the same statements with regard to tattoos and veils. In an environment in which the local and the global, the real and the virtual, as well as the pure and the impure tend to get easily confused, tattoos and veils suffer just as much as nudity. What is it that tattoos, nudity, and veils want today? If it is neither a utopian modernity nor the critique of this modernity nor the nostalgic search for a past (or for authenticity or for a lost nature), is there anything that they positively stand for? The answer is difficult and easy at the same time. Barcan characterizes the postmodern situation with regard to nudity in such a way that it fits perfectly well into the schemes of contemporary veiling and tattooing: "a desire for the real, fetishization of the real, resignation to the fact that the real is always elusive, fun in fakery, and celebration of the delights of role-play and performance" (255). We are here a long way from classical nudism which abhorred theatralization and once even pondered to ban "nude gymnastics or athletics because dancing itself blurred the distinctions between 'natural' and 'theatricalized' ('unnatural') conditions" (Toepfer 1997: 69). Today the theatralization seems to be everything; and the theatre has become a reality. Barcan offers an answer with regard to nudism and I think that her answer is also fitting for the other two elements (tattoos and veils): The old concept of nudism that used to be ideologically loaded "has by and large mutated into a 'lifestyle' [and] this is certainly the discourse used by the vast majority of nudists to describe their practice" (84). The natural and innocent kind of nakedness propagated by classical nudists (which is often still called "naturism") has been transformed into *cultural* nudity. This is a general trend: Barcan finds that "contemporary depilation practices aim to transform 'nakedness' (nature) into 'nudity' (culture)" (143).

Nilüfer Göle comes to the very similar conclusions in her article on veiling in which she traces the phenomenon back to Pierre Bourdieu's notion of habitus: "Rather than employing the concept of social classes, which emphasizes economic exploitation for some, it is more useful to refer to this stratification through the concept of habitus that encompasses lifestyles" (Göle 2000: 480). In many (though not in all) cases,[2] the veil has been pushed through a movement leading from *religion* to culture and this movement can indeed be described as parallel with the shift of nudism from *nature* to culture. Just like nudity is no longer an expression only of nature, the veil is no longer *only* an expression of religious belief but appears as an ambiguous signifier engaging in *cultural* play instead of criticizing culture and attempting to replace it with religion. Or, to make the parallelism more distinct, nudism is no longer a matter of "nudist religion" with utopian exercises such as Kneipp water cures, gymnastics, and vows of purity, but has moved from a rather austere religion to "nude culture" in which even tattoos have begun to play an interesting role.

Nudism has become "nude culture" incorporating all mediatized and commercial aspects of nudity. Tattoos have lost their anti-civilizational agenda and have become "tattoo culture," which, in return, contributes to "nude culture" because the nude body is now more than ever covered with traces of culture and civilization. Chapter 7 has shown that while conventional (predominantly male) tattoos tended to create a social sect or a caste, female body graffiti creates an environment. Any ambiguity contained in this constellation is paralleled by the paradox of "veil-culture": Is it in favor or against liberation? Does it work against objectification or does it objectify? Does it eroticize or de-eroticize the body? Does it prevent fantasies or promote fantasies?

## BEING COOL

Both veiling and (naturist) nudism have once been invented in order to desexualize the body. The postmodern situation has definitely foiled this project by reducing them (at least generally) to a matter of lifestyle in which the only moral or aesthetic category able to hold the complex mixture of attitudes together is perhaps the category of coolness. When it comes to coolness, Aliaa El Mahdy with her red ballet shoes leads the way. Normally, innocent nudity strives to be total, while "partial and bizarre attire become invested with considerable erotic valence because they represent a compromise between control and freedom" (Blank 1973: 23). Partial nudity has been defined as a "transit," which is more erotic than both nudity and clothing. Jennifer Blessing "sees striptease as an institutionalization of the transitional state between the (supposed) artifice of clothing and the (supposed) purity of nudity" (quoted from Barcan 2004: 29). How does El Mahdy reconcile the claims of innocent nudity with eroticism? She refrains from the absolute, but does not exclude the component of the innocent. There are definitely sexual connotations in this picture because, finally, El Mahdy's project is one of sexual liberation, an agenda that nudists "from the nudist beach" shy away from today. However, at the same time, she refrains from the imagery of nudity in consumer culture which tends to equate nudity with sex. In the end, her attire comes along as a gesture distorting references to a nudist utopia while integrating at the same time moral conflicts and taboos. The overall impression is that of a tantalizing paradox. If this picture has any merits, they can be traced to the cool attitude with which El Mahdy manages to juxtapose incompatible options; and this might be an indication of what this "lifestyle" is striving for.

Aliaa El Mahdy perceives clothes (as well as veiling) as items that sexualize and objectify the normally not sexualized body. There she is indeed in company not necessarily with Third Wavers but rather with classical European nudists from the 1920s who insisted that "shamefaced petit bourgeois and religious attitudes toward the body had to be discarded" (J. Williams 2007: 25). In this sense, El Mahdy merely repeats European pre-war nudist experiments whose intention was to provoke a "Catholicism that considered nudism as yet another example of the same moral decadence perceived in cinema, nightlife, and the visual culture of the 'gay twenties'" (Peeters 2006: 459). Similar to what happened in Muslim Brotherhood Egypt in the twenty-first century, nudism represented "a moral threat that Catholics in the 1920s could also perceive in mainstream cinema, dance culture, café visiting, and even sunbathing at the seaside" (ibid.).[3]

Nudists believe that the body is no object of shame and that freedom from clothes is an act of liberation. Many have argued that shame is an artificial feeling of inferiority and that "no one shall be able to hide weaknesses behind clothes" (J. Williams 2007: 64). It is thus coherent that El Mahdy reverts to nudism which, in Western culture, is a classical way to help "people to rise above their primitive urges, liberate themselves from bourgeois morality" (64).

El Mahdy is in a rush—she attempts to push Egyptian society through a span of nude culture that reaches from interwar nudism to contemporary Slut Walks. However, the project does not seem impossible. What Third Wave feminists and classical nudists of the 1920s have in common is that they want to use the nude and non-objectified body to reform society. The difference between both is that Girl Power sexualizes society, even if the act of sexualization is meticulously controlled. Nudists strive to overcome sexuality and instate the equality of men and women because, without sexual connotations of the nude body, objectification will be impossible. This decontextualization of the body "implies that the more naked the body becomes . . . , the more the body assumes an abstract identity. Modernity signifies a tendency toward the abstractness of form" (Toepfer 1997: 1).

# NOTES

1. "For the racist, nakedness signals rawness, animality, dumb flesh and is repeatedly invoked, socially and legally, as the sign of the inhuman and the other. For the critical race theorist, nakedness is deconstructed as an entirely socialized and juridicized concept yet nonetheless reproduced as that which irreducibly indexes skin's visual legibility" (Cheng 2009: 102).

2. An exception are the Gulf States in which, according to an empirical study we conducted in 2013 in Kuwait, the insistence on religion (as opposed to culture) with regard to veiling remains very important (Botz-Bornstein and Abdullah-Kahn 2014). For the exceptional status of Kuwait see also the section The Veil in Kuwait in chapter 3.

3. Peeters speaks about Catholic Belgium.

# Bibliography

Abdrabboh, Bob. 1984. *Saudi Arabia: Forces of Modernization.* Brattleboro, VT: Amana Books.

Abu-Lughod, Lila. 1986. *Veiled Sentiments: Honour and Poetry Among the Bedouin.* Berkeley: University of California Press.

Abu-Lughod, Lila. 1990. "The Romance of Resistance: Tracing Transformations of Power through Bedouin Women" in *American Ethnologist* 17:1, 41–55.

Abu-Lughod, Lila. 2002. "Do Muslim Women Really Need Saving? Anthropological Reflections on Cultural Relativism and Its Others" in *American Anthropologist* 104:3, 783–790.

Abu-Zeid, A. 1965. Honor and shame among the Bedouin of Egypt" in Peristiany, J. (Ed.), *Honor and Shame.* London: Weidenfeld and Nicolson, 256–257.

Adorno, Theodor. 1973. *Negative Dialectics.* Trans. by E. B. Ashton. New York: Continuum Press.

Afshar, Haleh. 2008. "Can I See Your Hair? Choice, Agency and Attitudes: The Dilemma of Faith and Feminism for Muslim Women Who Cover" in *Ethnic and Racial Studies* 31:2, 411–427.

Agamben, Giorgio. 2011. *Nudities.* Trans. by D. Kishlik and S. Pedatella. Stanford: California University Press.

Ahmed, Leila. 1982. "Western Ethnocentrism and Perceptions of the Harem" in *Feminist Studies* 8:3, 521–534.

Ahmed, Leila. 1992. *Women and Gender in Islam: Historical Roots of a Modern Debate.* New Haven: Yale University Press.

Ahmed, Leila. 2011. *A Quiet Revolution: The Veil's Resurgence, from the Middle East to America.* New Haven, CT, and London: Yale University Press.

Ahmed, Sara and Jackie Stacey. 2001. *Thinking through the Skin.* London and New York: Routledge.

Al Mahadin, Saba, and Peter Burns. 2007. "Visitors, Visions, and Veils: The Portrayal of the Arab World in Tourism Advertising" in Rami Farouk Daher (ed.), *Tourism in the Middle East: Continuity, Change and Transformation.* Bristol, UK: Channel View.

Alsanea, Rajaa. 2007. *Girls of Riyadh.* New York: Penguin Press.

Alvi, Sajida S. 2003. "Muslim Women and Islamic Religious Tradition: A Historical Overview and Contemporary Issues" in Sajida Alvi, Homa Hoodfar, and Sheila McDonough (eds.), *The Muslim Veil in North America: Issues and Debates.* Toronto: Women's Press, 145–180.

Amara, Fadela. 2004. *Ni Putes ni soumises.* Paris: La Découverte.

Anderson, Benedict. 1983. *Imagined Communities.* London: Verso.

Anderson, Jon W. 2005. "Wiring Up: The Internet Difference for Muslim Networks" in Miriam Cooke and Bruce Lawrence (eds.), *Muslim Networks from Hajj to Hip Hop*. Chapel Hill and London: University of North Carolina Press, 252–263.
Anzieu, Didier. 1995. *Le Moi-peau*. Paris: Dunier.
Armstrong, Myrna L. 1991. "Career-Oriented Women with Tattoos" in *Image: Journal of Nursing Scholarship* 23, 215–220.
Atkinson, Michael and Kevin Young. 2001. "Flesh Journey: Neo Primitives and the Contemporary Rediscovery of Radical Body Modification" in *Deviant Behavior* 22, 117–146.
Badran, Margot. 2009. *Feminism in Islam: Secular and Religious Convergences*. Oxford: Oneworld.
Bailey, David A. and Giliane Tawadros (eds.). 2003. *Veil: Veiling, Representation and Contemporary Art*. London: Iniva.
Balasescu, Alexandru. 2007 *Paris Chic, Teheran Thrills*. Bucharest: Zeta Books.
Barcan, Ruth. 2004. *Nudity: A Cultural Anatomy*. Oxford: Berg.
Barkman, Adam. 2012. "Is a Tattoo a Sign of Impiety?" in R. Arp (ed.), *Tattoos and Philosophy*. Oxford: Wiley-Blackwell, 121–129.
Barry, Brian. 2006. "Democracy Needs Dialogue and Deliberation—Not Political Blocs" in H. Afshar (ed.), *Democracy and Islam, Hansard Society Democracy Series*, http://www.democracyseries.org.uk/sites/democracyseries.org.uk/files/HANSARDpercent20DEMpercent20ISLAMpercent20FINAL.pdf. Last accessed 2 August 2013.
Barthes, Roland. 1993. *L'Empire des signes*. Geneva: Skira.
Baudrillard, Jean. 1979. *De la séduction*. Paris: Galilée. Engl.: *Seduction*. Trans. by B. Singer. Montreal: New World Perspectives, 1990b.
Baudrillard, Jean. 1990. *Cool Memories (1980–1985)*. New York: Verso.
Baudrillard, Jean. 1993 [1976]. *Symbolic Exchange and Death*. London: Sage.
Baudrillard, Jean. 1994 [1981]. *Simulacra and Simulation*. Ann Arbor: University of Michigan Press.
Baumgardener, Jennifer and Amy Richards. 2000. *Manifesta: Young Women, Feminism and the Future*. New York: Farrar, Straus and Giroux.
Baumgardener, Jennifer and Amy Richards. 2004. "Feminism and Femininity: Or How We Learned to Stop Worrying about the Thong" in Anita Harris (ed.), *All about the Girl: Culture, Power, and Identity*. New York: Routledge, 59–67.
BBC News. 1997. "Men Cringe as Adverts Show 'Girl Power.'" November 13, http://news.bbc.co.uk/2/hi/business/30378.stm. Last accessed 2 August 2013.
Beeler, Karin. 2006. *Tattoos, Desire and Violence: Marks of Resistance in Literature, Film and Television*. Jefferson, SC: McFarland.
Berg, Charles. 1951. *The Unconscious Significance of Hair*. London: George Allen and Unwin.
Bergson, Henri. 1938. *La Penseé et le mouvant*. Paris: Quadrige.
Bergson, Henri. 1988. *Matter and Memory*. Trans. by N. M. Paul and W. S. Palmer. New York: Zone Books.
Blank, Leonard. 1973. "Nakedness and Nudity: A Darwinian Explanation for Looking and Showing" in *Leonardo* 6:1, 23–27.
Bodnar, Judit. 2007. "Becoming Bourgeois" in Mike Davis and D. Bertrand Monk (eds.), *Dreamworlds of Neoliberalism: Evil Paradises*. New York: New Press, 140–151.
Boehn, Max von. 1937. *Dolls and Puppets*. Edinburgh: Harrap.
Boodakian, Florence Dee. 2008. *Resisting Nudities: Study in the Aesthetics of Eroticism*. New York: Peter Lang.
Booth, Marilyn. 2010. "The Muslim Woman as Celebrity Author and the Politics of Translating Arabic: Girls of Riyadh Go on the Road" in *Journal of Middle East Women's Studies* 6:3, 149–182.
Botz-Bornstein, Thorsten. 1997. "Iki, Style, Trace: Shuzo Kuki and the Spirit of Hermeneutics" in *Philosophy East and West* 47:4, 554–580.
Botz-Bornstein, Thorsten. 2011. *The Cool-Kawaii: Afro-Japanese Aesthetics and New World Modernity*. Lanham, MD: Lexington Books.

Botz-Bornstein, Thorsten. 2012. "Barbie and the Power of Negative Thinking: Of Barbies, Eve-Barbies, and I-Barbies" in *Kritikos: Journal of Postmodern Cultural Sound, Text and Image* 9 (online).

Botz-Bornstein, Thorsten. 2014. "Revelation and Seduction: Baudrillard, Tillich, and Muslim Punk" in the *International Journal of Baudrillard Studies* 11:1.

Botz-Bornstein, Thorsten and Noreen Abdullah-Khan. 2014. *The Veil in Kuwait: Gender, Fashion, Identity.* New York: Palgrave.

Bouhdiba, Abdelwahab. 1974. *Sexuality in Islam.* London: Routledge.

Bradley, John R. 2005. *Saudi Arabia Exposed: Inside a Kingdom in Crisis.* New York: Palgrave Macmillan.

Braunberger, Christine. 2000. "Revolting Bodies: The Monster Beauty of Tattooed Women" in *NWSA Journal* 12:2, 1–23.

Brooks, Geraldine. 1996. *Nine Parts of Desire, the Hidden World of Islamic Women.* London: Penguin.

Brown, Brené. 2006. "Shame Resilience Theory: A Grounded Theory Study on Women and Shame" in *Families in Society* 87:1, 43–52.

Cabreros-Sud, Veena. 1995. "Kicking Ass" in Rebecca Walker (ed.), *To Be Real: Telling the Truth and Changing the Face of Feminism.* New York: Anchor Books, 41–48.

Canales, Jimena and Andrew Herscher. 2005. "Criminal Skins: Tattoos and Modern Architecture in the Work of Adolf Loos" in *Architectural History* 48, 235–256.

Caplan, Jane. 2000. *Written on the Body: The Tattoo in European and American History.* London: Reaktion Books.

Carrington, Victoria. 2009. "I Write, Therefore I Am: Texts in the City" in *Visual Communication* 8:4, 409–425.

Carroll, Lynn and Roxanne Anderson. 2002. "Body Piercing, Tattooing, Self-Esteem, and Body Investment in Adolescent Girls" in *Adolescence* 37, 627–637.

Cheng, Anne Anlin. 2009. "Skins, Tattoos, and Susceptibility" in *Representations* 108:1, 98–119.

Clark, Kenneth. 1956. *The Nude: A Study in Ideal Form.* New York: Pantheon.

Clarke, Lynda. 2003. "Hijab According to the Hadith: Text and Interpretation" in Stacy Alvi, Homa Hoodfar, and Sheila McDonough (eds.), *The Muslim Veil in North America: Issues and Debates.* Toronto: Women's Press, 214–286.

Connor, Marlene Kim. 1994. *What Is Cool? Understanding Black Manhood in America.* New York: Crown.

Cooke, Miriam. 2000. *Women Claim Islam: Creating Islamic Feminism through Literature.* New York: Routledge.

Cover, Rob. 2003. "The Naked Subject: Nudity, Context and Sexualization in Contemporary Culture" in *Body and Society* 9:3, 53–72.

de Bary, William Theodore, Wing-tsit Chan, and Burton Watson (eds). 1960. *Sources of Chinese Tradition* vol. I. New York: Columbia University Press.

de Cenival, Marie. 2013. "Vive les féministes à poil!" in *Le Monde*, 26 July.

DeCaires Narain, Denise. 2004. "What Happened to Global Sisterhood? Writing and Reading 'the' Postcolonial Woman" in Stacy Gillis, Gillian Howie, and Rebecca Munford (eds.), *Third Wave Feminism: A Critical Exploration.* New York: Palgrave Macmillan, 240–251.

Delaney, Carol. 1994. "Untangling the Meanings of Hair in Turkish Society" in *Anthropological Quarterly* 67:4, 159–172.

DeMello, Margo. 2000. *Bodies of Inscription: A Cultural History of the Modern Tattoo Community.* Durham, NC, and London: Duke University Press.

Derrida, Jacques. 1979. *Spurs: Nietzsche's Styles.* Trans. by Barbara Harlow. Chicago: University of Chicago Press.

Derrida, Jacques. 1981. *Dissemination.* Trans. by B. Johnson. London: Althone.

Derrida, Jacques. 1987. *The Truth in Painting.* Trans. by G. Bennington. Chicago: University of Chicago Press.

Derrida, Jacques. 1993. *Khôra.* Paris: Galilée.

Derrida, Jacques and Helene Cixous. 2001. *Veils.* Trans. by G. Bennington. Stanford, CA: Stanford University Press.

Dinerstein, Joel. 1999. "Lester Young and the Birth of Cool" in Gena Dagel Caponi (ed.), *Signifyin(g), Sanctifyin(g), and Slam Dunking: A Reader in African American Expressive Culture*. Cambridge, MA: University of Massachusetts Press, 239–278.

Dobie, Madeleine. 2001. *Foreign Bodies: Gender, Language, and Culture in French Orientalism*. Stanford, CA: Stanford University Press.

Dodd, Peter C. 1973. "Honor and the Forces of Change in Arab Society" in *International Journal of Middle East Studies* 4:1, 40–54.

Du Bois, W. E. B. 1997. *The Souls of Black Folk*. Boston, New York: Bedford.

Earle, Sarah and Keith Sharp. 2007. *Sex in Cyberspace: Men Who Pay for Sex*. Aldershot, UK: Ashgate.

El Fani, Nadia and Caroline Fourest. 2013. *Nos seins, nos armes! [Our Breasts, Our Weapons!]* (documentary film).

El Guindi, Fadwa. 1981. "Veiling Infitah with Muslim Ethic: Egypt's Contemporary Islamic Movement" in *Social Problems* 28: 465–485.

El Guindi, Fadwa. 1999. *Veil: Modesty, Privacy and Resistance*. Oxford: Berg.

El Mahdy, Aliaa. Personal blog: http://arebelsdiary.blogspot.de. Last accessed 3 February 2012.

El Saadawi, Nawal. 1997. *The Nawal El-Saadawi Reader*. London: Zed.

Elmusa, Sharif S. 1997. "Faust without the Devil? The Interplay of Technology and Culture in Saudi Arabia" in *The Middle East Journal* 51:3, 345–357.

Enloe, Cynthia. 1990. *Bananas, Beaches and Bases: Making Feminist Sense of International Politics*. Berkeley: University of California Press.

Esposito, John L. and Dalia Mogahed. 2007. *Who Speaks for Islam? What a Billion Muslims Really Think*. New York: Gallup Press.

Fanon, Frantz. 1967. *A Dying Colonialism*. Trans. by H. Chevalier. New York: Grove Press.

Fares, B. 1938. "Ird" in *Supplement to the Encyclopaedia of Islam*. Leiden: E. J. Brill, 96–97.

Fisher, Jill A. 2002. "Tattooing the Body, Marking Culture" in *Body and Society* 8:4, 91–107.

Fleming, Juliet. 1997. "The Renaissance Tattoo" in *RES: Anthropology and Aesthetics* 31, 34–52.

Fraiman, Susan. 2003. *Cool Men and the Second Sex*. New York: Columbia University Press.

Frampton, Kenneth. 1983. "Towards a Critical Regionalism: Six Points for an Architecture of Resistance" in Hal Foster (ed.), *The Anti-Aesthetic: Essays on Postmodern Culture*. Port Townsend, WA: Bay Press, 16–30.

Franks, Myfanwy. 2000. "Crossing the Borders of Whiteness? White Muslim Women Who Wear the Hijab in Britain Today" in *Ethnic and Racial Studies* 23:5, 917–929.

Frenske, Mindy. 2007. *Tattoos in American Visual Culture*. New York: Palgrave Macmillan.

Gadamer, Hans-Georg. 1989 [1975]. *Truth and Method*. London: Sheed and Ward.

Gatens, Moira. 1996. *Imaginary Bodies: Ethics, Power and Corporeality*. New York: Routledge.

Gladwell, Malcolm. 1997. "The Coolhunt" in *The New Yorker* March 17. http://www.gladwell.com/1997/1997_03_17_a_cool.htm. Last accessed 2 August 2013.

Goffman, Erving. 1963. *Stigma: Notes on the Management of Spoiled Identity*. Englewood Cliffs, NJ: Prentice Hall.

Gökariksel, Banu and Ellen McLarney. 2010. "Muslim Women, Consumer Capitalism, and the Islamic Culture Industry" in *Journal of Middle East Women's Studies* 6:3, 1–18.

Gökariksel, Banu and Anna Secor. 2012. "'Even I Was Tempted': The Moral Ambivalence and Ethical Practice of Veiling-Fashion in Turkey" in *Annals of the Association of American Geographers* 102:4, 847–862.

Göle, Nilüfer. 2000. "The Forbidden Modern: Civilization and Veiling" in L. Schiebinger (ed.), *Feminism and the Body*. Oxford: Oxford University Press, 465–489.

Gori, Roland. 2013. *La Fabrique des imposteurs*. Paris: LLL les liens qui libèrent.

Grace, Daphne. 2004. *The Woman in the Muslin Mask: Veiling and Identity in Postcolonial Literature*. London: Pluto Press.

Griffin, Christine. 2004. "Good Girls, Bad Girls" in Anita Harris (ed.), *All about the Girl: Culture, Power, and Identity*. New York: Routledge, 29–43.

Grosz, Elizabeth. 1994. *Volatile Bodies: Towards a Corporeal Feminism*. Bloomington: Indiana University Press.

Grumet, Gerald. 1983. "Psychodynamic Implications of Tattoos" in *Journal of Orthopsychiatry* 53, 482–492.

Gupta, Roxanne Kamayani. 2008. "Going the Whole Nine Yards: Vignettes of the Veil in India" in Jennifer Heath (ed.), *The Veil: Women Writers on Its History, Lore, and Politics*. Berkeley: University of California Press, 60–74.

Haddad, Yazbeck Yvonne. 2007. "The Post-9/11 Hijab as Icon" in *Sociology of Religion* 68:3, 253–267.

Hamburger, Ernest. 1966. "Tattooing as a Psychic Defense Mechanism" in *International Journal of Social Psychiatry* 12, 60–62.

Hammadou, Ghania. 1999. "Veils of My Youth" in *Transition* 80, 60–71.

Hammond, Andrew. 2005. *Pop Culture Arab World: Media, Arts, and Lifestyle*. Santa Barbara: ABC-Clio.

Harlow, Megan Jean. 2009. "Suicide Girls: Tattooing as Radical Feminist Agency" in *Communication and Critical/Cultural Studies* 5: 245–267. Also available at http://www.k-state.edu/actr/wp-content/uploads/2009/12/3harlowsuicidegirlcedaword.pdf.

Hassan, Riffat. 1999. "Feminism in Islam" in A. Sharma and K. Young (eds.), *Feminism and World Religions*. New York: State University of New York Press, 248–278.

Hatem, Mervat. 1988. "Egypt's Middle Class in Crisis: The Sexual Division of Labor" in *Middle East Journal* 42, 407–422.

Heath, Jennifer (ed.). 2008. *The Veil: Women Writers on Its History, Lore, and Politics*. Berkeley: University of California Press.

Heidegger, Martin. 1959. "Aus einem Gepräch über die Sprache: Zwischen einem Japaner und einem Fragenden" in *Unterwegs zur Sprache*. Tübingen: Neske.

Heidegger, Martin. 1976. *Einführung in die Metaphysik*. Frankfurt: Klostermann.

Henry, Astrid. 2004. *Not My Mother's Sister: Generational Conflict and Third-Wave Feminism*. Bloomington: Indiana University Press.

Herskovits, Melville J. 1941. *The Myth of the Negro Past*. New York: Harper.

Heywood, Leslie and Jennifer Drake. 2004. "'It's All about the Benjamins': Economic Determinants of Third Wave Feminism in the United States" in S. Gillis, G. Howie, and R. Munford (eds.), *Third Wave Feminism: A Critical Exploration*. New York: Palgrave Macmillan, 13–23.

Hijabtrendz. http://www.hijabtrendz.com/2008/04/29/hijab-fashion-trend-alert. Last accessed 27 July 2012.

Hirschmann, Nancy J. 1997. "Eastern Veiling, Western Freedom?" in *The Review of Politics* 59:3, 461–488.

Hirsi, Ayaan A. 2007. *Infidel*. New York: Free Press.

Hobsbawm, Eric J. 1990. *Nations and Nationalism since 1780: Programme, Myth, Reality*. Cambridge: Cambridge University Press.

Holland, Samantha. 2004. *Alternate Femininities: Body, Age and Identity*. Oxford: Berg.

Holt, Grace Sims. 1972. "'Inversion' in Black Communication" in T. Kochman (ed.), *Rappin' and Stylin' Out: Communication in Urban Black America*. Urbana and Chicago: University of Illinois Press, 152–159.

Homsi, Eymen. 2011. "Genuflection and Empire" in Kari Jormakka (ed.), Architecture in the Age of Empire: 11th International Bauhaus-Colloquium. Weimar: Verlag der Bauhaus-Universität, 300–315. Available on http://www.eymenhomsi.com/wp-content/uploads/2012/01/genuflection.pdf. Last accessed 2 August 2013.

Hoodfar, Homa. 2001. "The Veil in Their Minds and on Our Heads: Veiling Practices and Muslim Women" in E. A. Castelli (ed.), *Woman, Gender, Religion: A Reader*. Basingstoke, UK: Palgrave, 420–440.

Hoodfar, Homa. 2003. "More Than Clothing: Veiling as an Adaptive Strategy," in Stacey Alvi, Homa Hoodfar, and Sheila McDonough (eds.), *The Muslim Veil in North America: Issues and Debates*. Toronto: Women's Press, 3–39.

Hopkins, Susan. 2002. *Girl Heroes: The New Force in Popular Culture*. Annandale, Australia: Pluto Press.

Huizinga, Johan. 1970. *Homo Ludens*. London: Temple Smith.

Huxley, Aldous. 1974. *The Art of Seeing*. London: Chatto & Windus.

Ink-ography. http://ink-ography.blogspot.com. Last accessed 30 September 2011.

Ivekovic, Rada. 2004. "The Veil in France: Secularism, Nation, Women" in *Economic and Political Weekly*, 39:11, 1117–1119.

James, Paul and Freya Carkeek. 1997. "This Abstract Body: From Embodied Symbolism to Techno-Disembodiment" in David Holmes (ed.), *Virtual Politics: Identity and Community in Cyberspace*. London and Thousand Oaks, CA: Sage, 107–124.

Johnson, Rebecca. 2007. "*Kawaii* and *Kirei*: Navigating the Identities of Women in *Laputa: Castle in the Sky* by Hayao Miyazaki and *Ghost in the Shell* by Mamoru Oshii" in *Rhizomes: Cultural Studies in Emerging Knowledge* 14 (online).

Jolly, Margaret. 1996. "*Woman Ikat Raet Long Human Raet O No?* Women's Rights, Human Rights and Domestic Violence in Vanuatu" in *Feminist Review* 52, 169–190.

Jullien, François. 2007. *The Impossible Nude: Chinese Art and Western Aesthetics*. Chicago: University of Chicago Press.

Kang, Nancy. 2012. "Painted Fetters: Tattooing as Feminist Liberation" in R. Arp (ed.), *Tattoos and Philosophy*. Oxford: Wiley-Blackwell, 65–80.

Kant, Immanuel. 1965. *Critique of Pure Reason*. Trans. by N. Kemp Smith. New York: St. Martin's Press.

Kant, Immanuel. 1976. *Critique of Practical Reason, and Other Writings in Moral Philosophy*. Trans. by L. White Beck. New York: Garland.

Kant, Immanuel. 1991. *Metaphysics of Morals* [*Metaphysik der Sitten*, 1796]. Cambridge: Cambridge University Press.

Kaplan, E. Ann. 1983. *Women and Film: Both Sides of the Camera*. New York: Methuen.

Kar, Mehrangiz. 2006. "Death of a Mannequin" in L. A. Zanganeh (ed.), *My Sister, Guard Your Veil; My Brother, Guard Your Eyes: Uncensored Iranian Voices*. Boston: Beacon Press, 29–37.

Karim, Jamillah. 2005. "Voices of Faith, Faces of Beauty: Connecting American Muslim Women through *Azizah*" in Miriam Cooke and Bruce Lawrence (eds.), *Muslim Networks from Hajj to Hip Hop*. Chapel Hill and London: University of North Carolina Press, 169–188.

Karim, Jamillah. 2006. "Through Sunni Women's Eyes: Black Feminism and the Nation of Islam" in *Souls: A Critical Journal of Black Politics, Culture and Society* 8:4, 19–30.

Kearney, Mary Celeste. 1998. "'Don't Need You!' Rethinking Identity Politics and Separation for a Grrrl Perspective" in J. S. Epstein (ed.), *Youth Culture: Identity in a Postmodern World*. Molder, MA: Beachwell, 148–188.

Keyes, David. 2011. "Saudi Arabia's Religious Police Outlaw 'Tempting Eyes'" in The Daily Beast, November 19. http://www.thedailybeast.com/articles/2011/11/19/saudi-arabia-s-religious-police-outlaw-tempting-eyes.html. Last accessed 3 March 2013.

Khaleel, Mohammed. 2005. "Assessing English Translations of the Qur'an" in *Middle East Quarterly*, Spring, 58–71. http://www.meforum.org/717/assessing-english-translations-of-the-quran/#_ftnref58. Last accessed 2 August 2013.

Killian, Caitlin. 2003. "The Other Side of the Veil: North African Women in France Respond to the Headscarf Affair" in *Gender and Society* 17: 4, 567–590.

Kissack, Terence. 2000. "Alfred Kinsey and Homosexuality in the '50s" in *Journal of the History of Sexuality* 9:4, 474–491.

Knight, Michael Muhammad. 2004. *The Taqwacores*. New York: Soft Skull Press.

Kofman, Sarah. 1980. *L'Énigme de la femme: La femme dans les textes de Freud*. Paris, Galilée. Engl.: *The Enigma of Woman*. Trans. by Catherine Porter Ithaca, NY: Cornell University Press, 1985.

Kofman, Sarah. 1982. *Le Respect des femmes*. Paris: Galilée. Parts of the book are contained in English translation as "The Economy of Respect: Kant and Respect for Women" in R. M. Schott (ed.), *Feminist Interpretations of Immanuel Kant* (University Park, PA: Pennsylvania State University Press, 1997), 355–372; "The Economy of Respect: Kant and Respect for Women" in *Social Research* 49, 1982, 383–404; "Rousseau's Phallocratic Ends" in *Hypatia* 3:3, 1989, 123–136 .

Kotani, Mari. 2006. "Metamorphosis of the Japanese Girl: The Girl, the Hyper Girl, and the Battling Beauty" in F. Lunning (ed.), *Mechademia 1: Emerging Worlds of Anime and Manga*. Minneapolis: University of Minnesota Press, 162–169.

Krakow, Amy. 1994. *Total Tattoo Book*. New York: Warner Books.

Kressel, Gideon M. 1992. "Shame and Gender" in *Anthropological Quarterly* 65:1, 34–46.

Laborde, Cecile. 2006. "Female Autonomy, Education and the Hijab" in *Critical Review of International Social and Political Philosophy* 9:3, 351–377.

Lacan, Jacques. 1982. "The Meaning of the Phallus" in J. Mitchell and J. Rose (eds.), *Feminine Sexuality: Jacques Lacan and the École Freudienne*. London: Macmillan, 74–85.

Lafontaine, Laurene M. 2008. "Out of the Cloister: Unveiling to Better Serve the Gospel" in Jennifer Heath (ed.), *The Veil: Women Writers on Its History, Lore, and Politics*. Berkeley: University of California Press, 74–89.

Lautman, Victoria. 1994. *The New Tattoo*. New York: Abbeville Press.

Lazreg, Marnia. 2009. *Questioning the Veil: Open Letters to Muslim Women*. Princeton, NJ: Princeton University Press.

Leach, Edmund. 1958. "Magical Hair" in *Journal of the Royal Anthropological Society* 88, 147–164. Reprinted in *The Essential Edmund Leach*, vol. 2. New Haven, CT: Yale University Press, 2001, 177–201.

Lee, Wendy Lynne. 2012. "Never Merely There: Tattoos as a Practice of Writing and Telling Stories" in R. Arp (ed.), *Tattoos and Philosophy*. Oxford: Wiley-Blackwell, 151–164.

Lent, John A. 1999. *Themes and Issues in Asian Cartooning: Cute, Cheap, Mad, and Sexy*. Bowling Green, OH: Bowling Green State University Popular Press.

Lewis, Reina. 2010. "Marketing Muslim Lifestyle: A New Media Genre" in *Journal of Middle East Women's Studies* 6:3, 58–90.

Lingis, Alphonso. 1984. *Excesses: Eros and Culture*. Albany: State Universiy of New York Press.

Linke, Uli. 1999. *German Bodies: Race and Representation after Hitler*. London: Routledge.

Lokke, Maria. 2013. "A Secret History of Women and Tattoo" in *The New Yorker*, 16 January (online).

Loos, Adolf. 1962. "Ornament und Verbrechen" in *Sämtliche Schriften*. Vienna: Herold, 276–288.

Lorber, Judith. 2002. "Heroes, Warriors, and 'Burqas': A Feminist Sociologist's Reflections on September 11" in *Sociological Forum* 17:3, 377–396.

Lyotard, Jean-François. 1994. *Lessons on the Analytic of the Sublime*. Trans. by Elizabeth Rottenberg. Stanford, CA: Stanford University Press.

MacCormack, Patricia. 2006. "The Great Ephemeral Tattooed Skin" in *Body and Society* 12:2, 57–82.

MacLeod, Arlene Elowe. 1993. *Accommodating Protest: Working Women, the New Veiling, and Change in Cairo*. New York: Columbia University Press.

Magnet, Shoshana. 2007. "Feminist Sexualities, Race and the Internet: An Investigation of Suicidegirls.com" in *New Media Society* 9, 577–601.

Mahmood, Saba. 2005. *Politics of Piety: The Islamic Revival and the Feminist Subject*. Princeton, NJ: Princeton University Press.

Majid, Anouar. 1998. "The Politics of Feminism in Islam" in *Signs: Journal of Women in Culture and Society* 23:2, 321–361.

Majors, Richard and Janet Mancini Billson. 1992. *Cool Pose: The Dilemmas of Black Manhood in America*. New York: Lexington Books.

Masood, Maliha. 2008. "On the Road: Travels with My *Hijab*" in Jennifer Heath (ed.), *The Veil: Women Writers on Its History, Lore, and Politics*. Berkeley: University of California Press, 213–229.

Massad, Joseph A. 2007. *Desiring Arabs*. Chicago: University of Chicago Press.

Mazrui, Ali A. 1997. "Islamic and Western Values" in *Foreign Affairs* 76:5, 118–132.

McCaughey, Martha. 1997. *Real Knockouts: The Physical Feminism of Women's Self-defense*. New York: New York University Press.

McLuhan, Marshall. 1964. *Understanding Media: The Extensions of Man*. New York and Scarborough, Ontario: Prentice Hall.

Mernissi, Fatima. 1991a. *The Veil and the Male Elite: A Feminist Interpretation of Women's Rights in Islam*. New York: Basic Books.

Mernissi, Fatima. 1991b. *Women and Islam: A Historical and Theological Enquiry*. Oxford: Blackwell.

Mifflin, Margot. 1997. *Bodies of Subversion: A Secret History of Women and Tattoo*. New York: Juno Books.

Mill, John Stuart. 1985. *The Subjection of Women*. London: Dent/Everyman.

Miller, Jean-Chris. 1996. "But What Does It Mean? Symbolism in Tattoo" in *Tattoo Review* 8:50, 44–49.

Minces, Juliette. 1982. *The House of Obedience: Women in Arab Society*. London: Zed Press.

Miori, Daniel. 2012. "To Ink or Not to Ink: Tattoos and Bioethics" in R. Arp (ed.), *Tattoos and Philosophy*. Oxford: Wiley-Blackwell, 193–205.

Mir-Hosseini, Ziba. 2007. "The Politics and Hermeneutics of Hijab in Iran: From Confinement to Choice" in *Muslim World Journal of Human Rights* 4:1, np.

Moallem, Minoo. 1999. "Transnationalism, Feminism, and Fundamentalism" in C. Kaplan, N. Alarcon, and M. Moallem (eds.), *Transnationalism and Fundamentalism*. Durham, NC: Duke University Press, 320–348.

Moallem, Minoo. 2005. *Between Warrior Brother and Veiled Sister: Islamic Fundamentalism and the Politics of Patriarchy in Iran*. Berkeley and Los Angeles: University of California Press.

Mohanty, Chandra Talpade. 1988. "Under Western Eyes: Feminist Scholarship and Colonial Discourses" in *Feminist Review* 30, 65–88.

Mohanty, Chandra Talpade. 2003. *Feminism without Borders: Decolonizing Theory, Practicing Solidarity*. Durham, NC: Duke University Press.

Moore, Molly. 2006. "Dutch Convert to Islam: Veiled and Viewed as a 'Traitor' a Woman's Experience Illustrates Europe's Struggle with Its Identity" in *Washington Post Foreign Service*, 19 March, A21.

Moors, Annelies. 2009. "'Islamic Fashion' in Europe: Religious Conviction, Aesthetic Style, and Creative Consumption" in *Encounters* 1, 175–201.

Moors, Annelies and Emma Tarlo (eds.). 2007. *Fashion Theory* 11:2/3 (special double issue "Muslim Fashions").

Moreira, Paul. 2012. "Interview" in *Ragemag*. Ragemag.fr/sexe-islam-revolutions-paul-moreira. Last accessed 1 March 2013.

Muchembled, Robert. 1983. "Le corps, la culture populaire et la culture des élites en France" in A. E. Imhoff (ed.), *Leib und Leben in der Geschichte der Neuzeit*. Berliner historische Studien, vol. 9. Berlin: Dunker and Humblot.

Mule, Pat and Diane Barthel. 1992. "The Return to the Veil: Individual Autonomy vs. Social Esteem" in *Sociological Forum* 7:2, 323–332.

Murphy, Robert F. 1964. "Social Distance and the Veil" in *American Anthropologist* 66:6-1, 1257–1274.

Mutahhari, Murtaza. *On the Islamic Hijab*. Extracts retrieved from http://www.rafed.net/en/index.php/women-world-magazine/woman-and-society/hijab?start=100. Last accessed 8 August 2013.

Naficy, Hamid. 2003. "Poetics and Politics of Veil, Voice and Vision in Iranian Post-Revolutionary Cinema" in David A. Bailey and Gilane Tawadros (eds.), *Veil: Veiling, Representation and Contemporary Art*. London: Iniva, 136–156.

Nietzsche, Friedrich. 1974. *The Gay Science*. London: Vintage Books.

Nussbaum, Martha. 2010. "Veiled Threats" in the *New York Times*, 11 July. http://opinionator.blogs.nytimes.com/2010/07/11/veiled-threats/. Last accessed 13 March 2013.

O'Brian, Wendy. 2004. Qu(e)erying Pornography: Contesting Identity Politics in Feminism" in Stacy Gillis, Gillian Howie, and Rebecca Munford (eds.), *Third Wave Feminism: A Critical Exploration*. New York: Palgrave Macmillan, 97–109. 122–135.

Ochsenwald, William. 2007. "Islam and Loyalty in the Saudi Hijaz, 1926–1939" in *Die Welt des Islams, New Series* 47:1, 7–32.

Ogi, Fusami. 2001. "Gender Insubordination in Japanese Comics (Manga) for Girls" in John A. Lent (ed.), *Illustrating Asia: Comics, Humor Magazines, and Picture Books*. Honolulu: University of Hawai'i Press, 171–186.

Ohashi, Ryosuke. 1992. "'Iki' und 'kire' als Frage der Kunst im Zeitalter der Moderne" in *Aesthetics* 3:5, March, 105–116.

Olgun, Ayse. 2005. "Kadin Modacilar Erkek Patronlara Kazan Kaldirdi" in *Yeni Safak* 20. http://yenisafak.com.tr/arsiv/2005/eylul/20/g07.html. Last accessed 2 August 2013.

Owen, A. Susan, Sara R. Stein, and Leah R. Vande Berg. 2007. *Bad Girls: Cultural Politics and Media Representations of Transgressive Women*. New York: Peter Lang.

Patai, Raphael. 1976. *The Arab Mind*. New York: Scribner.

Peeters, Evert. 2006. "Authenticity and Asceticism: Discourse and Performance in Nude Culture and Health Reform in Belgium, 1920–1940" in *Journal of the History of Sexuality* 15:3, 432–461.

Perry, Albert. 1933. *Tattoos: Secrets of a Strange Art Practiced by the Natives of the United States*. Fort Worth, TX: Lucky Horseshoe Stock Tattoo.

Pitts, Victoria. 2003. *In the Flesh: The Cultural Politics of Body Modification*. Gordonsville, VA: Palgrave Macmillan.

Pountain, Dick and David Robins. 2000. *Cool Rules: Anatomy of an Attitude*. London: Reaktion.

Prosser, Jay. 2001. "Skin Memories" in Sara Ahmed and Jackie Stacey (eds.), *Thinking through the Skin*. London and New York: Routledge, 52–68..

*The Qur'an*. Yusuf Ali's, Saheeh's and Pickthall's translations can be found on http://quran.com.

Rahnavard, Zahra. *Beauty of Concealment and the Concealment of Beauty*. Extracts retrieved from http://www.rafed.net/en/index.php/women-world-magazine/woman-and-society/hijab?start=100. Last accessed 8 August 2013.

Rahnavard, Zahra. *Message of the Hijab*. Extracts retrieved from http://www.rafed.net/en/index.php/women-world-magazine/woman-and-society/hijab?start=100. Last accessed 8 August 2013.

Rank My Tattoos. http://www.rankmytattoos.com. Last accessed 30 September, 2011.

Read, Jen'Nan Ghazal and John P. Bartkowski. 2000. "To Veil or Not to Veil? A Case Study of Identity Negotiation among Muslim Women in Austin, Texas" in *Gender and Society* 14:3, 395–417.

Redeker, Robert. 2011. "Viagra and the Utopia of Immortality" in T. Botz-Bornstein (ed.), *The Philosophy of Viagra: Bioethical Responses to the Viagrification of the Modern World*. Amsterdam, New York: Rodopi, 71–76.

Redfern, Catherine and Kristin Aune. 2010. *Reclaiming the F Word: The New Feminist Movement*. London: Zed Books.

Rhouni, Raja. 2010. *Secular and Islamic Feminist Critiques in the Work of Fatima Mernissi*. Leiden: E. J. Brill.

Ricœur, Paul. 1969. *Le Conflit des interprétations: Essais d'herméneutique*, vol. 1. Paris: Seuil.

Richie, Donald. 1980. *The Japanese Tattoo*. New York and Tokyo: Weatherhill.

Rose, Gillian. 1993. *Feminism and Geography: The Limits of Geographical Knowledge*. Minneapolis: University of Minnesota Press.

Rosenberg, Jessica and Gitana Garofalo. 1998. "Riot Grrrl: Revolutions from Within" in *Signs: Journal of Women in Culture and Society* 23:3 (Special Issue on Feminisms and Youth Cultures), 809–841.

Ross, Chad. 2004. *Naked Germany: Health, Race and the Nation*. Oxford: Berg.

Rousseau, Jean-Jacques. 1835. *Œuvres complètes de J. J. Rousseau: Lettres écrites de la montagne*. Paris: Furne.

Rousseau, Jean-Jacques. 1979 [1762]. *Emile: or, On Education*. Introduction, translation, and notes by Allan Bloom. New York: Basic Books.

Rowe-Finkbeiner, Kristin. 2004. *The F-Word: Feminism in Jeopardy—Women, Politics, and the Future*. Seattle: Seal Press.

Rubin, Arnold. 1988. *Marks of Civilization*. Berkeley: University of California Press.

Saadallah. Sherin. 2004. "Muslim Feminism in the Third Wave: A Reflective Inquiry" in
Stacey Gillis, Gillian Howie, and Rebecca Munford (eds.), *Third Wave Feminism: A Criti-
cal Exploration.* New York: Palgrave Macmillan, 216–226.
Sakaranaho, Tuula. 2008. "'Equal but Different': Women in Turkey from the Islamic Point of
View" in Anitta Kynsilehto (ed.), *Islamic Feminism: Current Perspectives.* Tampere Peace
Research Institute Occasional Paper No. 96. Tampere, Finland: University of Tampere
Press, 47–56.
Sallon, Hélène. 2013. "Grimé en femme, un Egyptien 'teste' le harcèlement sexuel" in *Le
Monde*, 11 May.
Sandikci, Özlem and Güliz Ger. 2007. "Constructing and Representing the Islamic Consumer
in Turkey" in *Fashion Theory* 11:2/3, 189–210.
Sandikci, Özlem and Güliz Ger. 2010. "Veiling in Style: How Does a Stigmatized Practice
Become Fashionable?" http://ssrn.com/abstract=1507461. Last accessed 2 August 2013.
Sanders, Clinton. 1989. *Customizing the Body: The Art and Culture of Tattooing.* Philadelphia:
Temple University Press.
Scott, James C. 1990. *Domination and the Arts of Resistance: Hidden Scripts.* New Haven, CT:
Yale University Press.
Scott, Joan Wallach. 2007. *The Politics of the Veil.* Princeton, NJ: Princeton University Press.
Secor, Anna J. 2002. "The Veil and Urban Space in Istanbul: Women's Dress, Mobility and
Islamic Knowledge" in *Gender, Place and Culture: A Journal of Feminist Geography* 9:1,
5–22.
Sedghi, Hamideh. 2007. *Women and Politics in Iran: Veiling, Unveiling, and Reveiling.* Cam-
bridge: Cambridge University Press.
Sedira, Zineb. 2003. "Mapping the Illusive" in David A. Bailey and Gilane Tawadros (eds.),
*Veil: Veiling, Representation and Contemporary Art.* London: Iniva, 56–70.
Shadid, W. and P. S. van Koningsveld. 2005. "Muslim Dress in Europe: Debates on the
Headscarf" in *Journal of Islamic Studies* 16:1, 35–61.
Shail, Andrew. 2004. "'You're Not One of Those Boring Masculinists, Are You?' The Ques-
tion of Male-Embodied Feminism" in Stacy Gillis, Gillian Howie, and Rebecca Munford
(eds.), *Third Wave Feminism: A Critical Exploration.* New York: Palgrave Macmillan,
97–109.
Shirazi, Faegheh. 2001. *The Hijab in Modern Culture.* Gainesville, FL: University of Florida
Press.
Shirazi, Faegheh. 2010. "Islam and Barbie: The Commodification of *Hijabi* Dolls" in *Islamic
Perspective* 3, 10–27.
Siegel, Deborah. 2007. *Sisterhood, Interrupted: From Radical Women to Grrls Gone Wild.*
Gordonsville, VA: Palgrave Macmillan.
Sobh, Rana, Russell Belk, and Justin Gressel. 2011. "Conflicting Imperatives of Modesty and
Vanity among Young Women in the Arabian Gulf" in D. W. Dahl, G. V. Johar, and S. M. J.
van Osselaer (eds.), *Advances in Consumer Research* 38.
Sokoloff, William W. 2001. "Kant and the Paradox of Respect" in *American Journal of Politi-
cal Science* 45:4, 768–779.
Soueif, Ahdaf. 2003. "The Language of the Veil" in David A. Bailey and Gilane Tawadros
(eds.), *Veil: Veiling, Representation and Contemporary Art.* London: Iniva, 108–118.
Southgate, Nick. 2003. "Coolhunting, Account Planning and the Ancient Cool of Aristotle" in
*Marketing Intelligence and Planning* 21:7, 453–461.
Stearns, Peter N. 1994. *American Cool: Constructing a Twentieth Century Emotional Style.*
New York: New York University Press.
Strathern, Andrew. 1975. "Why Is Shame on the Skin?" in *Ethnology* 14:4, 347–356.
Suicide, Missy. 2004. *Suicide Girls: Beauty Redefined.* Pasadena, CA: Ammo Books.
Suicide Girls. http://suicidegirls.com. Last accessed 30 September 2011.
Swedenburg, Ted. 2002. "Islamic Hip-Hop versus Islamophobia" in T. Mitchell (ed.), *Global
Noise: Rap and Hip-Hop Outside the USA.* Middletown, CT: Wesleyan University Press,
57–85.
Syed, Ibrahim B. "Is Head Cover for Women Mandatory In Islam?" *Islamic Research Founda-
tion            International.            *http://www.irfi.org/articles/women_in_islam/

is_head_cover_for_women_
mandator.htm. Last accessed 4 May 2013.

Taliaferro, Charles and Mark Odden. 2012. "Tattoos and the Tattooing Arts in Perspective" in R. Arp (ed.), *Tattoos and Philosophy*. Oxford: Wiley-Blackwell, 3–13.

Talvi, Silja. 2000. "Marked for Life: Tattoos and the Redefinition of Self" in Ophira Edut (ed.), *Body Outlaws: Young Women Write about Body Image and Identity*. Seattle: Seal Press, 211–218.

Tanizaki, Jun'ichirō. 1962. *Tattoo* in Ivan Morris (ed.), *Modern Japanese Stories: An Anthology*, 90–100. Rutland, VT, and Tokyo: Tuttle.

Tao of Tattoos. http://www.tao-of-tattoos.com. Last accessed 30 September 2011.

Tarlo, Emma. 2007. "Islamic Cosmopolitanism: The Sartorial Biographies of Three Muslim Women in London" in *Fashion Theory* 11:2/3, 1–30.

Taylor, Jocelyn. 1995. "Testimony of a Naked Woman" in Rebecca Walker (ed.), *To Be Real: Telling the Truth and Changing the Face of Feminism*. New York: Anchor Books, 219–237.

Taylor, Mark C. 1995. *Skinscapes in Pierced Hearts and True Love: A Century of Drawings for Tattoos*. New York and Honolulu: The Drawing Center and Hardy Marks Publications.

Taylor, Mark C. 1997. *Hiding*. Chicago: University of Chicago Press.

Taylor, Pamela K. 2008. "I Just Want to Be Me: Issues in Identity for One American Muslim Woman" in Jennifer Heath (ed.), *The Veil: Women Writers on Its History, Lore, and Politics*. Berkeley: University of California Press, 119–138.

Todd, Jane Marie. 1986. "The Veiled Woman in Freud's 'Das Unheimliche'" in *Signs: Journal of Women in Culture and Society* 11:3, 519–528.

Toepfer, Karl. 1997. *Empire of Ecstasy: Nudity and Movement in German Body Culture 1910–1935*. Berkeley: University of California Press.

Toepfer, Karl. 2003. "One Hundred Years of Nakedness in German Performance" in *The Drama Review* 47:4, 144–188.

Vandoodewaard, William. 2011. "Art, Nakedness, and Redemption." http://www.reformation21.org/articles/art-nakedness-and-redemption.php. Last accessed 2 August 2013.

Van Nieuwkerk, Karin. 2008. "Biography and Choice: Female Converts to Islam in the Netherlands" in *Islam and Christian-Muslim Relations* 19:4, 431–447.

Velliquette, Anne M., Jeff B. Murray, and Elizabeth H. Creyer. 1998. "The Tattoo Renaissance: An Ethnographic Account of Symbolic Consumer Behavior" in *Advances in Consumer Research* 25, 461–467.

Verharen, Charles C. 1997. "The New World and the Dreams to Which It May Give Rise: An African and American Response to Hegel's Challenge" in *Journal of Black Studies* 27:4, 456–493.

Virilio, Paul. 2009 [1980]. *The Aesthetics of Disappearance*. New York: Semiotext(e).

Walker, Rebecca. 1998. "Foreword" to Ophira Edut (ed.), *Body Outlaws: Rewriting the Rules of Beauty and Body Image*. Emerville, CA: Seal Press, viii–xviii.

Wassef, Nadia. 2001. "On Selective Consumerism: Egyptian Women and Ethnographic Representation" in *Feminist Review* 69, 111–123.

Weinberg, Martin S. 1965. "Sexual Modesty, Social Meanings, and the Nudist Camp" in *Social Problems* 12:3, 311–318.

Weinsheimer, Joel. 2003. "Meaningless Hermeneutics?" in B. Krajewski (ed.), *Gadamer's Repercussions: Reconsidering Philosophical Hermeneutics*. Ewing, NJ: University of California Press, 158–168.

West, Cornel. 1993. *Keeping Faith: Philosophy and Race in America*. New York: Routledge.

Williams, John Alden. 1979. "Return of the Veil in Egypt" in *Middle East Review* 11:3, 49–54.

Williams, John Alden. 1980. "Veiling as a Political and Social Phenomenon" in J. L. Esposito (ed.), *Islam and Development: Religion and Sociopolitical Change*. Syracuse, NY: Syracuse University Press, 71–86.

Williams, John Alexander. 2007. *Turning to Nature in Germany: Hiking, Nudism, and Conservation, 1900–1940*. Stanford, NY: Stanford University Press.

Williams, Rhys and Gira Vashi. 2007. "*Hijab* and American Muslim Women: Creating the Space for Autonomous Selves" in *Sociology of Religion* 68:3, 269–287.

Williams, Terry. 1994. "Foreword" to Connor, xiii–xix.

Witz, Anne. 2000. "Whose Body Matters? Feminist Sociology and the Corporeal Turn in Sociology and Feminism" in *Body and Society* 6:2, 1–24.

Wolf, Naomi. 1995. "Brideland" in R. Walker (ed.), *To Be Real: Telling the Truth and Changing the Face of Feminism*. New York: Anchor Books, 335–340.

Woodhull, Winifred. 2003. "Global Feminisms, Transnational Political Economies, Third World Cultural Production" in Stacy Gillis and Rebecca Munford (eds.), *Third Wave Feminism and Women's Studies* Special issue of the *Journal of International Women's Studies* 4:2, 76–90.

Wurtzel, Elizabeth. 1998. *Bitch: In Praise of Difficult Women*. New York: Doubleday.

Yeğenoğlu, Meyda. 1998. *Colonial Fantasies: Towards a Feminist Reading of Orientalism*. Cambridge: Cambridge University Press.

Zahedi, Ashraf. 2008. "Concealing and Revealing Female Hair: Veiling Dynamics in Contemporary Iran" in Jennifer Heath (ed.), *The Veil: Women Writers on Its History, Lore, and Politics*. Berkeley: University of California Press, 250–265.

Zaslow, Emilie. 2009. *Feminism, Inc.: Coming of Age in Girl Power Media Culture*. New York: Palgrave Macmillan.

Žižek, Slavoj. 1992. *Looking Awry: An Introduction to Jacques Lacan through Popular Culture*. Cambridge, MA: MIT Press.

Zuhur, Sherifa. 1992. *Revealing Reveiling: Islamic Gender Ideology in Contemporary Egypt*. Albany: State University of New York Press.

# Index

# About the Author

**Thorsten Botz-Bornstein** was born in Germany and studied philosophy in Paris and Oxford. As a postdoctoral researcher based in Finland he undertook extensive research on Russian formalism and semiotics in Russia and the Baltic countries. He has also been researching in Japan, in particular on the Kyoto School and on the philosophy of Nishida Kitarô. At present he is Associate Professor of Philosophy at the Gulf University for Science and Technology in Kuwait. His publications are *Place and Dream: Japan and the Virtual* (Rodopi, 2004); *Films and Dreams: Tarkovsky, Sokurov, Bergman, Kubrik, Wong Kar-wai* (Lexington Books, 2007); *La Chine contre l'Amérique: Culture sans civilisation contre civilisation sans culture?* (L'Harmattan, 2012); *Vasily Sesemann: Experience, Formalism and the Question of Being* (Rodopi, 2006); *Aesthetics and Politics of Space in Russia and Japan* (Lexington Books, 2009); *The Cool-Kawaii: Afro-Japanese Aesthetics and New World Modernity* (Lexington Books, 2010); *The Veil in Kuwait: Gender, Fashion, Identity* (with Noreen Abdullah-Khan, Palgrave, 2014); and *Transcultural Architecture: Limits and Opportunities of Critical Regionalism* (Ashgate, 2015). He is also the editor of *The Philosophy of Viagra: Bioethical Responses to the Viagrification of the Modern World* (Rodopi, 2011); *Inception and Philosophy: Ideas to Die For* (Open Court, 2011). *Re-ethnicizing the Minds? Tendencies of Cultural Revival in Contemporary Philosophy* (Rodopi, 2006). *The Crisis of the Human Sciences: False Objectivity and the Decline of Creativity* (Cabridge Scholars Publishing, 2010); and *Culture, Nature, Memes* (Cambridge Scholars Publishing, 2008).